Bodily Communication

This
Book
Belongs
to

....

....

Bodily Communication

Michael Argyle

Methuen & Co Ltd

London

First published in 1975 by Methuen & Co. Ltd
11 New Fetter Lane, London EC4P 4EE
Reprinted twice
Reprinted 1981
Copyright © 1975 by Michael Argyle

Printed in Great Britain by
Richard Clay (The Chaucer Press) Ltd
Bungay, Suffolk

ISBN 0 416 55290 0

Contents

Preface

Bodily, or non-verbal, communication has been the object of a great deal of research in recent years, and a lot of very interesting findings have emerged. These are of great theoretical interest to psychologists, linguists, sociologists, and others, and they have a number of important social applications. In this book I have tried to examine the biological and cultural roots of bodily communication, the different purposes for which it is used (e.g. expressing interpersonal attitudes, supporting speech), to examine the different bodily signals (e.g. facial, gestural), and to explore the wider theoretical and practical implications. I have done my best to write a book that is both scholarly and popular – scholarly in that all of the assertions are based on sound evidence and some of the main sources given, popular in that it is intended to be intelligible and interesting to the general reader.

I learnt a great deal from Robert Hinde, Edmund Leach, John Lyons, Mike Cullen, and other members of the Royal Society group on non-verbal communication – which produced *Non-Verbal Communication*, edited by Hinde and published in 1972. I also gained a great deal from Erving Goffman, Ralph Exline, Albert Scheflen, Irenäus Eibl-Eibesfeldt, Paul Ekman, Stuart Altmann, Kenneth Pike, and others, who attended a number of small conferences on this topic at Long Island, at Oxford, and at Amsterdam, during 1969 and 1970.

A number of recent publications have been particularly useful to me – Ekman and Friesen's paper on 'Categories, origins, usage and coding' (*Semiotica*, 1969), Mehrabian *Nonverbal Communication* (1972), Knapp, *Nonverbal Communication in Human Interaction* (1972), Harré and Secord, *The Explanation of Social Behaviour* (1972), Birdwhistell, *Kinesics and Context* (1970) and recent papers by Kendon and Exline.

I am grateful to the Social Science Research Council for a series of grants which have made the research at Oxford in this field possible. And I am indebted to all those who have been members of our research group, and particularly to John Breaux, David Clarke, Peter Collett, Mark Cook, Jean Graham, Roger Ingham, Adam Kendon, Mansur Lalljee, Brian Little, Robert McHenry, Kimiko Shimoda, Mary Sissons, Ederyn Williams, and Marylin Williams, and to Ann McKendry for typing the manuscript.

Michael Argyle

Department of Experimental Psychology,
South Parks Road,
Oxford.

Acknowledgements

The author and publisher would like to thank the following for permission to reproduce copyright material:

Plates E. P. Dutton & Co Ltd for plate 1; Weidenfeld and Nicolson for plates 2 & 3; Macmillan Publishing Co Inc for plate 4; William Collins and Sons Ltd for plates 5, 6 & 7; *Scientific American* for plate 11; Plenum Press for plate 12; B. H. MacDermot Esq. and Robert Hale & Co for plate 13; American Heritage for plate 14; Prentice-Hall Inc and Dr A. E. Scheflen for plates 15, 16 & 17; University of Chicago Press for plate 18; The Open University for plates 19 & 20.

Figures Penguin Books Ltd for figure 2.1; Wolfe Publishing Ltd for figure 4.3; University of Pennsylvania Press for figure 11.2; Pergamon Press for figure 12.3; Edicom N. V. for figure 13.1.

Acknowledgements

The author and publisher would like to thank the following for permission to reproduce copyright material:

Part 1

*The biological &
cultural background*

I

Introduction

Bodily communication, or non-verbal communication, NVC, plays a central part in human social behaviour. Recent research by social psychologists and others has shown that these signals play a more important part, and function in a more intricate manner, than had previously been realized. If we want to understand human social behaviour we shall have to disentangle this non-verbal system.

At least we know what these signals are – gestures, head movements and other bodily movements, posture, facial expression, direction of gaze, proximity and spatial position, bodily contact, orientation, tones of voice and other non-verbal aspects of speech, clothes, and bodily adornment. Each of these can be sub-divided into a number of further variables, for example different aspects of gaze – looking while listening, looking while talking, mutual gaze, length of glances, amount of eye-opening, pupil expansion, etc. It is a matter of sheer empirical research to find out what effects, if any, these variables have. For example head-nods are very important, foot movements are not. We shall describe the detailed working of each kind of signal in Part III.

We have a good idea of the different messages which are conveyed by different bodily signals – emotional states, attitudes to other people, information about the self and supporting speech by providing illustrations, feedback, and synchronizing signals, and in sign-language replacing it. It is used as well in ritual and ceremony, art and music, propaganda and politics. It has been suggested that in some spheres there has been a cultural swing away from the previous emphasis on language. The alternative kinds of communication are discussed in Part II.

Research on communication in animals has found that they use signals which are rather similar to those used by men – involving for example facial expressions, posture, tones of voice, direction of gaze, and changes in bodily colouring. This provides important evidence about the evolutionary origins of NVC. Cross-cultural studies of human societies show that some aspects of bodily communication are very similar in all cultures – the facial expressions for emotions for example. Others – for instance symbolic gestures – vary greatly. However, men are able to communicate by means of language, and much human NVC is closely linked to speech, supporting and sustaining it in various ways. Human NVC differs from that of animals in another way: while animal signals are simply responses which trigger responses in other animals, much human NVC is intended to communicate, and the signals used have common meanings to both senders and receivers. We shall inquire whether these sets of meaningful signals have a structure in the ways that languages do. We shall consider why NVC is used at all, and what the difference is between verbal and non-verbal versions of the same message.

The results of this inquiry have implications beyond the sphere of social psychology. There are fairly radical implications for other areas of study concerned with human behaviour – linguistics, philosophy, politics, and theology for example. The main point here is to suggest that too much importance has been attached to language in the past – we shall show that language is highly dependent on and closely intertwined with NVC, and that there is a lot which cannot be expressed adequately in words. There are also practical implications in a number of areas – treatment of mental patients, education, design of communication systems, race relations, and international affairs, for example.

Definitions and distinctions

By a *sign* or signal we shall mean an element of the behaviour, appearance, etc., of one organism that is received by the sense organs of a second organism and affects its behaviour. We exclude simply mechanical influences: if A pushes B over this is a mechanical effect (though it will probably be a communication as well). Signs normally act at a distance, though we shall consider certain forms of bodily contact as signs. Some signals are intended to communicate – these will be called *communications*. Signals are a quite distinctive class of behaviour, because they have *meanings* – they might stand for other objects or events, or create expectations of behaviour to follow.

The distinction between communication proper, and other signs

When a man raises his programme at an auction sale to make a bid, he consciously intends to send a message to the auctioneer: he is using a shared code, and the auctioneer perceives him correctly as a person intending to send a particular message. It is clearly different when an animal or person in a certain emotional state displays visible signs of that emotion, such as trembling or perspiring, which are then perceived by others: this is an observed sign, but there is no intention to communicate. For communication proper there are goal-directed signals, whereas signs are simply behavioural or physiological responses. In communication there is awareness of others as beings who understand the code which is being used.

Unfortunately it is very difficult to decide whether a particular non-verbal signal is intended to communicate or not: as we shall see there are communications which are

6 The biological & cultural background

motivated, without conscious awareness of intention. One criterion is whether or not the signal is modified as a function of the conditions (e.g. when telephoning instead of communicating visibly), or whether the signal is repeated if it has no effect. Another criterion is whether or not the sender varies his signal in order to elicit the correct response from the receiver (Wiener *et al.*, 1972).

The same signal can be used as a communication or a sign; for example a person may attempt to communicate that he is upper class by using an accent which is used by real upper class people, and which normally acts as a sign. A non-verbal signal may be partly communication, partly sign; for example facial expression of emotion is partly innate and spontaneous, partly controlled by the desire to conform to cultural requirements.

Conscious versus *unconscious communications*

A person may succeed in dominating another by the use of such non-verbal signals as standing erect, with hands on hips, not smiling, and speaking loudly. A person may indicate that he has come to the end of a sentence by looking up, and returning his hand to rest, or indicate that he wants to go on speaking by keeping a hand in mid-gesture. In none of these cases are those involved usually aware of the signals being used or of what they mean. They are probably all cases of communication, but unconscious on both sides. We shall consider the special features of consciously controlled behaviour later.

Similar considerations apply to the perception of signs: a girl is attracted by a boy, so her pupils expand, acting as a signal which in turn attracts him, though he is not aware that this signal is doing it. Most animal communication appears to be like this. An animal responds to a situation, and this response triggers off responses in other animals. Although these signals do not appear to be goal-directed in most cases, it can be argued that they are part of a goal-directed evolutionary process that has produced this signalling system.

Again the distinction between conscious and unconscious signals is a matter of degree and there can be intermediate degrees of conscious insight. For example a person may successfully communicate his social status by the clothes he wears, but verbally categorize these clothes only as 'nice', or 'suitable'. Other cases of unconscious communication occur in primitive rituals where the symbolism, for example of red gum for menstrual blood, has a powerful emotive and possibly therapeutic effect without anyone being consciously aware of this symbolism.

We can distinguish between communications where the sender and receiver are aware or unaware of the signal, as follows:

sender	*receiver*	
aware	aware	verbal communication, some gestures, e.g. pointing
mostly unaware	mostly aware	most NVC
unaware	unware, but has an effect	pupil dilation, gaze shifts and other small non-verbal signals
aware	unaware	sender is trained in the use of e.g. spatial behaviour
unaware	aware	receiver is trained in the interpretation of e.g. bodily posture

Verbal versus *non-verbal*

Verbal behaviour usually consists of speech, but also sometimes of writing, or gestures standing for letters or words. However, speech is accompanied by an intricate set of non-verbal signals, providing illustrations and feed-back and helping with synchronization. Some of these are really part of the verbal message itself – the *prosodic* signals of timing, pitch, and emphasis in particular. Other non-verbal signals are independent of the speech contents, including the *paralinguistic* signals of emotional tone of speech. However, non-verbal signals are often affected by verbal coding; for example symbolic acts or objects used in rituals may be named or have specific meanings, and patterns of non-verbal behaviour, e.g. styles of behaviour like 'charm', 'dignity', and 'presence', may be verbally categorized. On the other hand some non-verbal signals stand for emotions, attitudes, or experiences which are not easily expressable in words. Last, as noted above, the distinction verbal/non-verbal does not correspond to vocal/non-vocal, since there are hand-movements which stand for words, and vocalizations which do not.

The number of decoders who can interpret signals

Many communications and signs can be interpreted more or less accurately by most members of a culture. Other signals can be understood only by those with special training. Deaf-and-dumb language, or the gestures of, for instance, tic-tac men, are like this. In the field of signs psychoanalysts can make interpretations from observed behaviour which cannot be made by laymen. Mahls (lecture at Long Island) gives examples of inferring the commitment of a patient to analysis from the distance she moves onto the couch, and her attitude to the analyst from her bodily posture. We shall discuss later whether such inferences are correct. Those who have read this book will be in a position to make new inferences from minor non-verbal signals about emotional states, interpersonal attitudes, etc. Some aspects of behaviour are unique to individuals, and therefore cannot be interpreted at all, except by those who know them well or have made a special study of their behaviour.

Cases of mis-match between encoder and decoder

Often there is a close matching between encoding and decoding. A gives a hitch-hike sign, which is clearly understood by B. C likes D; he looks D in the eye; D realizes that

C likes him, though neither is more than dimly aware of the communication involved.

A variety of complications are produced when signaller (S) and receiver (R) are at cross-purposes.

(1) R misunderstands S's signal. There is always some degree of failure, through S sending misleading or inadequate signals, or R failing to interpret them correctly. This becomes acute when S and R belong to different cultural groups, e.g. different age groups. Here S and R are not using a shared code.

(2) Signs are taken for communications, or vice versa. S communicates that he likes R (when he doesn't), or is upper class (when he isn't), and this is interpreted by R as a valid sign of S's true feelings or social status. S may emit signals that he likes R (when he does), and R thinks that this is a managed communication, when it is really quite spontaneous.

Theoretical problems about bodily communication

(1) *What are the origins of NVC?*

For animals NVC is largely innate; the problem is to unravel the evolutionary processes which have led to the development of the social signals used by particular species – bird-song, the bees' dance, primate facial expressions, and the like. In man we want to know how much of this innate system is left; are facial expressions for emotions innate and universal, for example?

Clearly learning is important too, since there are extensive cultural variations in NVC. In which case, how are these signals and their interpretations learnt? For hand signals with conventional meanings it is likely that children learn them by direct imitation or instruction. In the case of signs

for, age, class, etc. the interpretation could be learnt by observation. Other kinds of NVC are more difficult to account
for. How do people learn to use the rather intricate signals
connected with synchronizing speech for example, since
they are apparently unaware of what these signals are? And
how do the non-verbal signals used in rituals acquire their
meanings, which cannot be put into words by those using
them or by those being influenced?

(2) *Why is NVC used?*

In the case of animals there is no problem: patterns of NVC
have evolved which are essential to survival – they attract
mates, give warning of predators, and so on. In the case of
humans it is not obvious why we need to use NVC at all,
since we have the power of language, which on the face of
it is a far more elaborate, subtle, and flexible means of communication than grunts, head-nods, etc. What is it that
NVC can do which language can't do as well? There are
various possibilities. Perhaps NVC, being more primitive
and direct, has a more powerful effect. Perhaps it is useful
to be able to use a second channel so that both the verbal
and non-verbal channels can be used at the same time, without being confused with one another. Perhaps there are
some things which language is not well adapted to express.
Or perhaps there are some things which it is better not to
make too explicit or attend to fully. These are fundamental
questions of communication and social behaviour, which it
is important to settle. Perhaps the most basic question
concerns the difference between messages with the same
basic meaning, expressed verbally and non-verbally.

A number of writers have stressed the importance of non-
verbal communication. McLuhan (1962) suggests that its
importance has increased as a result of television, Susanne
Langer (1942) suggests that it is the key to understanding
music, myth, and ritual. Political writers have drawn at-

tention to the increasing use of symbolic political behaviour, accompanied by a distrust of language in some circles.

(3) *The meaning of non-verbal signals*

In discussions of communication it is usually supposed that there is an encoder, a message, and a decoder. We need to discover the meaning of particular signals to encoders and decoders. This is straightforward when the message contains information of a cognitive kind, as in gesture languages. Other cases are not so easy. What is the meaning of a head-nod in a conversation, where this is not consciously noted but has the effect of allowing another person to carry on talking? It has perhaps a 'behavioural meaning', though a person knowledgeable about NVC might give it a cognitive meaning of the kind 'you have permission to carry on talking'. What is the meaning of a piece of music, which arouses certain emotions, images, and motor responses? Again the meaning could be said to lie in the reactions of beholders, or perhaps in the intentions of the composer, if these can be discovered. What is the meaning of a ritual, which is full of complex symbolism, and whose effect may be initiation or healing? In the case of language, however, it is not enough to define meaning as the reactions of language users; words *denote* sets of acts or objects, and they *connote* the abstract idea of those sets. Verbal discussion and reasoning depends on the existence of these shared abstract meanings where one concept is related to other concepts. Do non-verbal signals have shared connotations in a similar way?

We want to know how well NVC functions as a communication system, how much information of different kinds is conveyed, and how accurate the information is that is received. There may be errors because the encoding is done inaccurately or with intent to deceive, or because the decoding is performed wrongly, or because little information is extracted from the message. When there is deliberate deception, is the decoder able to see through it? And how often are there mismatches, whereby communications proper are mistaken for signs, and vice versa?

(4) *How does bodily communication function, considered as a sign system?*

Recent developments in linguistics have made a number of research workers hopeful that similar principles might prove successful in unravelling NVC, and it has become fashionable to refer to 'body language'. We shall have to examine different kinds of NVC very carefully to see the respects in which they do and do not resemble languages proper. For example, does NVC have a two-level structure of a few meaningless basic units (like phonemes) which can be combined into a large number of meaningful units (like words)? Are there rules of combination and sequence, corresponding to grammatical rules? Can we make a useful distinction between language and speech, competence and performance, between the underlying system, with its meaningful set of all-or-none relationships, and the variable, statistical approximations to this found in specific performances? Can users of the system produce an indefinitely large set of original messages?

If NVC does not function like a language then we need to find out exactly how it does function as a system of communication.

Methods of research for the study of NVC

Most research in psychology is done by means of laboratory experiments. However, laboratory experiments in social psychology have come under fire from several directions in recent years, so much so that it has become fashionable to speak of 'the crisis in social psychology'. The main lines of criticism are that laboratory experiments are artificial, so that they generate spurious phenomena or fail to include important features of the real world, that the people studied are treated as passive 'subjects' who are not allowed to do more than behave like machines or rats, that experimenters unconsciously influence subjects to produce the results they expect, that no account is taken of the variety of reasons for subjects responding the way that they do, and that laboratory experiments do not enable us to discover rules or systems such as grammar in linguistics. However, those doing research on NVC have been well aware of these difficulties for some time, have done their best to evade them, and have been critical of artificial laboratory research in which subjects sit in cubicles, press buttons, and where both verbal and non-verbal communication are eliminated (Argyle, 1969).

The laboratory arrangements used depend on the approach of the investigator. In the Oxford laboratory most research takes place in a large, furnished room, which can be observed through a one-way screen, and where video-tape recordings can be made. The subjects are well aware that this is a laboratory, but they are not told the purpose of a particular experiment until afterwards. They are asked to take part in some familiar social task, such as an interview or other type of conversation.

Whether we use laboratory experiments or not, it is essential to use scientific research methods of a rigorous kind, which enable us to test alternative hypotheses. It is no use lapsing into a kind of woolly humanism, with a broad and generous vision of human nature, but failing to collect empirical data which will advance our knowledge. Indeed as knowledge in any field becomes more extensive, the hypotheses to be tested become increasingly complex, and the methods of testing need corresponding increases in subtlety.

One approach is to study people in field situations where they are unaffected by the activities of the investigator. It is also possible to do field experiments, which are open to some of the previous objections, but which make causal inferences possible. For example, in an investigation described later, an actor stopped a lot of people in Paddington station to ask them the way: his apparent social class was varied experimentally, and the behaviour of the respondents filmed. Some laboratory techniques also make use of unsuspecting subjects, for example in some experiment subjects think they are in a waiting room talking to others in the same position.

It is important to note the distinction between discovery and proof. Experiments are ideally suited to proof – by holding variables constant, by careful manipulation of experimental variables and measurement of dependent variables. However experiments do not always lead to the discovery of new ideas, indeed they may prevent it, by restricting attention to a certain very limited set of variables or procedures. Discovery occurs more often as a result of more informal and less well controlled research – clinical case studies, anthropological field studies, and intensive study of particular field situations for example. These are 'rich' sources of data, in that they do not exclude anything in the way that experiments do. We can also learn from unusual situations, such as initiation rites in primitive societies, encounter groups, or modern drama, where certain aspects of social behaviour are exaggerated; the study of such abnormal phenomena may help us to understand familiar ones more clearly.

In this book we are interested in a variety of very different issues about NVC – for example, its evolutionary origins, whether it is culturally universal, what particular signals mean, how it is related to speech, whether deception can be penetrated, why it is used at all, and its structure as a communication system. Each of these issues needs different research procedures, and different issues arise in each case about how satisfactory these methods are.

One kind of research is concerned with decoding, that is finding the meaning of non-verbal signals to recipients.

There are numerous problems here – the difficulty of using staged rather than genuine stimuli (for example of emotions), the need to provide a credible setting, the difficulty of finding aspects of meaning beyond those the decoder can report (such as behavioural or unverbalizable reactions), and the need to distinguish between communications and signs.

Another kind of research concerns encoding, for example asking subjects to behave as if they were happy. Problems include the inadequacy of posed expressions, and the difficulty of including unconscious signals. Psychoanalysts can provide interpretations for unconscious signals, but they cannot provide convincing proof that these interpretations are correct. Research on encoding can be pursued by studying the effects of varying some of the conditions of communication, such as the visibility of the sender.

An alternative approach is the ethological method of studying sequences of behaviour without experimental interference. This has been successful in the study of animal communication, and the statistical probability that one act will lead to another can be measured. The method has also been successful in studying the sequences of NVC that accompany speech. A number of investigators have analysed these processes in great detail, by the frame-by-frame study of short periods of film. While interactors are not aware of signals of very short duration, it is clear that such signals are of importance here. In order to disentangle the causal processes at work, some progress can be made by means of statistical analysis, but it is probably necessary to resort to some kind of experimentation

Investigators who believe that NVC is a structured system of communication like a language have used different, and non-statistical approaches. Linguists commonly work with 'idealized data' to arrive at the language system. Birdwhistell (1970) has concentrated on trying to establish the basic 'vocabulary' of non-verbal signals. Garfinkel (1963) introduced deliberate rule-breaking as a method of checking the existence of social rules. Goffman (1971) has been searching for repeated sequences of behaviour, with the same underlying structure.

There are a number of other kinds of research in NVC which will be described later. Examples include comparing different species of animals in order to discover evolutionary changes, cross-cultural comparisons to find how far NVC is invariant and how far dependent on culture, and the study of NVC in children, mental patients, and others.

The practical implications of NVC research

Research into human behaviour usually has practical consequences or applications, often in directions not thought of by the original investigators. Here are examples of some applications which have been made already, or which could be made in the near future. These will be developed in more detail in Chapter 19.

(1) *Education, social skills training and therapy*

At present education places a great deal of emphasis on words, books, and verbal communication. Training in social skills is now being given in various quarters – for interviewers, teachers, and other performers of professional social skills, and also in some schools. Much of this training emphasizes the use of bodily communication.

(2) *Communication between people of different cultures, classes, ages etc.*

Difficulties of communication are often due to differences in the use of non-verbal signals, and this can lead to misunderstanding and hostility. Education and training can prevent that.

(3) *Problems of communication by telephone or video-phone, and for the blind and the deaf*

In each of these cases some of the normal means of bodily

communication are absent. Special skills have to be developed to compensate; and research on NVC can suggest how this can be done.

(4) *Understanding social behaviour in everyday life*

Our understanding of social behaviour in everyday life is often inadequate, since it is based on an incorrect model of man. Just as our behaviour is not primarily the product of rational conscious decisions, nor is our social behaviour primarily based on the exchange of verbal propositions. Since most of our NVC is unconscious, people are not aware of the important roles it plays in social behaviour. It seems to me very desirable that this should be more widely known, in the hope that people will become more sensitive to what is going on about them, and more highly skilled in coping with it.

References

ARGYLE, M. (1969) *Social Interaction*. London: Methuen.

BIRDWHISTELL, R. (1970) *Kinesics and Content*. Philadelphia: University of Pennsylvania Press.

GARFINKEL, H. (1963) Trust and stable actions. In O. J. Harvey (ed.) *Motivation and Social Interaction*. New York: Ronald.

GOFFMAN, E. (1971) *Relations in Public*. London: Allen Lane.

LANGER, S. K. (1942) *Philosophy in a New Key*. Cambridge, Mass.: Harvard University Press.

MCLUHAN, M. (1962) *The Gutenberg Galaxy*. Toronto: University of Toronto Press.

SCHEFLEN, A. E. (1965) The natural history method in psychotherapy: communicational research. In L. A. Gottschalk and A. H. Auerbach (eds.) *Methods of Research in Psychotherapy*. New York: Appleton-Century-Crofts.

WIENER, M. *et al.* (1972) Nonverbal behaviour and nonverbal communication. *Psychological Review* 79: 185–214.

2

Non-verbal communication in animals

In the last few years research on animal communication has made great advances and has discovered the basic principles and laws. This is of great importance, since it must be assumed that human communication, both verbal and non-verbal, has developed out of these more primitive forms. By comparing different animal systems, the principles of communication in general may be found.

Research workers studying animal and human behaviour have recently come to see that there are a number of close similarities between the social behaviour of humans and that of apes and monkeys; in particular, both groups use very similar non-verbal signals. Research on human and non-human primates has converged in the discovery of common signals and systems of communication. Animals conduct their entire social life by means of non-verbal communication. They make friends, find mates, rear children, co-operate in groups, establish leadership hierarchies, and get rid of their enemies entirely by the use of NV signals. This elaborate signalling system has mainly been built up in the course of evolution, as a result of its value for the survival of the species.

A lot about communication processes which cannot be learnt from humans can be learnt from studying animals. The NV system is revealed in simpler form, without cultural elaboration. The evolutionary development of particular signals can be studied by comparing communication in closely related species. The way signals or modes of communication function in the total social life of a group can be discovered from detailed field studies.

In this chapter we shall use 'communication' in a broad sense to include any behaviour on the part of one animal that affects the behaviour of another animal. Animal A is in some state (emotional or other); this is encoded into a signal, which is decoded by animal B. This can be described as conveying 'information' to B in that B can now predict A's behaviour, knows which species A belongs to, and so on.

It is very difficult to decide whether animals 'intend' to communicate, and this will be discussed later (p. 47f). A more important distinction is between those acts which have been adapted as social signals during evolution, and those which primarily serve some other purpose. In many cases it is clear that animals do not intend to send signals – they may send them even though no other animal is present; such communication includes visible physiological changes, like signs of excitement or fatigue. Similarly it is not necessary to suppose that the recipient is consciously aware of a signal. Its affect may be directly physiological; for example, when a pregnant female mouse smells a strange male she aborts some of the embryos, thus controlling population under conditions of over-crowding. Other signals, such as the bees' dance (see p. 25f), involve more cognitive processing.

In almost all cases of animal communication, a signal by A 'triggers' a response by B, which is not a result of direct physical contact or energy transfer. Thus a small signal like a shift of gaze can have a considerable physical effect, such as flight.

Signals can be studied experimentally, for example varying different aspects of dummy birds or fish can reveal which aspect of the signal is important. David Lack (1939) found that if the breast feathers of a robin were dyed brown those birds were attacked less by other robins, and experiments by Tinbergen (1951) using dummies showed that birds recognized predators from the shape of their wings. In some cases a complex and repeated set of signals is found, like the song of an individual bird or a 'courtship' sequence. This is a more elaborate kind of communication, which has some parallels with the syntax of human speech.

The effects of experience on the use of NVC have been studied through experiments in which animals have been reared in isolation, either from adults or peers, or for certain periods, to find out what is learnt from whom and when. When signals are learnt they can form a local tradition, such as a dialect.

Animal communication can also be studied as a formal system. We can study the different ways in which signals have meaning, how they are interpreted, how they are used in social behaviour, whether they have a syntax, and so on. Each system of animal communication possesses certain 'design features', which enables it to function for a particular species in its particular environment. Such design features can be compared with those of human language and human non-verbal communication.

The different non-verbal messages used by animals

(1) *Emotions and interpersonal attitudes*

There are a number of basic social relationships between animals – between mates, parents and children, friends, and so on. A complete set of NV signals is used to manage these relationships. We will illustrate these signals where possible by reference to the non-human primates.

Sexual. A female of most non-human primate species signals her sexual readiness by her visible physiological condition, especially the blue swelling on her buttocks. She may present to the male, or the male may try to mount, after which copulation takes place. Sexual behaviour involves a carefully co-ordinated sequence of NV acts by the two partners. Birds and other species engage in much longer sequences of courtship behaviour: the male attracts the female by his song and his appearance; there are elaborate joint rituals, in which the male may feed the female, or build her a nest.

Maternal–infantile signals. Mothers embrace and suckle their infants, later allowing them to cling on underneath or ride on top. Most species have a special call, and some have a special facial expression for recalling their young. Infants produce the complementary pattern of clinging, sucking, riding, and running to mother when frightened. They use special cries when they are separated from and united with their mother.

Affiliative behaviour between siblings and friends, young and old, takes several forms. A lot of time is spent in grooming – taking turns to extract small pieces of dead skin or insects from one another's coats, while lip-smacking and showing the appropriate facial expressions. Animals also spend time in bodily contact, in families and between friends.

Young animals play a lot: the invitation to play consists of the 'playface', and the play consists of imitation, chasing, fighting, and mounting. In grooming and play there are long sequences of interaction, in which one act leads to another with a certain probability. When two animals meet they usually greet one another, by lip-smacking, touching, smelling, embracing, or mounting each other, or even by shaking hands.

Submission and appeasement. When one animal admits the dominance of another it may signal submission in various ways. It may just turn and flee, screeching, urinating, and looking over its shoulder. It may make appeasement signals by cowering, curling up, holding out a hand, facing away and lowering the eyes, presenting for copulation, or inviting grooming. Some species, like cats and dogs, show 'defensive threat', perhaps when there is conflict between flight and attack. The hair or feathers are erected, there are self-protective responses such as eye closing, and some aggressive signals like barking.

As well as giving submissive or threat signals which actually change a relationship, animals may make briefer gestures which merely communicate or recognize an existing relationship, and thus make social life proceed more smoothly, and prevent aggression. It has been observed that monkeys may express dominance by such gestures as a brisk, striding gait, and sitting calmly; submission is expressed by grimacing and retracting the testes.

Establishing and maintaining contact. Members of a group of animals often keep in contact by means of 'contact calls'. This is common in birds, but is also found in primates, sheep, sea lions, and squirrels. Animals come to recognize the calls of their mates, parents, and children, and in some species of birds couples sing duets together. These calls are interesting in that they are spontaneous and not a response to a particular stimulus.

Threat to member of own species. Various dominance questions, such as access to food and females, are settled by threat displays between pairs of males. Usually they do not fight, but simply make terrifying displays at one another. These threat displays consist of a number of NV signals:

facial expression: bared teeth, lowered eye brows, staring eyes

posture: tense, head lowered, forelegs bent, swaying
movement: slow approach
bodily state: hair bristling
bodily contact: hit, bite
vocalization: barking or grunting

Attack. Sometimes an animal will actually attack a member of its own group, of another group, or another species. This may take the form of charging, slapping, scratching, stamping on the back, hair-pulling, biting, lifting, and slamming down.

Flight. When an animal is frightened it engages in various forms of flight and avoidance – running away screaming, putting its arm across its face, hiding, or creeping away quietly.

Interspecies signals. Many animals live in a co-operative relationship with other species, for example 'cleaner' fish eat the parasites on certain other fish. Special signals are developed to enable such co-operation to take place. More often different species are in conflict with each other – one is a predator, or they are in competition for the same territory.

Threat signals are used, which are similar to those used within the species, though these are more likely to lead to an actual attack. Some birds attack predators by 'mobbing' – a special call leads to a collective attack on an enemy.

(2) *Identity signals*

An important aspect of animal communication concerns identity. It is necessary to recognize the species of another animal, which group he belongs to, his sex and social status, which individual he is, and where he is.

First, it is necessary to know whether another animal belongs to the same species, to one of several different species of predators which have to be treated differently, to one of several species of prey, or to a species with which relations of co-operation or peaceful co-existence have developed. Mammals recognize another's species mainly by various crucial aspects of his appearance and by vocalizations. Insects, however, recognize their own species by their distinctive pheromones (taste or smell signals), while birds recognize species both by shape and by song. The essential and universal components of a song can be established by acoustic analysis; some birds have an innate capacity to sing and to recognize their species tune.

In other species of birds, like the chaffinch, there is a basic song found in different groups, but there are also detailed differences of 'dialect'. In these species there is a period of imitative learning, in the nest, or for a period each year, from the father, from both parents, or from the whole group of neighbours. These differences of dialect make it possible for birds to distinguish between members of different groups, and it is assumed that this is the biological function of imitative variations on the basic song.

When recognition is a visual matter, there is usually no difficulty in perceiving the sex and age of another animal. Its social status can also be perceived from such signals as, in the case of some monkeys, an upright posture and a raised tail. Birds too can distinguish sex differences, and to some extent age differences, from bird-song. Some insects can signal social status by pheromones.

Particular individuals can be distinguished from others of the same species or group by their individual appearance or call. For example a sea-bird returning to a colony of 2,000, can recognize and be recognized by its own family by distinctive calls. The calls vary in pitch, tone quality, loudness, combinations of these, and changes in time, providing thousands of different versions of a basically similar call. The male and female bou-bou shrike learn to sing a duet which is in the group dialect but is also unique to that pair, so that they can recognize each other.

Bird-song contains another piece of information – where the singer is. Bird-song is used to claim territory, such as a particular tree, and has the function of attracting females and repelling males from that place. High-pitched song that is repeated over a long period gives very clear information about spatial position to other birds over a wide area.

These identity signals are included in calls which also convey other messages. The identifying elements may be particularly clear in the beginning of the call, while individual, group and species identification may be carried by different acoustic features of it.

(3) *The communication of information about the outside world*

Most animal communication is of the kinds already described – signalling internal emotional states, attitudes to other animals, and identity. However, animals can also communicate to a limited degree information about the outside world. This kind of communication comes nearest to human language. We shall discuss three examples.

(a) The bees' dance. A very interesting case of apparently symbolic communication was discovered by Von Frisch (1967) and has been the object of a great deal of detailed experimental research. It was found that when a worker bee returned to the hive after finding a good source of food she engaged in a dance which contained information about the position of the food, and that the other bees then flew out to where the food was. If the food was fairly near, she made a *round dance*; the other bees smelt the scent on her and were aroused so that they flew out in all directions in search of that scent. If the distance of the food was greater she did a figure-of-eight *tail wagging dance*; the change-over from one kind of dance to another took place at between 5 and 100 metres, differing between species of bee. In the tail-wagging dance distance is communicated by speed – the greater the distance the slower the dance. If the dance is performed on a

horizontal surface the axis of the dance points to the food. If, as is more usual, the dance takes place on a vertical surface, direction is indicated in a different way: if the food lies in a direction 45 degrees to the left of the sun, the axis of the dance lies 45 degrees to the left of the vertical, and so on. If the route to the food involves a detour, the direction given is the direct one. A similar though much more prolonged dance is given by scouts who have found a new site for the hive; they may dance for several days, changing direction with the orientation of the sun, until there is a consensus in the hive.

Later research has suggested that information about direction and distance is also contained in and may be transmitted by sound signals. More important is the possibility that the other bees do not make any use of information about distance and direction at all, but simply fly off to the known sites which have the same scent as that on the returning worker bee; they may then be helped by bee scent at the site. Experiments by Johnson (1967) and Wenner (1967) showed that inexperienced bees follow bee scent rather than the dance. Von Frisch, however, argues that their experiments were upset by the use of over-strong sugar solution which excited the bees and made them fly erratically, and he reports experiments in which bees distinguish a scented food-place from a scented place with no food. He also found that bees could follow the dance information over longer distances than those used by Johnson and Wenner, up to 4,400 metres. It does seem unlikely that this elaborate signalling system should have been developed if it is not used.

(b) *Alarm signals*. When enemies approach the territory the first animals to see them raise the alarm, in the case of primates by roaring, howling, or barking.

In some species of birds there are particular calls for particular kinds of predator, and these sometimes imitate the predator's call. The degree of danger may also be conveyed by the loudness of the call or its excitement. Response to such calls is innate – chickens keep quiet inside the egg when they hear the chicken warning call.

(c) *More elaborate signalling systems in animals.* A lot of interest has been aroused by recent attempts to teach chimpanzees symbolic communication. Gardner and Gardner (1969) taught a female chimpanzee, Washoe, to use about ninety signs from the American deaf and dumb language. Most of these signs are analogical, e.g. a tail-wagging sign means 'dog', but others are more arbitrary. Washoe was able to use combinations of two signs rather like a young child, but did not always get them in the right order; in most cases one of these words was one of twelve 'pivot words', like 'come gimme', 'please' etc. This suggests the use of a primitive syntax. We do not yet know whether syntaxes of animal behaviour are sequential, or require one of Chomsky's more complex grammatical models (see p. 374f). Premack (1970) taught another chimpanzee, Sarah, to use a smaller number of plastic shapes on a magnetized board. Here most of the signs were letters, or other arbitrary signs, standing for words. Sarah succeeded in learning to use more complicated sentences and concepts than Washoe, including the ideas of same and different, yes and no questions, and naming, and she could answer questions of different kinds.

While these experiments are of great interest, it is generally agreed that there are great differences between what Washoe and Sarah can do (so far) and human language.

We discuss later the theory that language had its origins in gesture (p. 256).

Different channels of communication

Taste and smell

Many animals have special glands which add scent to the

urine or excreta, or emit liquids or gases in other ways. The same species have receptors which are often extremely sensitive and able to detect these pheromones at very low concentrations. As a signalling system the use of pheromones has certain special properties.

(a) The signal persists over time, which is useful for marking a return route or a territory, but makes temporal patterning difficult. An animal can leave a signal after it has gone, or may use it itself; in these respects the use of pheromones is analogous to writing.

(b) Information is spread in all directions, slowly, and over a considerable distance; this is very valuable for certain species; the queen bee, for example, signals her continued survival by a secretion which circulates throughout the hive.

(c) Chemical signals contain rather little information; they are yes/no signals; little use is made of varying intensity, and they are not directional. Some species, however, have developed ways of adding to the information conveyed, for example by using several glands at once in different combinations, and changing the concentration.

A number of different signals can be sent in this way:

(1) Territories and trails can be marked.
(2) Repellent stimulants can lead to greater dispersal of members of the species.
(3) Other signals can lead to recruitment of more members of the group, for example among insects to co-operate over carrying a large food particle.
(4) Members of the group can be recognized, as can their sex, and sometimes their status.
(5) An alarm signal can be sent, as by some fish.
(6) Sexual availability is commonly signalled by smell, as by dogs.
(7) Information about food can be conveyed, as by bees.

These signals are nearly always discrete and stereotyped, rather than continuous.

Some species of primates use chemical communication. Lemurs have special scent organs, which are used to leave scent on trees, or to put scent on the tip of the tail, which is then waved in the face of another lemur. Chemical communication is used for sexual and aggressive purposes, for identification, in greetings, and for marking territory.

Tactile communication

This occurs in all animals and has certain special features.

(a) Many of the signals are not really signals at all, but basic social behaviour – for example aggressive, sexual, affiliative, and nurturant. Signals in other channels stand for or lead to tactile events. Tactile signals of various kinds are the most powerful means of establishing social relationships.

(b) This form of communication can only take place when animals are at very close quarters, so that other means of communication must be used before they change over to this channel.

(c) No specialized organs are needed either for transmission or reception.

(d) It is possible to send signals varying in intensity or rate to transmit quantitative information, as in the bees' dance.

The main form of tactile behaviour found in non-human primates is grooming, which is done mainly with the hands, helped by the teeth, tongue, and nose; it may be reciprocal. Aggressive bodily contacts are biting, striking and pulling fur. Presentation, mounting, and embracing occur not only between sexual partners, but in connexion with dominance and appeasement. Some kinds of monkeys, for example pigtail monkeys, spend a lot of time huddled together, with maximum bodily contact, and develop strong bonds with all the members of the group; they cling together particularly when frightened. Baboons, chimpanzees, and other non-huddling species use touch rather than bodily contact for reassurance and greeting. Greetings involve a wide variety of bodily contacts – genital and stomach muzzling, kissing, embracing, and grooming. All these bodily contacts may take a variety of forms depending on the social relationship between two animals; biting may be aggressive or playful, grooming may last for a longer or shorter time.

General visual communication

For most species of vertebrates, visual communication is the most important channel. All kinds of information can be communicated in this way, so there is no need to list the alternatives. Visual communication has a number of special properties, making it quite different from taste and smell.

(*a*) Very complex displays can be used, varying in pattern, colour, brightness, polarization, direction, and temporal pattern, though not all species can use all of these dimensions.

(*b*) Communication is immediate, and can cover a considerable distance, depending on the acuity of vision, and the power of the signals. It can be used to obtain immediate feedback on another animal's reactions.

(*c*) Visual signals can be switched on and off, and animals can control their signals to attract or avoid attention.

Visual signalling systems are adapted to the communication needs of a particular species in a particular environment. For example long-range signals are usually very stereotyped, and do not involve subtle discriminations. Highly graded signals are used at closer range. Infant monkeys have a distinctive appearance that elicits parental behaviour. Visual displays are minimized in species of birds most open to attack by predators. When two species use the same territory they may develop signals for spacing which can be received by both species.

Bodily appearance. The normal bodily appearance of an animal identifies its species, both to its own and to other species. It also communicates sex and age, and individuals can be recognized by other members of the group. Changes in bodily appearance signal information about an animal's internal state. Most female primates in oestrus can be readily identified by the highly visible blue swellings in the genitalia. A female may turn the coloured area towards a male, and this acts as a release for sexual activity. Some fish and birds can change their colour and size under the influence of temporary emotional states. Males in a state of sexual arousal display penile erection. In all states of emotional arousal, including sexual and aggressive, primates display other autonomic reactions – raised hair, dilated nostrils, sweating and panting, as well as postural and facial signals. Perspiration and other odours may be released at the same time.

Spatial behaviour. This varies between different species and environments. Infants cling to their mothers, and gradually venture to greater distances from her as they get older. Members of some species huddle together, especially when frightened. Some species, like langurs and baboons, have a 'personal space' like humans. Typical distances between two baboons of different classes vary: for example, two females sit closer than two males. Kummer (1968) interprets the spacing of baboons in terms of a balance of approach and avoidance forces – they keep to a certain degree of closeness as well as distance from one another. A more dominant male needs more space, and will only allow other animals to come to a certain distance. Approaching another animal can have different meanings depending on the other signals sent – it may be sexual, aggressive, or affiliative.

Michael Chance (in Chance and Jolly, 1970) maintains that the normal spatial arrangement in groups of primates is for the dominant males to be in the middle with their females near them and the others in concentric circles. Thelma Rowell (1972) argues that this happens only when food is provided, so that a circle is formed round the food. When a troop of monkeys is on the march the dominant males are near the front, mothers and infants are in the middle for protection, and other males take the rear to look after stragglers.

Facial expression. Unlike most lower animals, apes and monkeys have very expressive faces, and produce continual changes of expression with their changing moods and activities. These expressions are more definite than human expressions, they are not restrained, and there are a greater number of distinct expressions. Each species has about thirteen distinct expressions, and Jane van Lawick Goodall (1968) lists about twenty for chimpanzees. Facial expressions occur regularly in particular situations, from which their meaning can be deduced, and they are accompanied by characteristic vocalizations. Here are some of the facial expressions listed by Goodall:

TABLE 2.1. *Facial expression in primates* (from van Lawick Goodall, 1968)

Situation	Facial expression	Vocalization
relaxed situation in group	typical relaxed or alert face	soft grunt or groan
eating or approaching desirable food	mouth slightly opened at each sound; lips slightly retracted to show teeth	loud barking
social play	play face – mouth opened with teeth covered	'laughing' – soft panting sounds

TABLE 2.1.—contd

Situation	Facial expression	Vocalization
response to distant calls; when arriving in group	hoot face – lips pushed forward into trumpet	pant hoots and calls
prior to attack or copulation	glare	
when being attacked	mouth wide open, teeth exposed	screaming
mother cradles or retrieves infant	pout face – lips pursed and pushed forwards	hoot, whimper
when juveniles lose mothers	whimper face – like pout face but lips are withdrawn from teeth	whimpering
making submissive gestures after attack	grinning – lips parted and oblong expanse of closed teeth shown	squeak calls
conflict between aggression and restraint	yawning	

In addition to these changes of facial expression, individuals have quite distinctive faces, from which they can be identified.

Direction of gaze. This is not primarily a signal, but a means of receiving signals. However, the direction and manner of gaze reflect an animal's attitudes and hence become a social signal. Studying the gaze pattern in a group of monkeys can, as with spatial position, provide a key to the social structure. Mothers and their infants keep an eye on one another, as do mating males and females; when two animals have a close bond between them they look at each other, and keep close together. A direct stare is sent and received as a threat signal; looking away – 'cut-off' – is an appeasement, or submissive signal. Later we shall describe an experiment in which man communicated with monkey, using these signals. Michael Chance (1967) maintains that in many species there is an 'attention structure' whereby visual attention is directed to the dominant members of the group, so that subordinates can follow leaders, get out of their way, or desist from mating in response to a rapid approach movement. This mechanism, together with special vocalizations, enables members of the group to keep together in dense vegetation. Gaze also reveals direction of attention, or the particular animal to which other signals are directed. The significance of gaze depends on the facial expression that accompanies it – raised or lowered eyebrows, open or half-closed eyes, and so on.

Gestures. These are movements of the arm or other parts of the body which act as social signals. They may acquire meaning as intention movements – that is, by being the beginning of some larger sequence of behaviour – or via other mechanisms to be described later. Sometimes such gestures are made because an animal is too busy to do more, or because there are conflicting motivations. Thus an attack on another animal may be reduced to a gesture – hitting the ground for example – because the animal can't be bothered to do more than this. Sometimes they are used as apparently intentional social signals, as for example when an animal reassures another by touching it. Here are some of the more common gestures used by primates:

TABLE 2.2. *Gestures in primates*

Situation	Gesture
Threatening another animal	Fist shaking, stamping, slapping, banging, arm raising and waving, rocking
Conciliation, appeasement	Grooming invitation, touching, offering the hand, embracing

TABLE 2.2.—*contd*

Situation	Gesture
Sexual invitation, sub-mission	Presenting for copulation
Greeting	Bobbing, bowing, touching, kissing, grooming, presenting, mounting, hand-holding
Reassuring	Touching, patting, embracing, kissing

Posture. The way an animal sits or walks reflects its emotional state and social status. A high-status, confident animal sprawls in a relaxed position, and strides about in an up-right but relaxed manner. Animals lacking confidence are tense, sit with head drawn into shoulders and curled up, and walk cautiously. Some animals use the tail for communi-cation; confident baboons let their tails hang loosely, anxious baboons stick their tails up vertically. Other postures are used to invite grooming; the presenting position is the prelude to copulation. A gorilla leader may signal depar-ture by standing motionless and facing the direction to be taken (Rowell, 1972; see Figure 2.1).

Vocalization
This is used by many species of animals, and is the main channel for some birds, insects, and fish. For example a deafened turkey will kill her young since she takes them for predators on the evidence of vision alone. Sounds are produced in several different ways, by specialized organs, as in birds and porpoises, or in non-specialized ways as by insects which rub their legs together or gorillas who beat their chests. Sounds may be transmitted through air, water, through solids, or by direct contact. This channel of communication has several distinctive properties.

36 The biological & cultural background

Figure 2.1. Posture in monkeys (from Rowell, 1972: 88–91)

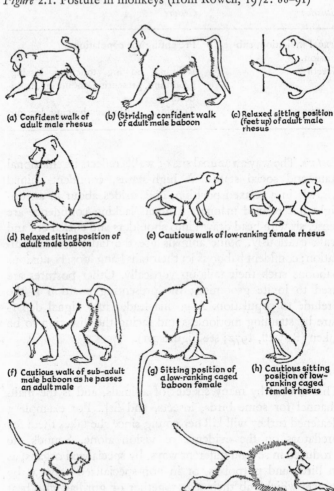

(a) Confident walk of adult male rhesus

(b) (Striding) confident walk of adult male baboon

(c) Relaxed sitting position (feet up) of adult male rhesus

(d) Relaxed sitting position of adult male baboon

(e) Cautious walk of low-ranking female rhesus

(f) Cautious walk of sub-adult male baboon as he passes an adult male

(g) Sitting position of a low-ranking caged baboon female

(h) Cautious sitting position of low-ranking caged female rhesus

(i) Adult female clutching infant

(j) Sub-adult male baboon chases and threatens another male

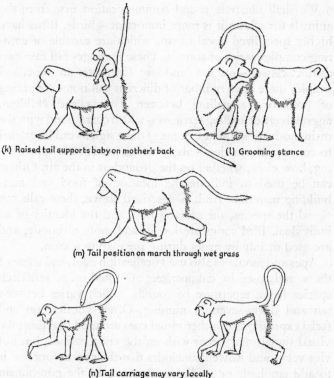

(k) Raised tail supports baby on mother's back

(l) Grooming stance

(m) Tail position on march through wet grass

(n) Tail carriage may vary locally

(a) Sounds are broadcast in all directions, they go round corners, through foliage, and reach animals whether they are listening or not. They can travel long distances, for example whales can communicate over distances of a hundred miles.

(b) High frequency sounds reveal clearly where they come from while low frequency sounds conceal it.

(c) Sounds fade rapidly, can be timed accurately, and so complex sequences may be sent.

(d) Sounds are heard by the sender, who can thus monitor the signals, for example when imitating another animal. Self-feedback is impossible with visual signals.

We shall illustrate sound communication first from the animals for whom it is more important – birds. Birds have highly specialized vocal organs which are capable of emitting complex series of sounds. These messages fall into two distinct classes – *call notes* and *song*. Call notes are short and simple; there are a number of different call notes – warning of predators, signalling between parents and children, aggressively defending territory – which correspond with the main motivational states. Some of these signals can be graded to convey information – about which predator is approaching, how close, whether on the ground or in the air. Others can be used to indicate the location of food and nest-building materials. And, as described above, these calls can signal the species, the social group, and the identity of an individual. Bird songs are longer and more elaborate, and are used mainly by males during the mating season.

Apes and monkeys also use vocalization a lot, and some of the sounds used by chimpanzees are listed on p. 32f. Each species has a repertoire of sounds, which varies between ten and thirty-seven in number. Often vocalization and facial expressions or other visual cues are used together; the visual signals may occur without the vocalizations, but not vice versa, and Rowell concludes that their main function is to add emphasis or to direct attention. In the non-human primates, as in man, most social behaviour makes simultaneous use of the visual and auditory channels; one of the main differences between these channels is that the visual depends on gaze direction, while vocalizations can be heard by anyone within range. In man the visual cues are normally subsidiary to the auditory ones while in apes and monkeys the reverse is the case. Non-human primates use a second type of vocalization, without gestures, when vegetation cuts off visual contact. These include infant-lost calls, contact calls within and between groups, and alarm calls. Some provide evidence of location, while others conceal it. They also signal the species and identity of the caller.

The origins of animal NVC

(1) *Evolution and inheritance*

The entire behaviour pattern of insects and other simple creatures is innate and is not dependent on environmental experiences. In animals higher in the evolutionary scale learning is progressively more important, though there is still a genetic basis. For example the call notes of many birds appear when infants are fostered from the egg by birds of another species. The cuckoo is a familiar case, but the same has been found with doves and canaries.

Animals have communication systems which clearly 'work' in their particular environment. Bees have means of letting the other bees know where the flowers are. Some birds and primates give warning calls about predators in a low register, since this conceals the position of the caller; birds who gave warning in a high note would be devoured by predators, so that the low call gene is favoured at the expense of the high call gene.

But how do certain signals come to be encoded in a particular way, and how do the recipients know what they mean? An answer can be given for the simpler forms of animal communication.

(*a*) *Intention movements.* These are part of a total pattern of behaviour, and the part comes to stand for the whole. A bird may spread its wings as a signal that it is about to depart. Bared teeth, indicating preparations to bite, become a threat display. Intention movements are perceived as standing for the whole since the rest of the pattern would be expected to follow. These signals are *iconic* or *analogical*, i.e. the signal is part of or is similar to what is referred to.

(*b*) *Displacement activities.* Animals are often in a condition of conflict and frustration – fear of a dominant animal keeps them away from the food, or else they can't jump far enough to get it. They then often engage in behaviour which appears to be irrelevant to the main drives operating. For example birds in an approach/avoidance conflict, motivated both to approach another bird and to fly away, fly backwards and forwards; when the conflict is high they engage in preening. Cleaning feathers or beak, drinking or eating, commonly occur in these conditions. The explanation is not agreed; it may be that when conflict inhibits the appearance of major patterns of motor behaviour, less important ones, hitherto inhibited, are allowed to appear; or it may be that a general state of arousal is produced which elicits irrelevant as well as relevant behaviour. If certain displacement activities regularly occur in some situation they can come to act as social signals. Goodall reports that chimpanzees when frustrated may scratch, yawn, groom, masturbate, rock, shake branches, slap and stamp, throw temper tantrums, or re-direct their aggression elsewhere. These different acts occur in different contexts: they groom when waiting for food, scratch when worried by the presence of a high-ranking animal. If they are used as signals they are *arbitrary*, in contrast to analogical, signals, since there is no similarity between signal and referent.

(*c*) *Autonomic displays*. Hair-erection, panting and sweating, and other bodily changes which result from heat-regulation or other autonomic activity, can be perceived by other animals and thus function as social signals.

(*d*) *Ritualization*. Once an act has acquired meaning in one of these ways, it may undergo evolutionary changes which make it more effective as a signal. These changes are known as ritualization. A signal varying in intensity may break up into a number of discrete signals – each with a precise meaning. This is found with the different degrees of threat used by primates – intermediate intensities are rarely used, and the typical intensities vary between species. Ritualization may make a signal more conspicuous, like the peacock's feathers used in courtship. Primates use ritualization rather little, since they have a complex social network, and most signals do not carry constant meanings but depend on relationships. However there are some examples of ritualized signals with precise, standard meanings. In baboons lip-smacking is derived from sucking, but has become a signal for concilia-tion or appeasement.

Ritualization leads to the development of *discrete*, digital stereotyped social signals, such as bird calls. These may be contrasted with signals which vary *continuously* along some dimension such as speed and loudness in a bird's warning call. Altmann (1967) has shown how analogical signals must always be continuous, since otherwise there could be large errors in communication.

We can illustrate the evolutionary origins of human signals from the development of some of the signals used by primates. The evolutionary history of a signal can be traced by studying the corresponding signals in closely related species, where the signals are thought to be earlier evolu-tionary forms. Van Hooff (1972) has traced the evolutionary origins of human smiling and laughing in this way. In primitive mammals one of the oldest facial expressions is the *bared-teeth scream* display: it is a defensive intention move-ment based on both biting and protective responses, and the animal may spit or hiss. In macaques and other monkeys the corresponding display is *the silent bared-teeth face*: this is a grin with the teeth fully exposed, and it is used by subordin-ate animals as an appeasement signal. In three lines of higher primates, chimpanzees, mandrills, and man, this signal changes its meaning and is used mainly as an affiliative and reassuring signal. Van Hooff suggests that this is the origin of the human smile. The origins of laughing are quite different. Many primates show the *play-face* or *relaxed open-mouth* display during social play. It is probably a ritualized intention movement based on gnawing which often occurs during mock-fighting in social play. Chimpanzees accompany the play-face with soft panting sounds or grunts, which may be parallel to the sounds of human laughter.

The evolutionary origin of vocalizations is more difficult to discover. Andrew (1963) has suggested that they are mainly a concomitant of facial expressions, combined with exhalation of air. For example most species of mammals have a pattern of responses designed to protect the sense organs in the face of sudden, frightening stimuli; the throat is constricted, air is expelled, making a loud noise, which later develops into an alarm call. This in turn divides for some birds and some primates into a series of sharp high-pitched calls which bring others to the spot to help with an intruder, and a short, low moan, which is difficult to localize, and gives warning of more dangerous predators. In species of monkeys which make high-pitched alarm calls, the more frightened it is, the further back it pulls the corners of its mouth, producing a more high-pitched scream. Another facial expression is the snarl, with bared teeth, an intention movement for attack, which becomes a threat signal; the sounds emitted with this kind of face are quite different, and themselves become threat signals.

When the signalling system used and the pattern of social life become more complex in the course of evolution, it is necessary for parallel developments to take place in the perception and recognition of signals. Greater sensitivity is required for rapid signals varying along several dimensions, and innate recognition of the actual repertoire of signals is needed. It is more difficult to learn the meaning of arbitrary than of analogical signals, so it is more important for these to be innate.

Analogical signals can be learnt more easily, at least by those animals that are capable of learning; nevertheless these are innately recognized for presumably there is natural selection for the ability to identify signals correctly, just as there is natural selection for suitable signals.

(2) *Learning*

Some animal signals are produced without environmental experience at all. This is true of the calls of some birds, and of other stereotyped and species-specific signals. However, there may be learning about which individuals the signals should be sent to, and in the correct recognition of these signals when emitted by others. W. H. Thorpe (1972) found that the chaffinch needed to hear itself singing, among other sounds, before its song stabilized, but it does not need to hear the adult song, so this is not a matter of imitation. The chaffinch's song is completely stabilized after the first breeding season. In some other finches the dialect of the local group is also acquired by imitation. Other species acquire the overall song pattern by imitation. This illustrates the whole range, from complete dependence of a signal on innate factors to complete dependence on environmental learning.

Where signals can be learned, it is possible for a tradition to be built up and passed on within a particular group. The development of a dialect for groups of birds is an example of this.

Meaning and syntax

Encoded meaning

Signals have meaning for the communicator through the fixed relationship between the signal and what it stands for. The encoded meaning for animals can be established by research into the relationship between some measurable aspect of the animal's state or situation, and the signals. When a bird signals the approach of a predator by imitating its call, this imitation stands for, 'means', the predator. When a bee indicates the location of the flowers, the speed of the dance stands for, means, the distance of the flowers. In both of these cases the signal refers to events in the outside world. Emotional displays on the other hand stand for the inner physiological state of the animal, and are indeed part of the state for which they stand. They can be said to refer to the full pattern of behaviour which might follow, as bared teeth stand for a bite, though the bite will only follow under certain conditions. Animal signals can also send information about the identity and spatial position of the animal, for instance as it does when a bird-song characterizes a species of bird; in this case the signal is related to the referent in yet another way.

Though most animal NVC has analogical meaning, based on intention movements, there are also arbitrary signals, derived from displacement activities and ritualization. Analogical signals are continuous, while arbitrary signals are usually discrete and digital. The meaning of a signal for the communicator is not always the same as its meaning for the recipient, for various reasons to which we now turn.

Decoded meaning

A signal can contain various kinds of information of use to a recipient, both about the specific position and future behaviour of the sender, about third parties such as predators, and about the location of food or other features of the world outside them. The decoded meaning for animals is established by studying the regular effect of a signal on the behaviour of the recipient, for example confining its behaviour to a smaller range of possible responses. It is possible to measure the amount of information encoded and decoded in a signal (in the information theory sense, in which one 'bit' of information represents a choice out of two alternatives). It has been estimated that the bees' dance contains about five bits, of which about half is actually received. However, the same message may be interpreted differently, and hence have different meanings, depending on the environmental setting and the identity of the recipient.

The message of the chaffinch's song can be said to contain

the information: 'I am the species *Fringilla coelebs*; I am owner of a territory; I am individual PDP8; I am in this particular part of my territory; I have no wife around.' An unmated female chaffinch may be attracted by such an announcement, an unmated male searching for a territory to occupy will keep away, a familiar neighbour may pay little attention or counter-sing, unless the other bird's song post were outside its recognized area, when it might evoke closer inspection. A young male chaffinch in its first spring on a newfound territory might repeat the song, adding it to his repertoire (Cullen, 1972). Indeed different dimensions of the same signal can evoke different responses from different recipients – while a bee may respond to the angle of dance, human beings may respond to the buzzing noise and thus avoid getting stung.

The function of a signal for the sender may be rather different from its meaning to a recipient – though the two evolve together as part of a total system of useful communication. An alarm signal has the biological function for the sender of protecting his descendants and other members of his group. The function of receiving the alarm signal is the more direct one of self-survival.

Syntactic structures

Human language has a three level structure: the lowest level consists of meaningless sounds or *phonemes*; these are combined, two or more at a time to form *morphemes* (the basic stems of words), which are combined in turn in sentences. Animal communication, however, appears to consist of meaningful elements – the alarm call, the yawn, and so on. It would be possible to break down such signals into smaller components themselves meaningless, since behaviour has a hierarchical structure, but they do not seem to consist of a limited class of basic elements as is the case with human language.

Animals use signals in combination either sequentially or

simultaneously. For example bees signal direction plus distance plus the nature of the scent. In most cases, however, the order of the signal is unimportant, so that there is no equivalent to grammar. However, there are some animal signals where the order does matter. The most obvious is bird-song, where the message consists of a definite tune, whose notes and phrases must be in the right order. Bird-songs are in fact more complex than they need to be for the information they appear to send; the reason for this is not yet known. Perhaps these signals say more than we think.

Another example of signals acting in combination is meta-communication: when a primate signals a playface, all accompanying signals carry a different meaning. A combination of different items of information is also involved when an animal interprets a signal by taking account of the perceived situation. John Smith (1969) has drawn attention to the fact that more messages can be sent than there are available signals. For example the herring gull's wheezing call is used (1) by young begging for food, (2) by young who have found a food source and want help in displacing the owner, (3) by adults before copulation.

Altmann (1967) has studied the sequences of social acts used by rhesus monkeys, and found that there are certain regular sequences, and others that never occur. Thus there are limitations on the sequential signals that can be sent. He also found that an animal's behaviour could be predicted better by taking account of up to four previous acts; probably the same is true of the reaction of others to it.

To what extent do these systems of animal communication resemble human language? Hockett (1960) has drawn up a list of sixteen 'design features', of which language possesses all, and different animal systems some. It includes, for instance, arbitrariness of symbols, ability to refer to objects distant in time and space, or to talk about the system itself. With this approach it follows that 'linguicity' is a matter of degree. Chomsky (1968) does not share this view: he considers that language has a complex grammatical structure, requiring innate neural structures, and that it is totally different from any animal communication. Nevertheless we have to recognize that animal communication has a certain degree of complexity, and that some cases appear to use a simple syntax. What we can learn from the bees and chimpanzees is that animal non-verbal communication can make some use of arbitrary signals, can refer to objects which are absent in time and space, and that simple combinations of two or three signals can be used.

Intentionality and direction of communication

Signals may be intended to communicate, as when one person speaks to another, or may convey information without intention, as when others overhear the conversation, or when one person observes the emotional state or the identity of another. Behavioural evidence that an animal intends to communicate with another comes from observed prevarication, and from the directing of the signal at another. Lorenz (1952) gives an example of an attempt at deception.

> 'I had just opened the yard gate, and before I had time to shut it the dog rushed up barking loudly. Upon recognising me, he hesitated in a moment of acute embarrassment, then pushing past my leg he raced through the open gates and across the lane where he continued to bark furiously at our neighbour's gate just as though he had been addressing an enemy in that garden from the very beginning.'

Signals can be directed in several ways; in primates the commonest is to face towards and look at the animal addressed. Subordinates avoid gaze to avoid interaction. Primates learn to direct signals, such as aggressive yawning, accurately at others. When a female presents to a male, she still looks round and directs her gaze at him (Pl. 8). Primates may communicate, in more than one direction as

48 The biological & cultural background

when a female presents to a male and threatens other females simultaneously.

Further reading

ALTMANN, s. a. (ed.) *Social Communication among Primates.* Chicago: University of Chicago Press, 1967.

HINDE, R. (ed.) *Non-verbal Communication.* Cambridge: Royal Society and Cambridge University Press, 1972.

SEBEOK, T. A. (ed.) *Animal Communication.* Bloomington: Indiana University Press, 1968.

References

ANDREW, R. J. (1963) The origin and evolution of the calls and facial expressions of the primates. *Behaviour* **20**: 1–109.

CHANCE, M. R. A. (1967) Attention structure as a basis of primate rank orders. *Man* **2**: 503–18.

CHANCE, M. R. A. and JOLLY, C. J. (1970) *Social Groups of Monkeys, Apes and Men.* London: Cape.

CHOMSKY, N. (1968) *Language and Mind.* New York: Harcourt, Brace.

CULLEN, M. (1972) Some principles of animal communication. In R. Hinde (ed.) *Non-verbal Communication.* Cambridge: Royal Society and Cambridge University Press.

GARDNER, R. A. and GARDNER, B. T. (1969) In A. Schrier and F. Stollnitz (eds.) *Behavior of Non-human Primates* Vol. 3. New York: Academic Press.

HOCKETT, C. F. (1960) Logical considerations in the study of animal communication. In W. E. Lanyon and W. N. Tavolga (eds.) *Animal Sounds and Communication.* American Institute of Biological Sciences: Washington, D.C.

GOODALL, J. VAN LAWICK (1968) The behaviour of free-living chimpanzees in the Gomb stream reserve. *Animal Behaviour Monographs* **1**: 161–311.

JOHNSON, D. L. (1967) Communication among honey bees with field experience. *Animal Behaviour* **15**: 487–92.

KUMMER, H. (1968) *Social Organisation of Hamadryas Baboons.* Basel: Karger.

LACK, D. (1939) The behaviour of the robin. *Proceedings of the Zoological Society of London* **109**: 169–78.

LORENZ, K. (1952) *King Solomon's Ring.* London: Methuen.

PREMACK, D. (1970) A functional analysis of language. *Journal of the Experimental Analysis of Behaviour* **14**: 107–25.

ROWELL, T. (1972) *The Social Behaviour of Monkeys.* Harmondsworth: Penguin Books.

SMITH, W. J. (1969) Messages of vertebrate communication. *Science* **165**: 145–50.

THORPE, W. H. (1972) Vocal communication in birds. In R. Hinde (ed.) *Non verbal Communication.* Cambridge: Royal Society and Cambridge University Press.

TINBERGEN, N. (1951) *The Study of Instinct.* London: Oxford University Press.

VAN HOOFF, J. A. R. A. M. (1972) A comparative approach to the phylogeny of laughter and smiling. In R. Hinde (ed.) *Non-Verbal Communication.* Cambridge: Royal Society and Cambridge University Press.

VON FRISCH, K. (1967) *The Dance Language and the Orientation of Bees.* Cambridge, Mass.: Harvard University Press.

WENNER A. M., WELLS P. H., and ROHLF, F. J. (1967). An analysis of recruitment in honey bees. *Physiological Zoology* **30** (4): 317–4.

3

Bodily communication in human society

Human non-verbal communication is similar at many points to animal communication, but it is also different in a number of ways. The most important difference is that humans use language to communicate. However, as we shall see, language is closely linked with, and supported by, bodily communication, which adds to the meaning of utterances, provides feedback, and controls synchronization (see Chapter 8). This means that there is often a choice of verbal or non-verbal methods of communicating, and it raises the question of why NVC should be used at all, since language has a larger vocabulary and can convey more complex messages. This crucial question will receive a number of different answers as we consider different kinds of NVC in Part II. It is also possible to send inconsistent messages, where the non-verbal contradicts the verbal component.

Unlike most animal signals, much human communication is learnt, though in certain spheres there are strong innate components – notably in the expression of emotions and interpersonal attitudes. While some human communication is spontaneous, and governed by lower levels of the central nervous system, some is more reflective, and dependent on higher cognitive processes. There is no hard and fast line between these two, and often more than one level is involved, as in the case of a partly controlled emotional expression.

Since signals and their meaning can be learnt, it is easy for human groups and cultures to develop their own sets of signals. These may consist of local variations on universal themes, as in the ways like or dislike are expressed. In the next chapter we will examine the extent of cultural variations in NVC, and also the extent to which there are universal components of human NVC. Human groups can develop quite new social signals, such as those used in games and work. These depend for their meaning on ideas, mostly verbalized ideas, and the signals are meaningful in the context of the goals, rules, and concepts of the game.

Bodily expression is also used in ceremonies and rituals, at political meetings and demonstrations, and in the arts. Symbolic expression is given to ideas and feelings which cannot be so effectively expressed in words.

NVC is partly governed by the higher cognitive centres, and it is influenced by language and ideas. Is it itself a kind of language, with similar properties of meaning and syntax? We shall see that different kinds of NVC operate somewhat differently, and their structures will be examined in Part II. Meanwhile we may note that NVC is used in human society in the following different ways:

supporting language
replacing language
expressing emotions
expressing interpersonal attitudes
conveying information about the person
in ceremony and ritual
in propaganda, at political meetings and demonstrations
in the arts

To study different aspects of human NVC a variety of research methods are needed, some of them not previously used in other fields of research. In this chapter we shall describe studies using the method of rule-breaking, which is a way of studying rule-systems. In the next we will describe cross-cultural and inter-cultural studies of bodily communication. Research on meaning has used a number of different methods, related to the assumptions of different investigators.

Social acts

A number of sociologists have distinguished between human social behaviour and other events in the natural world. Human social acts, it is said, are initiated and planned with certain goals in mind; the performance is subject to self-direction, follows rules, and is meaningful to the performer in that he can give a verbal account justifying it, or may try to make an anticipated account come true. Furthermore, many social acts, verbal and non-verbal, have a symbolic character, which makes them different from nearly all animal behaviour. NV acts, like verbal ones, communicate quite differently from sheer physical signals. For example, the *absence* of a NV act, for example, a refusal to shake hands, may constitute an extremely important social act. Small differences in the physical acts performed e.g. small differences in the direction of gaze, can produce very big differences in their meaning. In this respect NV signals are similar to verbal ones, where a change in one letter can totally alter meaning. Furthermore, the same physical act can have a quite different meaning in different cultures, just as a word can. Putting these two points together, doing nothing in the same situation may have a quite different significance in two different cultures.

Somewhat similar views are expressed by 'existential' or 'humanistic' psychologists who reject the reductionist analysis of other psychologists and treat persons as a whole with emphasis on subjective experiences of identity, commitment to values, freedom, creativity, and love. Both ethnomethodologists and humanistic psychologists set themselves up in opposition to those psychologists who favour mechanistic, behaviourist research. A distinction is sometimes drawn between the 'old paradigm' of S-R experimentation and Skinnerian theory, and the 'new paradigm' of collecting accounts from performers in real-life situations. It is further suggested that there may be two quite different processes at work – the biological and the symbolic. Rom Harré (in a lecture given at Oxford in 1972) observed that when two people get married the process involved is one of symbolic social acts, as described above; when the same couple become parents the process involved is a quite different, biological one. However, it is hard to see how there could be two quite different processes in this way, since there seems to be a continuity of different levels of human behaviour, and since there is no hard-and-fast line between human and animal behaviour.

However, recent psychological models of human social behaviour do justice to the nature of social action without postulating two different processes, and without making it necessary to abandon normal scientific research procedures. The author's 'social skill' model for example (1972), pictures social behaviour as (1) a hierarchical system, in which the lower-level elements are automatic and habitual, while the higher-level sequences are under cognitive control; and (2) planned, and subject to continuous monitoring, or corrective action, in the light of feed-back. People can give verbal accounts of their plans, but not of the smaller elements of which the plans consist. Stimulus-response models have been abandoned by the majority of psychologists as a result of the discovery of the importance of cognitive processes of perceiving and categorizing, problem-solving and thinking; some behaviour is accomplished by verbalized mediation, other behaviour by non-verbal cognitive processes.

An important event in this story was Chomsky's (1957) demonstration that the sequence of words in a sentence could not be explained as a series of S-R links. However, language is a product of two different kinds of process – it is partly the product of competence in constructing grammatically correct combinations of words, partly a product of associations between words and meanings, and between different words, according to blind statistical laws of learning. Here too there is a higher level of meaningful sentences and a lower level at which meaningless sounds are generated at high speed and without conscious attention.

Interaction between two or more people also takes place at different levels. It consists partly of the exchange of meaningful utterances, and of carefully planned reciprocity of behaviour. At a less reflective level one person may influence another by reinforcing his behaviour by small smiles and head-nods, of which both parties are normally completely unaware. Speech is synchronized by a series of small nods, gaze-shifts, and grunts, which often function outside the region of conscious control (see p. 165f).

The analysis of social acts given earlier supposes that social behaviour is all a matter of deliberate communication. However, this is simply not the case, as the account of NVC given in later chapters makes clear. An actor may communicate deliberately, or quite unintentionally. Communication may be unintentional because it is habitual, below the level of conscious attention and control, as is the case with the NV accompaniments of speech. It may be unintentional because the agent is primarily concerned with something else; for example, a member of a working group may work very fast, and this may constitute an important signal to other members of the group, although not intended as such. There may be unintentional 'leakage' of emotional states (p. 111). There is no sharp division between the behaviour that is intentional and that which is not – intentionality is a matter of degree. Newly learnt patterns of behaviour are often carefully planned, but become habitual, 'spontaneous' and unintentional when they are well-practised.

The same social act may be produced spontaneously or with conscious planning and monitoring. Vernon Allen (in a lecture at Oxford) reports that if children are asked to give the impression of 'understanding' or 'not understanding' in class, this is rather different from the real thing. Perhaps if they were more experienced or were better actors the difference would be less, but there is still a difference of process, in that the performance is the focus of the performer's attention in one case, but not in the other. Does this invalidate the social act approach, or Goffman's (1956) model of social behaviour as a dramatic performance? These approaches suggest in effect that spontaneous behaviour operates in a similar way to staged behaviour, and our social skills analysis takes a similar position: there is communication directed towards others, and there is continuous use of feedback and corrective action in both cases. The main objection to the social behaviour as drama model is that first, the parts are only partly scripted beforehand, and have to be made up as one goes along, and secondly, the part the actor is playing is his own personality, not that of another.

There are certain aspects of social behaviour, however, which fit the 'social act' approach rather well. We discuss 'self-presentation' in Chapter 7: it appears to be necessary for both animals and humans to signal their identity to other people, for them to communicate enough information about themselves for others to be able to respond to them appropriately. Such information consists of symbolic information indicating to which of various categories of person they belong. Presumably such self-presentation in birds is not a product of deliberate and reflective cognitive processes, and probably in many human beings it is not. However, self-presentation often involves quite careful planning, and a certain amount of deception. When this behaviour has been performed over a period of time it becomes spontaneous and unreflective.

It is also necessary for interactors to send enough information about the purpose of their behaviour to make it intelligible to possible onlookers; Goffman (1971) has called this 'body-gloss'. People are evidently aware of what their behaviour looks like to others, and they send additional NV signals to show that it has some acceptable and sensible purpose, or occasionally to communicate a misleading meaning, as in various kinds of deceptive behaviour. In these latter cases there is much more conscious awareness than in relaxed, and spontaneous behaviour.

The meaning of NVC

NV signals are bodily movements, which can be analysed in purely physical terms. However, their importance is in their meaning to the sender and the receiver. For example hissing is the noise made by blowing air out of the mouth in a certain way, a noise that can also be made mechanically by pumping air through a small metal pipe. When a human being makes this noise he usually does it to communicate, but the meaning of the noise is different in different parts of the world. In Japan it may be used to show respect for superiors, in England it signals contempt. Communication of all kinds can be looked at in terms of a sender who encodes and a receiver who decodes, so that the signal has a meaning for each of them.

It is possible to use a much simpler analysis – that stimuli from the sender evoke responses in the receiver, but the slightly more complicated model opens the way to two separate kinds of research into NVC – studies of encoding and of decoding. We can still speak of encoding whether the sender intends to communicate or not. Decoding may be quite a complex affair since most NVC is difficult to interpret: a person walks out of a lecture half-way through, someone else bursts into tears – it may require further social interaction, and perhaps verbal communication to make the meaning clear. It is usual to think primarily in terms of verbal meanings, e.g. to think of a frowning face with bared teeth as 'hostile'. The verbal aspects of meaning may be studied by open-ended interview, or by asking subjects to write free descriptions of NV signals: this has the advantage that the most 'salient' features of the signal can be located, i.e. the dimensions of meaning which are most important to the subject.

When the relevant dimensions of meaning are known, subjects can be asked to rate signals along a suitable series of seven-point scales, such as:

friendly	— — — — — — — hostile
inferior	— — — — — — — superior
appropriate	— — — — — — — inappropriate

While people can often provide such verbal labels for non-verbal signals, this is not the way in which they are normally handled. We react to a facial expression or tone of voice without giving it a name, just as a car driver can follow the direction of the road without verbalizations. There are three stages of response:

NV signal	(1) perception	(2) physiological reactions of various kinds; subjective feelings and images	(3) response preparation

Verbal labelling at (1) does not exhaust the way signals are received. One way of assessing the non-verbal meaning is to ask people to group stimuli. For example, the triad method consists of asking which two of three stimuli are most similar. Larger numbers of stimuli can be sorted or ordered and the results analysed to show the dimensions of meaning. Peter Stringer (1967) carried out a cluster analysis of facial expressions: subjects were asked to group together the expressions which looked most similar. The subjects can then be asked to name the groupings or dimensions which they are using: this takes further time and thought, showing that the original sorting was not based on verbal categories. So the perceptual coding at this stage may be wholly or partly non-verbal.

At stage (2) there may be verbal associations, but there are also visual images, expectations, and bodily responses of a mainly non-verbal kind. Stage (3) may involve verbal planning, but more often does not. Some signals evoke a behavioural response but seem to have little phenomenal meaning – as in the case of small head-nods and other signals supporting speech.

Another approach to the meaning of a social act or signal is to infer it from the antecedents and consequences, as is done for animal behaviour. One animal is frightened by seeing a predator and makes a cry which has the effect of warning other members of the group. Much human NVC is like this – for example a head nod has the behavioural consequence of permitting another person to carry on talking, but neither party may be aware of the head-nod. Murray Melbin (1972) extended this approach in a study of interaction between mental nurses and patients. For example 'banters' (by a nurse) occurred in five kinds of situations, mostly difficult behaviour on the part of patients; the main alternative in these situations was to stop the patient doing what he was doing. Melbin deduces that the meaning of banters is 'between the poles of suppression, forbearance, and the direct management of a challenging situation'. It is important to know what the main alternatives are, and their frequencies. Thus not to shake hands when 99 per cent of others do has a different meaning from not shaking hands when no one else did so. Zero reactions can be highly meaningful.

Structuralists in linguistics emphasize that the meaning of

a word depends on the other words in the language. For example, in English there are 'mat', 'rug', and 'carpet', while in French there are *'tapis'*, *'paillasson'*, and *'carpette'*, and none of the the French words correspond to the English ones (Lyons, 1973). Similarly in the non-verbal sphere, the meaning of a signal depends on the range of alternative signals commonly used by a particular person, or in a particular situation or culture. However, as Lyons points out, there is a common core of meaning, corresponding to the grouping of objects in the outside world. Similarly there are certain universals in the non-verbal sphere – the seven basic facial expressions for example.

Psychologists analyse the meaning of signals in terms of the words and images evoked by them. Students of semiotics, however, point out that signs have two kinds of meanings – denotation and connotation. They denote a class of objects or events; they connote the abstract set of ideas which defines this class; connotation depends on the linkage of this sign with other signs in the communication system. Thus a gesture illustrating a large fish both represents the class of large fish and connotes this particular kind of beast. Connotation involves linkages with other concepts – small fish, large animals etc., both between verbalized concepts and between images of these classes. Connotation often deals in terms of opposition (large *v.* small) and of hierarchies of classes (fish as part of the animal kingdom). Some bodily signals have meanings as parts of elaborate sign systems. Kenneth Pike (1957) has made the point that one could not understand what is going on at a religious service, a baseball game, a fishing expedition, or a scientific experiment unless one understood the ideas and plans in the minds of the participants, together with the whole set of concepts and rules connected with the religious service or baseball game.

The meaning of NV signals varies with the particular social setting within a culture. The significance of touching another person is different if that person is (*a*) one's wife,

60 The biological & cultural background

(*b*) someone else's wife, (*c*) a complete stranger, (*d*) a patient, (*e*) another person in a crowded lift, (*f*) another member of an encounter group, and so on. The meaning of a NV signal depends also on its position in time and its relation to other signals. A slap on the back might be received as hearty congratulations or as a physical assault, depending on what has taken place beforehand. The signals made during a meal, to ask someone to pass something, to indicate that one would or would not like more food, that one likes the food, that one has had enough, etc., would be meaningless and unintelligible without reference to the setting.

Ray Birdwhistell (1970) maintains that bodily signals have little or no meaning in themselves but acquire meanings in particular contexts (p. 251f). In the case of simple gestures, like raising the hand, this is true. However, there are several kinds of NV signals which do have fairly constant meanings – facial expressions for emotion, illustrative gestures and pointing, for example. The meaning of a NV signal may be different for different persons present. P smiles; another person may think that P likes him, or that P is in a good mood, or that P is a happy and well-adjusted person, or that P is a machiavellian personality who wants to get something out of him, and so on. The label which is given to a particular physical act depends on the culture, the situation, and the observer.

Later in this book we shall discuss kinds of NVC whose meaning is more complex than the cases discussed so far. Religious ritual is a case in point (p. 180f). These rituals arouse a number of images, for example red gum is associated with menstrual blood in one ritual we shall discuss. However, anthropologists maintain that rituals have a further meaning, symbolizing the unity of the tribe by the use of symbols which represent the tribe as a whole, such as flags and totems.

Art and music also consist of NVC; art and music have a primarily non-verbal meaning and cannot be translated into words. Many experiments have been done on reactions to art and music, and they are found to have several kinds of non-verbal meaning – arousing visual images, arousing and representing emotions, producing bodily movements, representing objects and events, and communicating deeper attitudes, emotions and attitudes to life (p. 384f).

The rules of NVC

It is becoming generally accepted that while certain aspects of human behaviour follow biological laws, other aspects are *rule governed*. We saw above that when two people get married the social behaviour involved follows rules. If a person didn't do the right thing at a wedding he would probably admit that he had made a mistake, or others would draw attention to his failure to follow the rules. Some jokes consist of breaking a rule, and their point is derived from the existence of the rule, everyone being aware of what should happen, although it did not happen. Rules are not the same as statistical norms, they are shared ideas about what ought to happen.

In the case of language, it is clear that if the rules of grammar are broken beyond a certain point there is a failure to communicate – though with lesser grammatical failures more or less successful communication does take place. It would be impossible to understand language simply by studying the statistical regularities in the words used. The underlying structure must be discovered. This consists of a limited vocabulary of words, falling into certain grammatical classes, combined in ways prescribed by the rules of grammar. Behind the imperfections of actual utterances there is a simple, ideal grammatical structure, which is capable of generating all proper sentences in the language. This underlying structure cannot be found from the statistical analysis of actual speech, but by inference from idealized speech samples, and by seeing if the rules found generate acceptable sentences. This distinction between the language system and actual speech, between *langue* and *parole*, competence and performance, is basic to modern linguistics.

Similar considerations apply to games. Unless players agree to keep to a set of rules there can be no game at all; in many games it is necessary to have an umpire or referee to see that the rules are kept. However, a Martian social scientist who studied cricket would not get very far simply by studying statistical tendencies. He would have to discover the rules of the game, to master the basic units of behaviour like *ball*, *over*, *innings*, and a number of key concepts (such as *no-ball*, *declare*, *out*).

What we are really interested in are the rules governing NVC in different social situations. Some of these rules are obvious, and could be stated by any member of the culture, for example, that men should wear trousers and should not wear hats indoors. Others are less obvious, but are written down in books of etiquette – that is, they are codified and verbalized by arbiters of proper social behaviour. One example is the rule that ladies should normally go first through doors; certain exceptions are allowed, for example when entering a restaurant where a table has to be secured. Similar rules operate outside the usual sphere of etiquette books: Goffman (1963) observes that kissing a wife goodbye at a bus-stop is normally done quite differently from kissing her goodbye at an ocean terminal. The number of different situations, each with its set of rules, is considerable; according to Barker and Wright (1954) there are about 800 public situations each with its distinctive rules in a small town in Kansas. There are rules about the following situations, and many others: playing games of different kinds, attending ceremonies like church services, lectures, and other educational meetings, going into shops, offices, and similar places, eating meals in various settings, entertaining and being entertained, attending committees, various work settings, being at home with the family, behaviour in the streets and other public places, and so on.

The trouble with some of these rules is that they are not all taken very seriously. As Marvin Harris (1968:590) observes:

'. . . it would conjure up a way of life in which men tip their hats to ladies; youths defer to old people in public conveyances; unwed mothers are a rarity; citizens go to the aid of law enforcement officers; chewing gum is never stuck under tables and never dropped on the sidewalk; television repairmen fix television sets; children respect their aged parents; rich and poor get the same medical treatment; taxes are paid in full; all men are created equal; and our defense budget is used for maintaining peace.'

If rules cannot be discovered by observing behaviour, how can they be studied? There are several methods of studying rules, but all of them involve some extension of traditional research methods. (*a*) The most important method is the deliberate breaking of possible rules, to see what effect this has. Garfinkel (1963) was the first person to do this: students behaved towards their parents as if they were lodgers, or made wrong moves at games such as placing a o at noughts and crosses on a line instead of in a square (Fig. 3.1). I have used a more experimentally controlled version of this method, carefully breaking rules by degrees (see p. 64). (*b*) Sometimes it is possible to gain access to the rule book.

Figure 3.1.

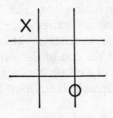

Obviously this can be done for actual games, but in real life there usually are no such books. Goffman (1963) studied etiquette books, but it can be objected that people often do not know or carry out the prescriptions of etiquette books. (c) Another method is studying the socially mobile. Garfinkel studied Agnes, a young lady who changed her sex, and became suddenly aware of the different rules followed by males and females. It would be perfectly easy to study less exotic cases of mobility, for example, between social classes or cultures. (d) However, the most widely used method has been patient observation of behaviour to discover the main units of performance, and regularities in their use, in particular situations. In a study of greetings for example, Harré suggested that greetings move through the following four phases in this order: (1) naming a stranger ('Ah, Dr Livingstone . . .'), (2) physical contact, (3) establishing his identity and status, and (4) using of a formula of admission. Suppose we suggested some more phases – (5) finding common bonds, and (6) explaining why we are meeting or being introduced. Careful research is now needed to find out how many of these elements are essential and under what conditions.

I have carried out several experiments on the rules of NVC. One experiment was about the rules governing interruptions, using the graduated rule-breaking method, and it produced quite unexpected results. The question was, does the acceptability of an interruption depend on the length of time the other person has been speaking, or on the grammatical point at which it occurs? Tapes were prepared in which interruptions took place. The length of utterance before the interruption was varied – 2, 5, 10, and 30 seconds, and the point in the sentence at which it occurred was varied as follows: at the end of the sentence, at the end of clause, in the middle of a clause. Ratings of the 'appropriateness' of the interruptor's behaviour by judges were as follows:

	Length of previous utterance (secs)			
	2	5	10	30
End of sentence	12·5	13·3	14·0	12·7
End of clause	11·7	7·5	7·7	6·1
Middle of phrase	4·4	5·9	3·5	4·2

Only the point in the sentence was a significant source of variance. This experiment is given as an example of the experimental study of rules. It provided evidence about the rules governing interruptions, which could not have been obtained by more informal methods.

Another experiment was concerned with the rules governing proximity and orientation in two-person conversations. The results are reported later (p. 320). We can note here that the rule operated in a statistical rather than an all-or-none manner, i.e. there is a range of acceptable proximity, and greater deviations are progressively disapproved of.

In another series of investigations we presented subjects with descriptions of a number of instances of rule-breaking, asked them to rate them along a series of rating scales, and analysed these ratings statistically. The main finding was that people distinguish quite sharply between two main classes of rules – those which are essential for a particular kind of social event to take place at all, and those which are merely conventions. It is much more disturbing for rules of the first kind to be broken. Here are some examples:

Guest at a meal
Totally disruptive: is unpleasant to the other guests, gets very drunk.
Only mildly disruptive: eats with the wrong implements, wears a hat (male).

Conversation
Totally disruptive: speaks an unknown language, is aggressive or not interested, replies to what is said by speaking on a different topic.
Only mildly disruptive: lies on the floor, sits too close or too far away.

Every situation has certain rules which are essential to that situation. Mann (1970) studied Australian football queues. These queues are very long, last for a whole night, and have evolved rules of their own. Members are allowed to operate in shifts, each person taking up to one hour off for three hours on; an individual can keep a place for two or three hours by leaving a sleeping bag or other property; those who break these rules are not allowed back in the queue; queue jumping of course is not allowed. These rules enable queuers to attain their goal of moving towards the gates in an orderly and fair way; it makes life in the queue tolerable and it encourages social integration.

It is interesting to inquire how systems of rules develop. Rules are a special kind of social norm – norms governing the co-ordination and sequence of social arts. There has been a great deal of research on the development of norms. We know that they develop in all groups, particularly on matters concerned with the main purpose or activities of the group, that the dominant members of the group are influential in deciding the norms, which can be regarded as the results of group problem-solving, that they are enforced by social pressures and persuasion, and by the rejection of deviates, and that they are more strongly enforced in cohesive groups. The distinctive feature of *rules* as opposed to other norms is that they regulate the co-ordination and sequence of social acts: when a rule is broken, the sequence of inter-action is dislocated and it is difficult for others to proceed. Examples are breaking the rules of games, making inappropriate moves in highly structured situations like auction sales and greetings, and producing the wrong sequence of verbal utterances, for example, replying to a question by a question or laughing where there is no joke. In a study of groups of adolescent boys (Sherif and Sherif, 1964) it was found that there were often rules such as 'going with a new girl is permissible so long as it is announced to the group in case there are any objections'. In studies of working groups it is found that there are rules about the allocation of the preferred jobs, about helping and reciprocation, and about slang words and non-verbal signals, for example in noisy factories.

There are are a number of unsolved problems about the formation of rules. For example, in certain cities, like Moscow and New York, there is a rule about which side of the pavement pedestrians shall walk, while in other cities, like London, there is no such rule. In Boston there used to be a rule governing whom one spoke to during each course of a dinner party: the hostess spoke to the person on her right during the first course and to the person to her left during the second course, and so on; all the other guests paired off and switched accordingly. But this rule is not normally used nowadays. It is by no means clear what the conditions are for a rule to be needed in such matters.

How can these rules be changed? Studies of changes in group norms show that these are changed as the result of an individual's deviating, and persuading the rest of the group that the new norm is to their advantage. The deviate may get his ideas from other groups, or may have thought of the change himself. He will be successful in persuading the other group members if he is of high status in the group, has conformed in the past, possesses persuasive social skills, and can show the others that they will gain from the change. Presumably there is a kind of natural selection in which rules survive which provide the greatest satisfaction to the majority of group members. It follows that there may be sets of social rules as yet unthought of, which might be even more beneficial. Perhaps we would simply do without some of our present rules, just as we manage without the 'Boston switch'.

Children have to learn the rules of their culture as do newcomers to the culture. Children receive some preliminary training in keeping rules by playing games. The rules of many situations are learnt quite easily since other people are in charge, and play counter-roles, which elicit rule-following behaviour directly. For example, if a doctor plays the doctor role is it quite clear what a patient should do. In some cases it may be necessary to explain the rules, for example, when a patient first starts psychotherapy, or a person joins a new church. There are books explaining some of the rules; Cavan (1970) studied the thirty-two books on etiquette directed to children kept by the San Francisco public library. She found that instruction is given on such matters as how to behave in public, respecting the rights of others, e.g. not asking certain kinds of personal questions, introducing and being introduced, inviting, accepting, and declining dates.

We have discussed so far those rules which are specific to particular social situations. Are there more general rules which apply to all situations throughout a culture? Just as the same language is used throughout a culture, so the same system of NVC is used. We shall discuss some of the differences between cultures in the next chapter.

Since there are so many different situations in a culture, each with its own rules, how do people know which rules they should follow? It depends on their 'definition of the situation'. People distinguish between situations by perceiving certain physical features of those situations. A concrete room which is chilly and damp, without paint or plaster, with a single weak electric light bulb, and a table and chair made of bare wood, is more likely to be the setting for an interrogation rather than a social conversation or an interview. Similarly the furniture and decoration can indicate whether a room is to be the setting for romance, work, or meditation, and can give clear indications of mood and of social status. These 'signals' are produced by furnishers, interior decorators, and everyone who arranges a room; they are decoded by those who enter it.

The physical setting can be deliberately manipulated to define the situation in a certain way. Various experiments have been made in the design of mental hospital environments.

Replacing tiles by carpeting reduces noise, making patients less irritable, makes the hospital seem more like home, while patients make greater efforts to be tidy and continent (Cheek *et al.*, 1971). An American abortion clinic has been studied, in which the furniture, the uniform of the staff, and an air of competence and cleanliness, create the impression that the clinic is a kind of hospital. This definition of the situation reassures nervous patrons and helps the reputation of the clinic. These techniques can be used to control the behaviour of other people.

Situations also vary in their sheer physical arrangements, affecting the distances and angles between people, who can see whom, and how well, and makes people walk or look in certain directions. The effects of these spatial factors on behaviour are discussed in Chapter 16.

A third aspect of situations is the nature of the task, or main activity. The rules of behaviour which are followed are quite different when the task is:

work or social activity
co-operative or competitive

and where the interactors are:

of the same or different status
of the same sex or different sex.

People at work may be related in different ways depending on the way the work-flow system is designed (Argyle, 1972). Party games, and encounter group exercises (see p. 297f), generate a range of social relationships and social behaviour not commonly experienced elsewhere.

Interaction is very difficult unless the nature of the situation is agreed, and also the relationship between the interactors. I tried the experiment of bringing pairs of people together and asking them to 'hold a conversation' for ten minutes, but without further instructions. In every case the first minute (approximately) was spent in deciding what kind of conversation to have. This was one of quite a limited class of conversations, e.g. (1) getting to know each other, (2) Oxford gossip, (3) serious discussion about work. Sometimes members of committees go to a pub after the meeting. Here the same individuals carry on discussing much the same issues, but with quite different rules operating – allowing hysterical laughter, spilling of beer, etc. It appears to be impossible to hold a conversation unless a regular cultural situation is selected, and all agree to abide by its rules. Particularly in 'formal' situations one does need to know the actual rules. The hero of the Hitchcock film *North by Northwest* managed to get himself arrested at an auction sale merely by bidding incorrectly – by bidding *less* than the last bidder instead of more. Guests at dinner at the older Oxford Colleges are sometimes perplexed by the rules governing how and when one may take snuff, pass the port, toast the Queen, mention a woman's name, go to the lavatory, or go home.

The study of rules opens up a number of new empirical issues, hitherto overlooked, such as under what conditions rules are formed, whether they form an interdependent system, whether they are represented by cognitive structures, what the characteristics of the different kinds of rule-breaking are. Traditional research into cause-effect relationships of variations within the rules is complementary to the study of rules, though often that has to be done first – and by proper research methods.

Further Reading

GOFFMAN, E. (1963) *Behavior in Public Places*. New York: Free Press.

HARRÉ, R. and SECORD, C. W. (1972) *The Explanation of Social Behaviour*. Oxford: Blackwell.

STONE, G. P. and FARBERMAN, H. A. (1970) *Social Psychology through Symbolic Interaction*. Waltham, Mass.: Ginn-Blaisdell.

References

ARGYLE, M. (1972) *The Psychology of Interpersonal Behaviour*. Harmondsworth: Penguin Books.

BARKER, R. G., and WRIGHT, H. F. (1954) *Midwest and its Children: The Psychological Ecology of an American Town*. Evanston, Ill.: Row, Peterson.

BIRDWHISTELL, R. L. (1970) *Kinesics and Context*. Philadelphia: University of Pennsylvania Press.

CAVAN, S. (1970) The etiquette of youth. *In* G. P. Stone and H. A. Farberman (eds.) *Social Psychology through Symbolic Interaction*. Waltham, Mass.: Ginn-Blaisdell.

CHEEK, F. E., MAXWELL, R. and WEISMAN, R. (1971) Carpeting the ward: an exploratory study in environmental psychiatry. *Mental Hygiene* **55**: 109–18.

CHOMSKY, N. (1957) *Syntactic Structures*. The Hague: Mouton.

GARFINKEL, H. (1963) Trust and stable action. In O. J. Harvey (ed.) *Motivation and Social Interaction*. New York: Ronald.

GOFFMAN, E. (1956) *The Presentation of Self in Everyday Life*. Edinburgh: Edinburgh University Press.

GOFFMAN, E. (1971) *Relations in Public*. London: Allen Lane.

HARRIS, M. (1968) *The Rise of Anthropological Theory*. London: Routledge and Kegan Paul.

LYONS, J. (1973) Structuralism and linguistics. In D. Robey (ed.) *Structuralism*. London: Oxford University Press.

MANN, L. (1970) The social psychology of waiting lines. *American Journal of Sociology* **75**: 340–54.

MELBIN, M. (1972) *Alone and with Others*. New York: Harper & Row.

PIKE, K. L. (1957) *Language in Relation to a Unified Theory of the Structure of Human Behavior*. 2nd revised edition. The Hague: Mouton.

SHERIF, M. and SHERIF, C. W. (1964) *Reference Groups*. New York: Harper and Row.

STRINGER, P. (1967) Cluster analysis of non-verbal judgements of facial expressions. *British Journal of Mathematical and Statistical Psychology* 20: 71–9.

4

Cultural differences & uniformities in bodily communication

We shall deal in later chapters with the detailed origins and the extent of cultural variation in facial expression, posture, gaze, and so on. Here we shall deal with the general principles involved. There are a number of very interesting and important issues here – the relative importance of biology and culture for NVC, the influence of thought and language and of other aspects of culture, whether there are non-verbal universals, and what the practical problems of inter-cultural communication are.

The biological and cultural origins of NVC

There has been considerable controversy about the extent to which emotional expression and other bodily signals are the same in all cultures and the extent to which they vary. However, the position has become very much clearer as the result of recent research, and the answer turns out to be rather different for different kinds of communication.

There is good evidence that some bodily signals are innate. Consider for example the facial expressions for emotions: first, these expressions are very similar in all the cultures in which they have been studied (p. 219f); secondly, they are found in young children, and have also been found in blind and deaf children, who could not have imitated

74 The biological & cultural background

them (Fig. 4.1); and thirdly, some human expressions are very similar to the facial expressions of non-human primates, and the evolutionary development of some of them has been traced (p. 41f). These considerations apply to the main facial expressions and to laughing and crying. Eibl-Eibesfeldt (1972) has found similar evidence of the universality of the 'eye-brow flash' – in which the eyebrows are raised to maximum extent for about one-sixth of a second, in greeting and flirting.

However there is some cultural variation even in these bodily signals. Cultures vary in the extent to which facial expressions are restrained or shown freely. In Japan the

Figure 4.1. Facial expressions of a child born deaf and blind. *a* relaxed, *b* smiling, *c* and *d* crying. (from Eibl-Eibesfeldt, 1970)

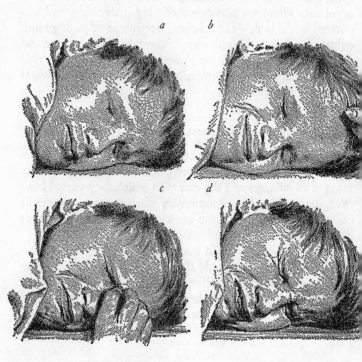

ideal is a controlled, expressionless face, and laughter or smiling may be used to conceal anger or grief. There are cultural variations in the situations in which these expres-

Figure 4.2. The eyebrow flash in different cultures. *a* Balinese, *b* French, *c* Papuan (Woitapmin), *d* Waika Indian. (from Eibl-Eibesfeldt, 1970)

sions are displayed; people may or may not weep at funerals, show joy when receiving honours, express grief when losing at games, and so on. Shimoda, Argyle and Ricci Bitti (in press) compared the perception of emotions by English, Italian and Japanese performers by subjects from these three countries. The percentages correct were as follows:

b

d

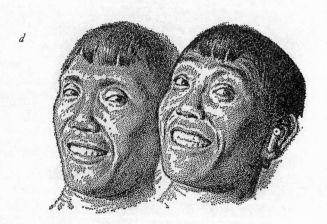

Judges	Performers		
	English	Italian	Japanese
English	63	58	38
Italian	53	62	28
Japanese	57	58	45

The English and Italians could judge their own and each other's emotions quite well, but not those of the Japanese; the latter could judge the others better than they were judged by them, but were not very good at judging Japanese emotional expression.

Gestural signals present a rather different picture, and are referred to by those who seek to emphasize the cultural component of communication. Thus LaBarre (1964) has listed the different hand movements with special meanings used in different cultures; a gesture from one culture would be meaningless in most other cultures; this is particularly true of gesture languages like those used in Italy and Greece. Some common bodily movements are used as social signals in a number of cultures, but with different meanings. For example sticking out the tongue may mean among other things mock terror used to ridicule, embarrassment, that the other is a fool, destruction of demons, wisdom, polite deference, negation, or provocative contempt. There is no common element among these meanings; evidently such bodily signals can be given a wide range of meanings. While some are arbitrary, the way they have been acquired can sometimes be traced. The tongue may be regarded as a phallic symbol in some cultures, while the lolling tongue of suicides may make the tongue an object of disgust.

On the other hand, we shall see later that there are a number of gestures with the same meanings in many cultures – pointing, clapping, raising the hand, shrugging the shoulders, and waving the hand, for example, (p. 260f).

We have seen that some bodily signals are primarily the product of biological evolution, while others are mainly the result of historical development. Let us consider a case where both factors are important – greeting signals. Greetings take an apparently wide variety of forms in different societies. Here is a list of some greetings used in primitive societies (from Krout, 1942).

Greeting signal	Culture
Clapping hands (highest form of respectful greeting)	People of Loango
Clapping hands and drumming ribs with elbows	People of Balonda
Yielding up one's clothes (as a sign of surrender in salutation)	Assyrians
Unclothing to the girdle	Abyssinians
Doffing hat or merely touching it; handshake	Americans and Europeans
Grasping hands and pressing thumbs together	Wanyiika people
Grasping hands and separating them with a pull so that a snapping noise is made by thumb and fingers	Nigerians
Engaging in a sort of scuffle in which each tries to raise to his lips the hands of the other; kissing beards	Arabs
Drawing hands from the shoulders and down the arms to the fingertips of the person greeted, or rubbing hands together	Ainus of Japan
Blowing into each other's hands or ears	Some preliterates
Stroking own face with other person's hands	Polynesians
Smelling each other's cheeks and joining and rubbing each other's noses	Mongols, Malayans, Burmese, Lapps
Snapping fingers	Dahomeans and others

Some other greetings are illustrated opposite.

Figure 4.3. Some forms of greeting (from Brun, 1969)

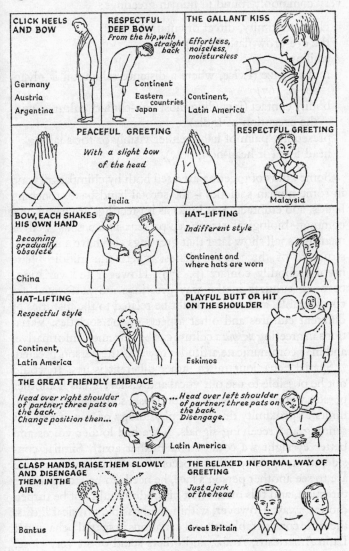

There are, however, a number of components which are very commonly found in human greetings:

close proximity, direct orientation
the eye-brow flash (p. 75)
smiling
mutual gaze (twice, where a distance salutation is given, see p. 167)
bodily contact (including most non-contact cultures, with the exception of India)
presenting palm of hand, either visibly or for shaking
head toss (or head-nod, bow).

Some kinds of greeting are used both by chimpanzees and in some human societies – the scrotal handshake, touching hands, and embracing. It looks as if greetings are based on a common biological structure, present in apes as well as men. We shall show later that greetings also have a universal structure of three main phases, where the middle phase involves bodily contact (p. 179). However the variations between cultures in the way greetings are performed are considerable, and can no doubt be related to the histories of different cultures and other aspects of the societies. Variations in greeting *within* a culture can be extremely informative, and may communicate attitudes towards the person greeted.

Spatial behaviour raises rather different issues. It would not be possible to use our vocal and visual signals if another person were too far away, or too close, so there are physical limits to proximity due to the physiology of our organs for sending and receiving signals. If we had louder voices and better eyesight we could stand further apart. Similar considerations apply to other aspects of spatial behaviour: if we are to see another person's face, he needs to be facing in our direction, and this means that his body should not be turned too far away. However, within the possible physical limits, there are considerable cultural variations in spatial behaviour: Latin Americans, Arabs, and others stand or sit very close, and with a more directly facing orientation: Scots, Swedes, English, and Americans, keep further apart, and prefer a more sideways position (p. 317f). These preferences are part of the cultures in question, can be traced to historical origins, related to the environment and ecology, and to the modal personalities in these cultures. It follows that the *same* signal, e.g. a proximity of two feet, has a *different* meaning for an Arab than for an Englishman, which leads to problems in inter-cultural encounters.

Cultures vary a great deal in the extent to which they make use of particular non-verbal signals. Touch is a good example. In India and China there is almost no bodily contact outside the family, even in greetings; there is also very little touching in Britain outside the family, apart from professional bodily contacts and involuntary contacts in crowds – both defined as non-social events. However, in parts of Africa people normally hold hands or intertwine their legs during conversation, as an extra channel of communication.

Similar considerations apply to a number of other channels of bodily communication – gestures, clothes, and smell are used far more in some societies than in others. Where a channel is not used, the information which it might otherwise convey has to be carried by other channels.

However, it is interesting to note that certain cultures make relatively little use of several channels, so that the whole non-verbal system must be operating less effectively than it might. For instance, in Britain several channels are under-used compared to other cultures:

Channel	Cultures using this channel more than in Britain
touch	parts of Africa, S.E. Europe
facial expression	Italy
gesture	Italy
clothes (males)	primitive societies, earlier historical periods in Britain
smell	Arabs

There are cultural differences in the use of NVC to communicate emotions, present information about the self, and so on. Emotions are expressed freely in Italy and Greece, by facial expression, gestures, and tone of voice. In Japan the opposite is the case; Britain is intermediate. Presentation of self can be done verbally and non-verbally. In some societies, for instance in India, it is done without restraint; in Britain there is a taboo on verbal self-presentation unless it is very indirect and discreet. The same is probably true of non-verbal self-presentation, and males in particular are very restricted in the range of clothes they can wear. Some cultures communicate interpersonal attitudes by the use of a large variety of personal pronouns. In Britain, Europe, and the U.S.A. there is a limited choice of forms of address, Christian name, surname, Mr, etc., but interpersonal attitudes have to be communicated entirely by NVC.

The influence of ideas and language

One of the main differences between men and animals is our possession of language and ideas, and these are some of the central features of cultures. First we will deal with the way people categorize events or other people, regardless of whether verbal labels are also used. It is possible to discover how a person classifies other people by the triad method, described above (p. 57), and the same method can be used for any set of signals.

Different cultures have different sets of words in particular areas. There may be a different set of colour words, corresponding to different regions of the spectrum; the same is found for the hot–cold dimension. Where we have one word for 'snow', 'parrot', or 'rice', other cultures may have several words. The general hypothesis is that there is a correlation between language and thought: Whorf (1956) maintained that language affects behaviour, either by creating cognitive categories, or by helping in perceptual coding, or by helping memory and recognition. The influence may run in the opposite direction: cultures may develop linguistic categories and distinctions which are important for them. Some of the best support for Whorf's hypothesis comes from experiments on the recognition of colours. It has been found that colours which are most consistently given the same name are recognized more efficiently. Similar results have been found in one of the main areas of NVC: a large number of photographs of an actress were used, representing different emotional states. Consistent verbal codability was found to be related to accuracy of recognition (Frijda and Van der Geer, 1961). The encoding of behaviour may also be influenced by verbal labels, and in each culture there are words which label NV acts or styles of behaviour, which may be unique to that culture. Examples are '*Machismo*' (Mexico) meaning flamboyant bravery, '*chutzpah*' (Yiddish) – outrageous cheek, 'honour' in Spain and elsewhere. Sub-cultures have such terms too – 'cool', 'weird', 'way-out' in the hippy sub-culture for example. It seems likely that the existence of the word helps both in the production of the behaviour, and also in its correct recognition. Similar labelling takes place in games: in cricket different balls may be labelled as 'full toss', 'googly', 'leg break', while the shot played may be labelled as 'cover-drive', 'cut', 'playing back'.

However, I think there is a danger of over-emphasizing the importance of these verbal labelling processes, since a great deal of social behaviour appears to be managed without much verbal mediation. The non-verbal signals which support speech by providing feedback and controlling synchronization do not seem to be verbally coded themselves (Chapter 8). There may be cognitive mediation, i.e. use of cognitive categories and constructs, but these need not have verbal labels.

Ideas and beliefs may be expressed through bodily

signals. Cultures may have ideals about postures, the use of gaze, and of course appearance. Particular non-verbal signals may be associated with certain social classes, racial groups, males or females, or with particular occupations, such as being a prostitute, priest, or soldier. Some gestures call up the ideas which they represent: a direct glance may be associated with the evil eye.

There are cultural differences in the way events are classified and related in the cognitive system, and these may not be reflected by language. Collett (1972) found, for example, that Arabs made more extreme judgements than Englishmen; the widely reported tendency of Arabs to exaggerate may be due to a general extremity of judgement. Some dimensions may be more important to one cultural group than to another; Africans in Nigeria classify each other primarily in terms of tribal membership, while Englishmen more often classify people on the basis of social class.

The perception and production of bodily signals is affected by courses of training or therapy in which there is instruction on labelling, feedback, and so on. There is no doubt that these various forms of training do make people more aware of NV signals, and that the effectiveness of social performance is increased. Providing verbal labels has various effects – it produces a concentration of attention on the labelled acts – patterns of gaze, pupil dilation, tones of voice, for example; it enables people to imagine alternative social acts, and brings behaviour more under deliberate control. However, after a time social behaviour becomes spontaneous and unreflective again though the cognitive system has been enriched by the period of conscious attention and verbalization.

Rules, structure, and other aspects of culture

We have seen that cultures develop rules and conventions, that is, standard and prescribed ways of behaving in particular situations. There are a number of situations which occur in virtually all cultures – eating a meal, buying and selling, religious services, working in a group, for example. The rules for these situations may vary greatly – consider buying and selling in Britain and North Africa. Some rules deal specifically with bodily communication – what posture to adopt and what clothes to wear at a formal meal, where to look when toasting someone's health (in Sweden), and so on. Some rules operate in many situations throughout a culture, such as rules about spatial behaviour, clothes, and the expression of emotions.

On the other hand each culture, and many sub-cultures, has situations which are unique to that culture, each with its rules.

'At Oxford University, for example, a faculty member can meet students at lectures, tutorials, discussion classes, departmental coffee, etc. He can meet his friends at sherry parties, college dinners, etc. In each of these situations it is generally understood how long the encounter will last (in some the actual time of day is fixed), what clothes shall be worn (e.g. whether a gown, suit etc.), how much of the time each person will talk, whether they stand or sit, and so on. This pattern of conventions varies sharply between different cultures and sub-cultures, and certain types of encounter may be unique to a particular culture. Visitors to the U.S.A. may have to learn what happens at a pyjama party, a bull session, a picnic, a baby shower, and may have to learn the elaborate rules which surround dating.' (Argyle, 1969, p. 190–1).

The social structure influences non-verbal communication. If the upper-status groups adopt one style of dress, behaviour, etc., and the lower-status groups use a different style, the signals in question become status symbols. They may be adopted by those seeking to rise in the system, so that the upper-status people have to adopt a different style, and there is a 'circulation of symbols' (p. 341f). Otherwise a person signals his social status by the particular style he selects. Similar considerations apply to membership of racial or other minority groups. American Negroes until about 1964 adopted a style which proclaimed that they were members of the Negro cub-culture, and low-status members of the general community – apart from high-status Negroes who engaged in rather conspicuous consumption. After 1964 a totally different style was adopted communicating total rejection of the white community and its symbols (p. 198f). European Jews had traditionally behaved in a quiet, meek, and deferential style; present-day Israelis have adopted an aggressive, self-confident manner in deliberate rejection of the traditional style. These social styles are brought about by the normal processes of historical social change. The imitation of models, and the effect of the mass media are important factors. The hippy style of appearance and behaviour appears to have started with Jack Kerouac, Allen Ginsberg and others in San Francisco in the early 1960s, was adopted by a number of pop singers who were greatly admired by young people, and spread all over the world.

The technology and material culture affect NVC in a variety of ways. McLuhan has suggested that prolonged TV watching will increase sensitivity to facial expressions and their meanings (p. 370f), though there is no empirical evidence that this is so, and it would be very difficult to obtain it now that TV is watched by so many. The use of the telephone might similarly be expected to increase sensitivity to tones of voice. The amount of overcrowding might be expected to affect spatial proximity – naturally people tolerate greater proximity in overcrowded cities – but perhaps their spatial behaviour led to the overcrowding.

Finally, broader aspects of national character are presumably related to, and partly expressed by, bodily communication. In cultures where extraversion or affiliative motivation are high (U.S.A., Australia), we would expect more proximity or more gaze, or other signals related to intimacy. In cultures in which 'face' and self-esteem are very important (Japan) we would expect more self-presentation behaviour, and greater control over the information emitted about the self. Both national character and bodily communication are affected by socialization experiences, though a lot remains to be found out here. For example, where babies are carried on their mother's back, they will spend less time looking at the mother's face, and may therefore have less motivation to look at faces later. Babies are carried in this way in Japan, and this could explain the relative aversion of gaze there.

The results of these cultural processes are different, but internally coherent cultural systems. For example in Japan there is less attention to faces, perhaps for the reason given above, and faces are also less expressive. There are thus related rules governing looking and the facial expression of emotion. In Arab culture on the other hand, faces are very expressive, language is stereotyped and often misleading, so a lot of attention is directed towards faces. We shall now describe the patterns of bodily communication in these two cultures.

Two case studies: the Japanese and the Arabs

The Japanese[1]

There are a number of very interesting features of NVC in Japan. To begin with there is more of it, and it has a greater degree of subtlety than elsewhere. This is partly the result of Zen teaching about the value of silence and perception without speech, partly due to the cultural homogeneity of the Japanese and the development of a code of prescribed behaviour, and partly because most social behaviour takes place inside small, closely knit groups, where people know each other extremely well. In conversation a lot is left unsaid, there are long silences, and there is a cultural ideal of talking little. This emphasis on non-verbal signals starts in the cradle: Cardill and Weinstein (1969) found that Japanese mothers spend more time with their infants and have more bodily contact, but vocalize less, than American mothers.

We will consider first the different kinds of information conveyed by NVC.

Supporting speech. Conversation includes a variety of expressive sounds which have no literal meaning, but which are used to convey surprise, agreement, etc. One of these is hissing, which means deference, another the word '*hai*', which literally means 'yes' but really indicates understanding rather than agreement. Japanese includes a lot of polite patter where the non-verbal accompaniments are most important.

Expression of emotions. Emotions must not be shown in public. This is particularly important for negative emotions, like sorrow or anger, but it also applies to positive emotions like joy.

Interpersonal attitudes. We saw above that Japanese emotions are hard to recognize, even by the Japanese. Hierarchical relations are very important in Japan, and people take great trouble to establish the correct relationship, by bowing, tone of voice, etc. There is a sharp contrast between behaviour to members of the family or work group, and to outsiders, who are treated with much more reserve.

Self-presentation is done partly by clothes, uniforms and badges, and the use of visiting cards, which clearly show rank and occupation. On the other hand there is little communication of individual characteristics, since situational rules are very important in Japan, and behaviour is more a product of situations then persons. This was observed by Ruth Benedict (1946), among others, and we have obtained some experimental evidence which supports this theory. Certainly social behaviour in many situations is formal and stereotyped, and social relationships fall into recognized categories. These patterns of behaviour often have verbal labels, for example:

Oyabum – koyum	Formal relationship with a person in the role of foster-parent.
Gimu	Obligations to parents, etc.

Ritual. There are a lot of traditional rituals – tea ceremonies, flower arrangement, etc. in which emphasis is placed on the correct use of subtle, and restrained NVC.

We will now consider the way particular non-verbal signals are used in Japan.

Facial expression. In public a poker face is the ideal, in private a faint smile. In many cases sorrow or displeasure must not be shown. The Japanese will smile or laugh rather than show negative emotions. While the restraint is the main difference between the Japanese and other cultures, the author and Kimiko Shimoda found that English and Italian subjects had great difficulty in judging even very expressive Japanese performers, which suggests that they may actually have different expressions for some emotions. (p. 77). While the Japanese facial musculature is the same as for non-orientals, the structure of the face, especially in the region of the eyes, is somewhat different.

Gaze. The Japanese do not look each other in the eyes much, but are taught to look at the neck. They avoid looking more than a very small amount at the faces of superiors. In public places eye-contact with strangers is avoided, but in a train or bus, for example, people will turn their heads from side to side, briefly scanning the others present.

Gesture. In addition to the usual gestures for emphasis and illustration, there are *temane* – gestures with arbitrary meanings. These are used at a distance, for example inviting a person to come, by extending the arm palm downwards and fluttering the fingers. Other gestures are used when words would be too direct, for example suggesting that someone is a liar by licking the forefinger and stroking an eyebrow.

Posture. The most interesting Japanese posture is bowing, which is a form of greeting, like a handshake. Bowing is used to establish relative status – the less important person bows lower; the more important can establish his superiority by bowing less low than the other, or there can be a competition in politeness; in any case each watches the other carefully as he bows himself.

Bodily contact. In public places there is very little bodily contact, not even hand-shaking. In crowded trains and buses on the other hand it is accepted, and people will sleep leaning on each other. In private there is a great deal of touching, keeping warm in winter, sleeping, and bathing together. There is less privacy than in many other cultures, but sleeping in the same room, or bathing together does not have the sexual implications it has elsewhere

Spatial behaviour. The differences between public and private behaviour were mentioned above. Spatial behaviour is affected by the design of rooms, and the need to keep warm. There are traditional rules that young people should walk behind their parents, and wives behind their husbands.

Clothes. There are special uniforms for almost every occupational group, for instance students and gangsters (dark glasses), as well as for policemen. There are costumes for hiking and for striking. Company badges indicate status in the firm.

Gifts play an important part in Japanese life. Gifts must be given, and returned, on a number of occasions. A typical Japanese might give and receive about twenty substantial gifts a month, and spend a substantial part of his income on it. The gifts are not personal, but impersonal objects of known price, bought at certain shops: the whole procedure can be seen as ritualized. While this is a burdensome system, it is impossible to escape from it without being socially ostracized. It is thought to help in the maintenance of social bonds (Morsbach, 1973).

The Arabs [2]

There have been a number of experimental and observational studies in the Lebanon, Saudi Arabia, Egypt, and other Arab countries, which show that there is considerable homogeneity in the style of social behaviour throughout this area. The main differences are between the town and traditional village cultures.

It has been found that the Arabs, like the Japanese, are very sensitive to non-verbal communication, partly since they too engage in a lot of stereotyped, formal behaviour, which needs to be supplemented non-verbally. However, Arab bodily communication is different in many ways, both from that of the Japanese and from that of the western world.

Expression of emotions. According to tradition interactors should control their emotions, with friendly faces and moderately pitched voices. Quite often, however, they break into violent expression of emotion, with unconcealed displays of sorrow, joy, or hostility, and men will cry and tear their clothes, or scream in public.

Interpersonal attitudes. In polite discourse there is a great deal of stereotyped conversation, which conveys little information. Interpersonal attitudes are conveyed mainly by tone of voice and other non-verbal signals. The Arabs are much concerned about their standing in the eyes of others, and make little distinction between status and affect. Outward appearances and honour are most important – shame is more important than guilt. Arabs use a lot of ingratiation – flattery and other displays of interpersonal affect – in order to manipulate others.

Self-presentation. Peter Collett found that Arabs have a high level of self-esteem, and this is sustained by expectations of praise and affection. The inflated self-image also gives rise to boasting, exaggeration, keeping up appearances, and not telling the truth about oneself, except to close kin. Arabs are upset by signs of minor criticism or scepticism, and are at the same time suspicious of each other.

Rituals. There is a lot of stereotyped behaviour at meals; when offered unwanted food it is necessary to refuse three times. And of course buying and selling are conducted by an often lengthy process of bargaining.

Gaze. A pair of Arabs in conversation in the laboratory look at each other more than two Americans or two Englishmen. Gaze and mutual gaze are very important to Arabs, and they find it difficult to talk to someone wearing dark glasses, or when walking side by side. Not facing directly enough is regarded as impolite.

Gesture. There is a rich vocabulary of gesture. Some gestures are used independently of speech; for example a hand is extended palm downwards and flipped upwards and over, meaning 'not my fault, but what are *you* doing about it'; holding tips of thumb and fingers of one hand pointing upwards in a pyramid and shaking the hand up and down from the wrist, means that someone is beautiful, or attractive, or that something is very well done. Other gestures are used to illustrate speech, including some where meaning is analogical but not self-explanatory. For example skimming the right fist with the left palm in a short horizontal motion away from the body expresses the hope for a violent end to the person under discussion. Other gestures are used for emphasis, accompanying conversation, such as moving a fist as if pounding a table.

Posture. Traditionally Arabs squat cross-legged, and also squat to urinate.

Touch. During conversation males will touch each other on the upper arm with the right hand, and will slap each other's right hands at a joke. On greeting two males will hold hands loosely for some time while going through the verbal part of the greeting. Males may embrace and kiss (hands, face or beard) after a long absence, at a wedding and other formal occasions. Females are not touched in public at all.

Spatial behaviour. E. T. Hall (1966) observed, and this has been confirmed experimentally by Watson and Graves (1966), that Arabs normally talk standing closer together and at a more direct angle than people in the West; close proximity during conversation is important to Arabs, though mutual gaze and shouting can compensate for it. In public places people do not grant each other the amount of personal space common in other cultures. Inside the home there is little personal privacy as Arabs do not like to be alone, but they like plenty of free space inside the house.

Clothes. The main point of interest is that Arabs keep themselves very well covered, in contrast to the non-Arab societies of the Sudan, who go stark naked in a similar climate. The women in particular are subject to powerful conventions about modesty; in many areas they still stay at home most of the time, and when they appear in public are completely covered and veiled, with face covered and only the eyes showing.

Tone of voice is an important clue to the real meaning of verbal utterances, whether they are friendly, sincere, superior, and so on. This is more important for Arabs than for westerners, since many verbal utterances are stereotyped and ambiguous. Arabs speak more loudly and are thought to be shouting by Europeans or Americans. Speech is often more colourful because of the flamboyant emotional expression and exaggeration.

Smell. E. T. Hall maintains that Arabs make a lot of use of smell, that they deliberately breathe on each other at close quarters, and smell one another's breath. However, it is not at all clear what useful information can be decoded from this source.

Cultural universals

Certain aspects of bodily communication are common to all cultures, either because they are innate, or because they are a result of universal human experiences. The extent of this universality is important because of the implications for inter-cultural communication. In the first place the same parts of the body are used in all cultures – facial expressions, gestures, spatial behaviour, etc. As we have seen there are cultural differences in the use that is made of different parts of the body – for example, the Japanese use the face less than we do, while Italians use the hands more. Furthermore, each part of the body is used for the same purposes in every culture – tone of voice is used to modify the meanings of utterances and to communicate interpersonal attitudes in all cultures; bodily appearance is used to convey information about the self – sex, age, social status, role, etc.

Secondly, a similar range of information is communicated non-verbally in all cultures – interpersonal attitudes, emotions, information about the self; NVC is used in support of speech, and in art and ritual. There is some cultural variation in the emphasis placed on these functions – the Japanese inhibit the communication of emotions, but make a lot of use of NVC to signal status and other interpersonal relations. Furthermore, NVC is used for the same reasons in all cultures – because speech is impossible or words not available, because words would be too direct or because bodily communication is stronger and more immediate. Some bodily signals have very similar meanings in all cultures – the facial expressions for emotion and common illustrative gestures, for example.

Non-verbal signals are used to manage much the same range of situations and relationships in all cultures, and these in turn are similar to those found in animal societies. The basic relationships are those within the family, between friends, in working groups, and in the community, with people who are liked and disliked, with people of higher, equal, and lower status, and with strangers. The common social situations are working, eating, buying and selling, passing time with friends etc. As we have seen a culture may have special defined variations in these situations and relationships, as the Japanese have the *Oyabum-koyum* relationship – in which an elder person becomes a kind of foster parent, demanding loyalty and obedience, but providing love and protection.

The basic principles of semiotics are also culturally universal. Meaning is usually analogical, both for signals like intention movements which are biologically innate, and for other signals like illustrative gestures, which are not. Other signals have arbitrary meanings; this is true of some innate signals with a complex evolutionary history of ritualization and displacement, like smiling and laughing. Yet other signals acquire arbitrary meanings as a result of historical associations, as with religious and political symbolism.

Inter-cultural communication

As we have seen in this book, there are cultural differences in the use of every aspect of non-verbal communication. These differences can easily produce misunderstanding and difficulties of communication when people from two different cultures meet. This is important not only for spies and tourists but also for diplomats and salesmen. Inside most countries there are further problems with cultural minority groups. As we shall see, one reason that they are disliked is because members of the majority cultures cannot understand the minority group's non-verbal behaviour. Traveller's tales about misunderstandings are endless, but they can be interpreted in terms of the kinds of differences discussed above. Here are a few examples.

Facial expression. Westerners find interaction with the Japanese very difficult, mainly because of their restrained facial expressions and habit of smiling and laughing unexpectedly.

Distance. E. T. Hall first noticed the difficulty of establishing an agreed distance with Arabs or Latin Americans at international meetings; they appeared to chase a retreating American or European, who would back to a more suitable distance, or rotate to establish a less directly facing position.

Bodily contact. Englishmen are amazed to see Italian youths holding hands and are startled when Arabs or Africans touch them.

Clothes. European missionaries were very upset that West African ladies did not wear clothes, and tried to make them do so, which was very disturbing since only disreputable women wore clothes at that period.

Gaze. Greeks (and probably others) are upset when coming

to England because people do not stare at them in public, and they feel that they are being ignored.

Tone of voice. Adams (1957) reports that the tone of voice which is interpreted as 'sincere' by Egyptians, sounds 'belligerent' to Americans.

Rules and rituals. Kenneth Pike (1967) reports the case of a missionary girl who got into difficulties with a cannibal chief because she tried to throw him on the floor (shook hands) and laughed at him (smiled). Westerners in Africa and the East often have difficulty in coming to terms with what they regard as dishonest bribery, but which is seen by the locals as the customary exchange of gifts.

Cognitive structures. Many visitors to the Middle East get into difficulties through misunderstanding the position of women, the role of religion, the importance of status, and other matters. A training scheme to deal with these problems is described below.

Social structure. Bennett and McKnight (1966) describe one of the difficulties in American–Japanese contacts: the Japanese treat the Americans as superiors, while the Americans try to treat the Japanese as equals rather than inferiors, leading to Japanese social withdrawal.

I have been studying prejudice towards members of minority groups in Britain from this point of view. The results so far suggest that in the case of many minority groups, though not all, there is a correlation between finding them difficult to interact with and disliking them. The pattern of difficulties is different in each case. Typical problems are 'difficult to communicate with', 'superior and overbearing', 'aggressive', 'impulsive', 'noisy', 'bad or different manners', and so on.

Various attempts have been made to train people for contacts with members of other cultures. A group at the

University of Illinois devised the 'Culture Assimilator' which is a programmed text to teach behaviour in another culture. The Arab Culture Assimilator consists of fifty-five problem episodes based on critical incidents dealing mainly with the role of women, the importance of religion in the Middle East, and interaction skills. The trainee assesses the causes of misperception or conflict for each problem, and is then told of the significance of his choice in terms of cultural concepts. Culture assimilators have been constructed for Greece, Thailand, and Honduras. Experimental before and after studies have shown positive but modest effects (Fiedler et al., 1971).

The Culture Assimilator is concerned with cognitive structures rather than NVC. Peter Collett (1971) trained a number of Englishmen instructing them to use some of the Arab non-verbal signals – closer proximity, more direct orientation, more looking, more smiling, and more touching. Arab subjects met a trained Englishman and a second, untrained, Englishman. The Arabs liked the trained Englishmen more, would like them for friends, and so on. The experiment was repeated with English subjects but they liked the two performers equally. An early experiment by Haines and Eachus (1965) found that subjects could be taught the non-verbal social skills of an imaginary new culture by means of role-playing with video-tape playback. Later research with role-playing has shown that it is most successful if combined with modelling, based on video tapes of skilled performers – who in this case would be natives of the culture in question. However, the adoption of the NV style of culture X by members of culture Y is only one solution to the inter-cultural problem. This may be the best solution under certain conditions. Another solution would be for each side to be aware of the curious habits of the other, and for both to make as much use as possible of those signals which are culturally universal.

The difficulties with immigrants could be met by educating both sides, at school. Peter McPhail (1972) has developed material for 'moral education'. One section consists of a series of cards describing conflict with members of racial or other minority groups, based on differences in customs or beliefs. For example 'A middle-aged Pakistani husband is walking in front of his wife on a narrow pavement beside the main road. Comments a man in a car "None of them know how to treat women"' (p. 367). These situations are used as the basis for role-playing, debate, art-work, or other classroom activities. Another set of the materials presents a number of problem situations in more detail, and include photographs, statistics, and sections of dramatic dialogue. One concerns the beginning of the Los Angeles race riot at Watts, another is on the relations between white doctors and Africans in South Africa. These are enacted and discussed in the classroom. Methods like this can probably increase sympathetic understanding for members of other cultural groups, and an awareness of some of the sources of conflict. However, to produce full awareness of differences in NVC may require films, and training in how to deal with members of other groups may require actual practice.

Notes

1. I am indebted to Dr Helmut Morsbach for information on this topic, cf. his paper 'Aspects of non-verbal communication in Japan.' Department of Psychology, University of Glasgow (1972). I am also indebted to Miss Kimiko Shimoda.
2. I am indebted to Dr Peter Collett for information on this topic. See Collett (1972).

Further Reading

EIBL-EIBESFELDT, I. (1972) Similarities and differences between cultures in expressive movements. In R. A. Hinde (ed.) *Non-Verbal Communication*. Cambridge: Royal Society and Cambridge University Press.

HALL, E. T. (1966) *The Hidden Dimension*. Garden City, New York: Doubleday.

LA BARRE, W. (1964) Paralinguistics, kinesics and cultural anthropology. In T. A. Sebeok (ed.) *Approaches to Semiotics*. The Hague: Mouton.

References

ADAMS, J. B. (1957) Culture and conflict in an Egyptian village. *American Anthropologist* 59: 225–35.

ARGYLE, M. (1969) *Social Interaction*. London: Methuen.

BENEDICT, R. (1946) *The Chrysanthemum and the Sword*. Boston: Houghton Mifflin.

BENNETT, J. W. and MCKNIGHT, R. K. (1966) Social norms, national imagery, and interpersonal relations. In A. G. Smith (ed.) *Communication and Culture*, New York: Holt, Rinehart & Winston.

BRUN T. (1969) *International Dictionary of Sign Language*. London: Wolfe.

CAUDILL, W. and WEINSTEIN, H. (1969) Maternal care and infant behavior in Japan and America. *Psychiatry* 32: 12–43.

COLLETT, P. (1971) On training Englishmen in the non-verbal behaviour of Arabs: an experiment in inter-cultural communication. *International Journal of Psychology* 6: 209–15.

COLLETT, P. (1972) Some psychological differences between Arabs and Englishmen relevant to Arab–English encounters: structure and content in cross cultural studies of self-esteem. *International Journal of Psychology* 7: 169–79.

EIBL-EIBESFELDT, I. (1970) *Love and Hate*. London: Methuen.

FIEDLER, F. E., MITCHELL, T., and TRIANDIS, H. C. (1971) The culture assimilator: an approach to cross-cultural training. *Journal of Applied Psychology* 55: 95–102.

HAINES, D. B. and EACHUS, H. T. (1965) A preliminary study of acquiring cross-cultural interaction skills through self-confrontation. Aerospace Medical Research Laboratories, Wright-Patterson Air Force Base, Ohio.

KROUT, M. H. (1942) *Introduction to Social Psychology*. New York: Harper & Row.

FRIJDA, N. H. and VAN DER GEER, J. P. (1961) Codability and recognition: an experiment with facial expressions. *Acta Psychologica* 18: 360–8.

MCPHAIL, P. (1972) *Lifeline*. London: Longman.

MORSBACH, H. (1973) The ritual of gift-giving in Japan. Paper given to British Psychological Society.

NAKANE, C. (1970) *Japanese Society*. London: Weidenfeld & Nicolson.

PIKE, K. L. (1967) *Language in Relation to a Unified Theory of Human Behavior*. 2nd revised edition. The Hague: Mouton.

SHIMODA, K., ARGYLE, M. and RICCI BITTI, P. (in press) The intercultural recognition of facial expressions by their national groups. *European Journal of Social Psychology*.

STOLUROW, L. M. (1965) Idiographic programming. *National Society for Programmed Instruction Journal* Oct.: 10–12.

WATSON, O. M. and GRAVES, T. D. (1966) Quantitative research in proxemic behaviour. *American Anthropologist* **68**: 971–85.

WHORF, B. L. (1956) *Language, Thought and Reality*. (ed. J. B. Carroll). Cambridge, Mass.: M.I.T. Press.

Part 2

The different uses of bodily communication

5
The expression of emotion

By emotions are usually meant such states as anxiety, depression, happiness, and so on. We may also include milder states or 'moods', feelings of pleasure and displeasure, different degrees of arousal or drowsiness, and the arousal and satisfaction of hunger, sex, and other drives. In each case there is subjective experience, a bodily state, and a pattern of non-verbal signals – in face, voice, and other areas. It is convenient to distinguish emotional states from interpersonal attitudes, though both may occur at once, for example a state of anger combined with being angry with (aggressive towards) someone. An emotional state is not in itself directed towards another person.

We saw above that as apes and monkeys go about their daily affairs they emit a constant stream of signals about their inner states, mainly by facial expressions and vocalizations (p. 32f). Human beings do the same, though we provide much less information, as a result of controlling our expressive behaviour. Why are these non-verbal signals sent? (1) Some are direct physiological reactions, in no sense intended to communicate. Examples are the facial expression for disgust when something nasty has been eaten, manifestations of organic states like drowsiness and excitement, and the disruption of behaviour in high degrees of arousal. (2) Some expressive signals have developed during evolution as social signals, which are sent spontaneously by animals and men. It is adaptive for animals to communicate, for example, a state of fear or anger. The complex evolutionary history of some of these expressions has been traced (p. 41f). However, it is not at all clear why it should be adaptive for humans to signal emotions like depression and anxiety – which some cultures like the Japanese try hard to inhibit. (3) Some emotional expressions can be regarded as social signals which are deliberately sent. This is only possible because there is a repertoire of expressions with agreed meanings. However, signals in this category very often do not reflect the emotional state actually experienced. The facial expressions and tones of voice for emotions are used for other purposes, such as accompanying speech in various ways (Chapter 8) and in rituals (Chapter 9).

William James maintained that the experience of emotion is the result of a person perceiving his own bodily and motor reactions – he feels his heart beating and observes himself running away so realizes he is afraid. Later research has found that there are indeed different bodily responses for some of their main emotions, like fear and anger, and for different degrees of arousal, and that people can discriminate such bodily states. However, other studies, for example with injections of adrenalin, have found that these bodily states are not sufficient in themselves to produce emotional experiences. Schachter (1964) found that subjects use environmental information to label their emotions: the *same* bodily state, induced by an adrenalin injection, was experienced as euphoria or anger depending on the behaviour of a confederate in the experimental situation. Tomkins (1962–3) has suggested that facial expression also helps to discriminate one emotion from another: as well as other bodily changes, an emotional state produces a specific facial expression which the person senses and which helps him to label the emotion. Shimoda has found some evidence for this theory (p. 219). A similar line of argument has been used by Bem (1967) in support of his theory that people perceive their attitudes by observing their behaviour – if they find themselves going to church they realize that they must be religious. Bem says that internal stimuli are not verbally labelled because they are not in the public domain, so people depend on public events like their own behaviour, which are verbally labelled. However, we have seen in this book that NV signals can be used whether they are verbally labelled or not.

The classification of emotions

The early research by Woodworth, Schlosberg, and others was done by asking subjects to identify verbally the emotions expressed by actors in posed photographs, showing the face only. This and later research is discussed on p. 214 ff. The present state of research on facial expressions suggests that people discriminate seven main groups – corresponding to happiness, surprise, fear, sadness, anger, disgust/contempt, and interest.

However, we shall see later that the face is not the only way in which emotions are expressed, and that the decoding of another's emotional state is based partly on his situation. I believe that a rather wider range of emotional reactions is expressed and interpreted though these cannot easily be identified from the face alone. Examples are:

amusement	good health	concentration
boredom	headache	puzzlement
guilt	nausea	sexual excitement
shame	fatigue	religious feeling
embarrassment	hunger	aesthetic feeling
impatience	thirst	patriotic feeling
self-satisfaction	self-confidence	

It remains for research to discover whether these states are signalled in a recognizable way.

What bodily signals are used to communicate emotional states? In later chapters we will deal with the detailed ways in which face, voice, and other areas convey emotions. The main areas are these:

Face: mouth, eyebrows, skin, facial movement
Eyes: amount of opening, pupil dilation, amount of gaze
Gesture: hand shape, hand movements, hands together, hands to face
Posture: tense or relaxed, erectness of posture, style of bodily movements
Tone of voice: pitch, speed, volume, rhythm, speech disturbances

Different parts of the body are able to convey different aspects of emotion. As we have seen the face is able to convey seven main emotions; Graham, Ricci Bitti and Argyle (1975) found that videotapes of head-only could be decoded more accurately than videotapes of the rest of the body. However, the body was just as good as the face for decoding five degrees of intensity of emotion. It seems likely that the feet can convey anger (by stamping), or degree of arousal.

Encoding emotions

The encoding of emotions can be studied by asking people to adopt the facial expression or tone of voice corresponding to happiness, sadness, etc. This may lead to exaggerated or conventionalized expressions. On the other hand there is a possible advantage in using posed expressions that performers will not restrain or disguise their expressions as they often do in real life. It has been found that a considerable range of facial expressions is produced by different people in the same emotional state. If a large sample of people pose expressions, only about 60 per cent are reliably recognizable by judges. However, there is a normal range of expressions for a particular emotion in the centre of which are expressions which would be regarded by most people as sad, happy, etc.

We discuss elsewhere the evidence for cross-cultural similarity in the facial expressions in emotion (p. 219f); the evolutionary origins of facial expressions and tones of voice (p. 41f) have been discussed already. Something is known about the physiological basis of emotional expression. It is partly due to different degrees of arousal, in which the individual is prepared for action, and has an increased heart-rate, rate of breathing, blood pressure, muscle tension, and skin temperature. There are also physiological differences between some of the main emotions. It has been found that anger and fear are quite different physiologically. Fear is accompanied by a high level of adrenalin, an increased heart-rate, muscular tension, and rate of breathing, but restricted flow of blood to the skin (hence white face) and to the muscles. Anger is accompanied by more adrenalin, more saliva, and increased flow of blood to the skin. The facial expressions for emotions are partly a direct result of these changes, but are partly social signals with a rather complex history. Tones of voice can be explained by the effects of facial expressions and tension in the throat.

Infants show the startle pattern to loud noises shortly after birth, and smile to a human face and voice at six weeks; they show delight and distress by three months, both by facial expression and by voice. They soon show reactions which are recognizable as disgust, anger, and fear. During the second year of life and later the emotional patterns displayed include distress (crying and hand in mouth), anger (temper tantrums), general activation (waving and other bodily motion) and frustration (scratching the body, teeth-grinding, kneading the feet). Laughter occurs in connexion with rough and tumble play, though it is not clear exactly what it signals. The same basic patterns of expression appear in blind children, though with greater variability. It looks as if emotional expression develops mainly in the course of maturation, but that there is also a little learning. Cultural variations in emotional expression prove that there must be some.

Cultural variations in emotional expression include (1) variations in the degree to which all such expression is restrained; (2) cultural conventions especially about laughing and crying in public; (3) cultural variations in the events which elicit emotional reactions: if the birth of twins will result in the twins and their mother being put to death, as at one time in the Niger delta, the birth of twins is not an occasion for rejoicing; (4) variations due to the fact that language and ideas may affect the way emotions are categorized: the Japanese make a clearer distinction than other cultures between 'sad' (e.g. because of a tragedy) and 'depressed' (an irrational mood).

The face is the single most important area for signalling emotions, and the face has evolved as a social signalling area. The skin reflects physiological states directly (red for anger, white for fear); the opening of the mouth reflects aggressive intentions, but also sexual ones by showing the tongue. Smiling has a more complex origin. Opening the eyes and raising the eyebrows gives better vision, while half-closing and lowering protects.

Tone of voice is also an important means of emotional expression. The grunts, barks, and screams of apes and monkeys are replaced in man by the tones of voice in which verbal utterances are delivered. We make far less use of emotional sounds like these grunts and screams, and do not keep up a constant signalling by this method for the benefit of those around us, but we do deliver our verbal utterances in tones of voice which indicate, among other things, our emotional state.

Gestures and other bodily movements form a third means of expressing emotions. Hand positions and movements can display quite specific emotions. These movements vary a lot from person to person, but when they occur are interpreted in the ways listed on p. 268. Emotions are also communicated, though far less distinctly, by other parts of the body. The body as a whole communicates the general tense–relaxed dimension which indicates the strength of whatever emotion is being expressed. Ekman and Friesen (1968) have found that emotions such as anxious and cautious can be identified to some extent from films of leg movement alone.

Lastly, emotions may be communicated by appearance, and particularly by clothes. A person in a particularly cheerful frame of mind is unlikely to dress in black unless he has to.

The expression of emotion is often the result of conflict between the basic biological pattern of expression, and cognitive attempts to control it. Dittmann (1972) suggests that attempts are made to control emotions when negative sanctions are feared. Such control often takes the form of inhibiting the expression of emotions; however, it may take the opposite form, as when a person expresses his suffering in order to influence others. It is very difficult to control the autonomic elements, such as perspiration and pupil expansion. Ekman and Friesen (1969), studying expression in mental patients, suggest that the hands and feet are less readily controlled than the face, and that there may be 'leakage' of emotional expression to these areas. There are two different possibilities here, first, that some areas are less easily controlled, or secondly that the information tries to seek an outlet, so that there is *more* expression in uncontrolled areas. In two patients they found that more negative emotions were communicated by the body than by the face, as estimated by judges – though as Mehrabian (1972) points out it is possible that these areas were more negative when there was no deception involved in the case of these patients. Another way in which concealed emotions may show through is in 'micromomentary expressions' which are in-visible to most observers. There can also be leakage into other channels, such as tone of voice or gesture; a nervous public speaker may be able to control his face and voice, but trembles or perspires visibly. When deception is being prac-tised most people avoid eye-contact, which can thus become a signal for deceptiveness (see p. 245).

Lanzetta and Kleck (1970) found a negative relation be-tween physiological measures of emotional arousal, and the expression of emotion, as measured by ability of judges to identify facial and postural cues correctly. A distinction has been made between 'internalizers' who show physiological arousal but little emotional expression, and 'externalizers' who do the opposite (Jones, 1960). These results were con-firmed by Buck et al. (1972), who also found that females tended to be externalizers and communicated emotions more clearly.

Decoding emotional expressions

The decoding or recognition of emotional expressions has been much studied but mostly by rather artificial research methods. For example subjects are shown still photographs of faces and asked to identify the emotions portrayed. This is not the way emotions are normally perceived; some, e.g. surprise, can probably only be recognized from a sequence of expressions; and it is impossible to tell from a still photo-graph how far the expression shown differs from the target person's normal appearance – which would be interpreted in terms of 'personality' rather than emotion. Emotions can be recognized better from a film than from static photographs, though photographs can be recognized at much better than chance level (Ekman et al., 1971). Another problem is that posed emotional expressions may be somewhat different from spontaneous ones, though in fact both are recognized equally accurately. In real-life situations people often make efforts to conceal their emotions, especially negative ones; this is only partly successful, but some of the pattern may not be displayed.

It is not really known how early children can recognize emotions. Probably they respond to smiling and frowning quite early. They probably respond to rough and gentle handling even earlier, and it is widely reported though not proved that they are sensitive to tense and relaxed arms holding them. The crying of another child elicits nurturance and smiling elicits smiling in nursery school children. The number of emotions which can be correctly identified from photographs increases with age – pain at 6–7, anger at 7, fear and horror 9–10, surprise 11, contempt 18 and later. This depends in part on the development of words and concepts for emotions. There are considerable individual differences between adults in ability to recognize emotions, and it is possible to train people quite easily to do this better (p. 368f).

We have seen that about 60 per cent of photographs of faces displaying emotional states are correctly recognized. If the 'best' photographs are used, accuracy may go up to 80 per cent, and higher than this for happiness, fear, and determination. Woodworth (1938) found which facial expressions can be distinguished most easily; anger may be confused with disgust and fear, but not with love or surprise.

The relative accuracy of judgements based on facial and vocal cues was studied by Davitz (1964) who played the film and sound tracks of performers who had been asked to read a neutral message lasting 10–15 seconds in six emotional styles. The relative accuracy scores were as follows:

Medium	Percentage recognition
sound film (voice + face)	59
sound track	47
silent film	56

The even higher accuracy scores reported earlier for still

photographs were based on carefully posed and selected photographs. However, different emotions are most easily recognized via different media.

Emotion	Medium			
	Voice	Face	Voice and face	
joy	42	86	81	
surprise	41	43	51·5	
fear	74	58	73	
disgust	34	52	51·5	
anger	56	62·5	61	Percentage
contempt	33	37	37	recognition

from E. A. Levitt in Davitz (1964).

In real-life conditions it seems likely that people respond to each other's emotional states without putting them into words.

Emotions are recognized from a whole pattern of non-verbal signals, which are usually consistent with each other, and also with the expectations created by the context, so that the task of the judge is easier than in these experiments. Experiments have been carried out on the perception of inconsistent signals. What happens is that one signal is discounted or reinterpreted, rather than that the two are averaged. The most common reason for such conflicting signals is a partly successful attempt to conceal an emotion. It is not known how such displays are perceived, but it is likely that if he notices them an observer places more weight on the signals for negative emotions, which are more likely to be concealed, and perhaps on the less well controlled signalling areas – hands, feet, skin, etc. When verbal and non-verbal signals are in conflict, it is very likely that more attention will be paid to the non-verbal component, as is the case with interpersonal attitudes.

Further information about a person's emotional states is derived from the situation he is seen to be in. Experiments have been carried out in which facial expressions and in-

formation about situations were both varied. In some early
experiments rather dramatic contexts were provided such as
'watching a hanging', and 'girl running from ghost'. Frijda
(1968) did a number of experiments in which subjects rated
on seven-point scales facial photographs alone, verbal descriptions of situations, and combined photographs and
situations. He found that the photographs made more con-
tribution to the combined ratings than the contexts,
especially when they were discordant. However, as Ekman
et al. observe, there are cases where the context will domi-
nate, and the source which is more important depends on
the clarity and the strength of the cues from each source.

Lalljee (unpublished study) found however that extremity
of facial expression was not of great importance; subjects
followed diverse strategies in interpreting conflicts between
facial expression and situation. They sometimes thought that
the facial expression masked the true emotion; this was done
more for happy faces than for sad ones, which were seen
as more authentic. Or they thought that the emotion had
some cause other than the situation described, or the situation was reinterpreted, for example when a happy face was
combined with an apparently sad situation.

The condition of the perceiver affects how he interprets
non-verbal cues for emotion. Hypnotized subjects were
made happy, anxious, or aggressive and shown some rather
vague pictures; their interpretations of the pictures reflected
their own emotional condition. A happy person thinks that
other people are happy. In real social situations there is a
further reason for this – a happy person produces at least a
temporary cheerful state in those that he meets – which he
sees as their emotional state, without realizing he has partly
induced it himself.

Davitz (1964) and his colleagues found that there is a
general ability to decode emotional expressions accurately,
whether these are communicated vocally, facially, or by
drawings. This ability correlated with the ability to encode

emotional expression, and also with verbal intelligence though not with thirty-three personality variables measured. Brian Little and Eleanor Stephens at Oxford (in press) presented triads of speech stimuli, where two were similar in emotional tone, and two in content. It was found that some subjects classified the stimuli primarily by the emotional tone of speech; these were people who classified persons mainly in terms of psychological constructs, i.e. in terms of personality attributes (e.g. introvert), as opposed to physical ones (e.g. tall) or roles (e.g. engineer), and who were presumed to be person-oriented as opposed to thing-oriented.

We may conclude that the non-verbal communication of emotions is largely innate, and is partly due to the direct effect of physiological states, partly to the development of social signals, whose adaptive purpose is to keep members of a group continually informed about the inner states of other animals. The main modification of this scheme in human culture is to restrain facial expressions, to replace vocal cries by the tone of voice used for conversations, and to introduce the use of conventional expressions in the absence of any emotional state.

Further Reading

DAVITZ, J. R. (1964) *The Communication of Emotional Meaning*. New York: McGraw Hill.

EKMAN, P., FRIESEN, W. V., and ELLSWORTH, P. (1972). *Emotion in the Human Face*. New York: Pergamon.

References

BEM, D. J. (1967). Self-perception: an alternative interpretation of cognitive dissonance phenomena. *Psychological Review* 74: 188–200.

BUCK, R. W. *et al.* (1972) Communication of affect through facial expressions in humans. *Journal of Social and Personality Psychology* 23: 362–71.

DITTMANN, A. T. (1972) *Interpersonal Messages of Emotion.* New York: Springer.

EKMAN, P. and FRIESEN, W. V. (1968) Nonverbal behavior in psychotherapy research. *Research in Psychotherapy* 3: 179–216.

EKMAN, P. and FRIESEN, W. V. (1969) Nonverbal leakage and clues to deception. *Psychiatry* 32: 88–105.

FRIJDA, N. H. (1968) Recognition of emotion. *Advances in Experimental Social Psychology* 4: 167–223.

GRAHAM, J. A., RICCI BITTI, P. and ARGYLE, M. (1975) A cross-cultural study of the communication of emotion by facial and gestural cues. *Journal of Human Movement Studies* 1: 68–77.

JONES, H. E. (1960) The longitudinal method in the study of personality. In I. Isore and H. W. Stevenson (eds.) *Personality Development in Children.* Austin: University of Texas Press.

LANZETTA, J. T., and KLECK, R. E. (1970) Encoding and decoding of nonverbal affect in humans. *Journal of Personality and Social Psychology* 16: 12–19.

LITTLE, B. R. and STEPHENS, E. (in press) Psychological construing and selective focusing on content versus expressive aspects of speech. *Journal of Consulting and Clinical Psychology.*

MEHRABIAN, A. (1972) *Nonverbal Communication.* Chicago: Aldine-Atherton.

SCHACHTER, S. (1964). The interaction of cognition and physiological determinants of emotional state. *Advances in Experimental Social Psychology* 1: 49–80.

TOMKINS, S. S. (1962–3) *Affect, Imagery, Consciousness.* New York: Springer.

WOODWORTH, R. S. (1938) *Experimental Psychology.* New York: Holt, Rinehart and Winston.

6

Communicating interpersonal attitudes

Animals find mates, rear their children, make friends, frighten off their enemies, establish dominance hierarchies and co-operate in groups, entirely by means of bodily signals. The human race has developed language, but it is used primarily for communicating information about other persons, objects, and ideas, rather than about feelings of one person towards his listener. Broadly speaking, NVC is used for one and language for the other. Animals developed special organs for sending and receiving bodily signals for establishing interpersonal relations, and man has inherited these organs. We shall describe below experiments which show that non-verbal signals have a much greater impact than equivalent verbal signals in communicating attitudes to other people. Though there is some cultural variation in the form of the bodily signals used, these are very similar in all cultures.

The dimensions of interpersonal attitudes

Two main dimensions of interpersonal relations have emerged from a number of investigations, as shown in Figure 6.1.

Figure 6.1.

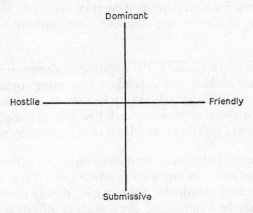

Affiliation includes a variety of positive social attitudes. Friendship, acceptance, and warmth between peers is one. There are similar attitudes inside families, for example, between parents and children.

Sexual attraction is similar to affiliation, and uses the same signals. However, rather stronger signals are sent, e.g. greater proximity and more mutual gaze, and additional signals are used, especially bodily contact.

Rejection, aggression is the opposite of affiliation. As with animals actual attacks are rare, except for small boys. In humans even the expression of hostility is often concealed, so that it may be hard to perceive this kind of attitude.

Dominance relationships occur where there are no clear differences of power or status between people. Dominance signals are also used to establish informal status differences where there is no objective basis for such differences, as in groups of primates. However, to establish a relationship which the other will accept requires some skill, or the other will simply leave – the relationship must be made sufficiently rewarding for him. Nurturant parental behaviour is a combination of dominance, affiliation, and protection of the child.

Submission, appeasement is the opposite of dominance. It includes the seeking of a dependent relationship by children and others. This behaviour may be used in later life in relation to older or more powerful people. It includes the admission of defeat and avoidance of aggression by another.

These are the broad dimensions of interpersonal attitudes; particular instances are often more complex. There may be combinations of attitudes, for example friendly dominance; there may be intermediate cases, such as affiliation tinged with sexuality; there may be conflict between verbal and non-verbal signals, as described below; and there may be deceptive signals.

Encoding interpersonal attitudes

In some cases the evolutionary history of a signal can be traced. We have seen how the smile developed from the silent bared-teeth face, used as an appeasement signal by monkeys (p. 41). Bodily contact may derive from grooming, one of the main kinds of primate affiliative behaviour. On the other hand gaze is used rather differently by humans and animals: in humans gaze is used to signal interest, attention, and liking, rather than hostility or aggression. Some of these signals are found in infants, and are the same in all cultures, so are probably innate, as in the case of the eye-brow flash (p. 75f). Blurton-Jones (1972) and others have found that children of 1–2 use a number of interpersonal gestures: they wave to indicate that they want to be with their mothers, they raise their arms if they want to be carried, they suck their thumbs when separated from their mothers. Infants also cry when separated from their mother, laugh when engaged in vigorous play with other children, smile when approaching another person, frown when attacking another child. The expression of interpersonal attitudes is also affected by culture and socialization. Arabs learn to use bodily contact in a wide range of social situations, where English children do not. Working-class children learn to use physical aggression towards those they dislike, while middle-class children learn to restrain it.

The encoding of interpersonal attitudes can be studied in various ways. Mehrabian (1972) asked experimental subjects to go and talk to a hat-rack, imagined to be a person of certain sex, status, etc.; he then measured the proximity, orientation, and posture adopted. Cook (1970) asked people to indicate on a series of plans how they would sit, and at what angle, in a variety of social encounters. In observational studies, for example of children, the particular occasions on which children send particular signals are noted, and the attitude signalled is inferred.

In one of Mehrabian's hat-rack experiments he found that liking or disliking the imagined other person, and supposing him to be of higher or lower status affected the subjects' gaze, proximity, and various aspects of their posture, as follows:

TABLE 6.1. Encoding interpersonal attitudes (from Mehrabian, 1968)

Positive attitude (males)   = 2·90 (gaze) − 1·35 (arms akimbo) − 1·34 (distance)
Positive attitude (females) = 5·89 (arms akimbo) − 1·07 (distance) + 0·40 (arm openness)
Addressee status (males)   = 6·00 (head tilt) + 3·25 (leg openness) + 2·50 (gaze) − 2·45 (arms akimbo)
                              − 1·16 (leg relaxation) − 0·89 (hand relaxation)
                              + 2·02 (gaze) − 3·69 (arms akimbo)

Addressee status (females) = 2·13 (head tilt)
                              − 2·74 (leg relaxation) − 4·64 (hand relaxation)
                              + 1·43 (arm openness)

From this and other studies we know which bodily signals are used to encode attitudes along the two main dimensions of interpersonal attitudes, as follows:

Bodily signal	Affiliation	Dominance
Bodily contact	Touches, strokes, holds (rather than hits)	—
Proximity	(1) Is within normal range (2) Closer proximity	—
Orientation	(1) If mutual gaze, a more direct orientation (2) But intimate friends sit side-by-side, and direct orientation at a table is competitive	Less direct
Gaze	More gaze, combined with smile; especially by males	Less gaze
Eyebrow	Raised rapidly in greeting and flirtation	—
Posture	(1) Lean forward (2) Open arms and legs (by females)	(1) More relaxed posture (2) Head tilted back (v. forward) (3) Hands on hips
Facial expression	Smiles	—
Tone of voice	Soft	Loud, assertive

Mehrabian found that dominance relations are partly communicated by a general pattern of bodily relaxation: the dominant person has his arms in an asymmetrical position, for instance one hand hooked over the back of a chair or in a pocket; he leans sideways; the legs are asymmetrical with one or both off the floor; the hands and neck are relaxed, and he leans backwards away from the vertical. However, dominance may involve a competition with other senders of dominance signals. There may be a rapid and subtle sequence of signals, which negotiate at the non-verbal level the precise relationship between two people.

Courtship signals are a variant of affiliative signals – like eyebrow-flash, gaze, smile, touch. Scheflen (1972) observes that they are quite widely used between males and females when no serious courtship is envisaged. There may be 'quasi-courtship', in which other signals indicate that the courtship is not serious – burlesquing it, keeping arms folded, or adopting a facial expression indicating lack of serious intention. We shall see later (p. 234) that pupil dilation acts as a signal for sexual attraction.

We have just seen that if A likes B he will use a number of different signals to communicate his attitudes – bodily contact, gaze, proximity, facial expression, soft tone of voice, direct orientation, bodily relaxation and open arm position. Normally a person would use some or all of these cues together, in an overall pattern of friendly or hostile NV behaviour. The author and Janet Dean (1965) suggested that these different signals could substitute for one another, so that if two people were, for example, placed further apart the loss of intimacy due to the greater distance would be compensated by more gaze, smiling etc. This was confirmed in a number of experiments in which gaze was measured at different distances. These experiments show that both gaze and mutual gaze increase with distance to a very marked degree, confirming the idea of the equivalence and substitution of signals. In other experiments it has been found that people look more when *not* talking and look less when discussing intimate topics, in both cases confirming the idea of an equilibrium level of intimacy, where increasing the strength of one signal reduces the strength of others. It is very likely that similar processes operate in the communication of other interpersonal attitudes.

We shall see below that when the verbal and non-verbal components of a message conflict more attention is paid to the non-verbal. But why do people send such messages and what other information may be conveyed by them?

Zaidel and Mehrabian (in Mehrabian, 1972) asked subjects

to enact three degrees of liking and three degrees of disliking, by speaking single words, using facial or vocal signals; these were then decoded by judges. It was found that the face communicated more information than the voice, and that variations in negative attitudes were conveyed better than variations in positive attitudes. The reason for this is probably that there are strong conventional restraints against expressing negative attitudes verbally. This may give rise to negative (NV) combined with positive (V) attitudes. Or when a girl says 'no, don't', her words may keep to the conventions, but her tone of voice express her real wishes. One reason for inconsistent messages then is the existence of social pressures which primarily affect verbal expression. For example non-verbal means of influence or persuasion are used when there are social conventions which make verbal influence unacceptable – as when a subordinate is dealing with a superior. The information that is received from all these inconsistent messages is primarily that the sender has the interpersonal attitude corresponding to the non-verbal signal. Inconsistent non-verbal messages may be used deliberately to indicate for example that although critical verbal remarks are being made the other is still accepted – as when a parent is dealing with a child.

In animals interpersonal signals reflect the real attitudes of the animals concerned. In human beings things are more complicated, and for strategic reasons signals are often sent which are not genuine. The most common form of deception is probably the expression of attitudes that are more friendly than the true attitude; this is partly to ingratiate superiors or others, from whom rewards are sought, partly to make life in social groups easier and pleasanter. Most dissimulation probably takes place in the face, since people are able to monitor their facial expression easily; it is not so widely known, however, that interpersonal attitudes are conveyed by a number of other non-verbal signals such as posture and orientation, which makes it possible to see through deceptive facial expression.

Most people can emit these interpersonal signals, and do so in much the same way. This is not surprising, since they are partly innate, partly learnt from the culture, which provides plenty of opportunities for observing these signals being used. In the Mehrabian experiments it was found that men were less effective encoders than women, and that people who were keen to be approved of were less effective. We have found that a proportion of mental patients are unable to display the ordinary signals, particularly for liking, and display a constant bored indifference, or hostility. These patients must have actually unlearnt, or learnt restraints for, the innate bodily signals used by young children.

Decoding signals for interpersonal attitudes

Interactors can perceive friendly, hostile, superior and inferior attitudes quite easily from facial expression, tone of voice, and the rest. This ability is studied by presenting video-tapes or real behavior, and asking subjects to judge what is being expressed along scales like

friendly — — — — — — — hostile

The first non-verbal signals to which infants respond are bodily contact, facial expression, and tone of voice. This perception is partly unlearnt, but there must also be some learning, since interpersonal attitudes are expressed somewhat differently in different cultures. Interpersonal attitudes are communicated by a combination of verbal and NV signals. Some experiments have studied the total effect of such combinations of cues. Albert Mehrabian (1972) carried out an experiment in which the relative effects of facial expression, tone of voice, and contents of speech were compared. The separate cues were initially equated for strength as in our experiment described below: tone of voice was studied by means of a band-pass filter which makes the verbal contents unintelligible. The results were that ratings of positive attitude (liking) = ·07 (verbal content) + ·38 (tone of voice) + ·55 (facial expression). In other words both of the non-verbal signals had much more effect than verbal content, and facial expression had more effect than tone of voice. The author and colleagues (Argyle, Alkema, and Gilmour, 1972) carried out a series of experiments in which verbal and non-verbal signals for friendly–hostile and dominant–submissive were compared. In the friendly–hostile experiments, three complete NV styles were constructed as follows:

Friendly: warm, soft tone of voice, open smile, relaxed posture
Neutral: expressionless voice, blank face
Hostile: harsh voice, frown with teeth showing, tense posture

These three styles were displayed by performers seen on video-tape counting from one to fifteen, to eliminate the verbal contents. These three performances were shown to a number of judges and rated on seven-point scales like:

hostile — ✗ — ✗ — ✗ — friendly
      A   B   C

The performances were modified so that they were judged as being approximately at A, B, and C in these scales. Similar work was carried out to develop three verbal messages, with almost identical ratings, when the typed versions were judged. These messages were as follows:

Friendly
'I enjoy meeting the subjects who take part in these experiments and find I usually get on well with them. I hope you

will be able to stay on afterwards to have a chat about the experiment. In fact, the people who came as subjects in the past always seemed to be very pleasant.'

Neutral
'I don't really mind meeting the subjects who take part in these experiments. Some of them are fairly nice. Others of course are rather tedious. You can come along afterwards and talk about the experiment if you like, but please don't stay too long. On the whole, I don't have very strong feelings about people who come as subjects in experiments.'

Hostile
'I don't much enjoy meeting the subjects who take part in these experiments. I often find them rather boring and difficult to deal with. Please don't hang around too long afterwards and talk about the experiments. Some people who come as subjects are really rather disagreeable.'

In the experiment proper the NV and verbal signals were combined in all nine combinations, e.g. friendly (NV), neutral (V) etc. The performers spoke the verbal message in the NV styles. These performances were then rated by fresh judges. Statistical analysis showed that the NV cues had about five times the effect of the verbal ones on the final ratings. When the two were in conflict the verbal messages were largely ignored. Very similar results were obtained with signals for superior–inferior (dominance–submission), and in studies by other investigators.

We found that conflicting signals have a special quality of their own. A friendly message spoken in a hostile way was seen as insincere, while a hostile message spoken in a friendly way was regarded as confusing. These conflicting signals are also found to be amusing, especially superior and hostile manners with conflicting messages. Sarcasm is another example – a pleasant message spoken in a hostile way:

again the non-verbal outweighs the verbal, but in this case by indicating that the *opposite* of the verbal message is implied.

Weitz (1972) found a very interesting case of verbal–non-verbal conflict, in the behaviour of whites towards blacks. There was a negative attitude between tone of voice (rated for *warmth* and *admiring*) and verbally expressed friendly attitudes towards a black subject; there were negative correlations between tone of voice and behavioural indices of friendship, such as proximity selected and intimacy of joint task selected. The most favourable tones of voice were used by subjects with moderately favourable attitudes. Those with the extremely favourable expressed attitudes were presumably concealing a basic hostility, which was revealed by their tone of voice.

Bugental and colleagues (1970) in a similar experiment found that tone of voice and verbal content did not add up, but that a positive message in either channel was discounted if the other was negative. However, facial expression had a greater effect than either tone of voice or contents of speech. And, contrary to our findings, children (not adults) regarded a negative script produced by a woman as negative even when accompanied by a positive face and voice.

In the present state of research it is not possible to give a quantitative measure of the weight given to each non-verbal signal. However, it seems likely that bodily contact of various forms is given most weight, followed by facial expression and tone of voice; posture comes next, orientation is probably weaker. Some of the main results of decoding experiments were given in the table on p. 123.

There are a number of complications about these results. The effects of orientation for example depend very much on the situation. In experimental situations, a more direct orientation communicates a more positive attitude; if two people are sitting at a table such an orientation is seen as hostile or competitive, and a side-by-side position as co-operative; two close friends will sit facing to eat, but side-by-side to drink or chat.

There are a number of interesting sex differences. Females adopt an open-arm, open-leg posture to males they like and males of higher status. With a much disliked male, male subjects adopted a less relaxed posture, with a more direct orientation and gaze than did females – suggesting greater vigilance in relation to physical threat. Similar results were obtained by Mark Cook (1970) at Oxford. He found that a strong positive attitude, as towards a close friend of the opposite sex, is expressed by proximity combined with a side-by-side orientation. A highly negative attitude for example to a person of the same sex in an argument is expressed by proximity combined with a direct orientation. Again it seems that in a hostile and competitive relationship people have to keep an eye on the other person, although in less intense relations there is *less* gaze. This is an example of two cues in different combinations generating special meanings – intimacy is signalled by a special combination of orientation and proximity.

How accurately are interpersonal attitudes perceived, and can people see through deceptive signals? Tagiuri (1958) found that members of groups could tell quite accurately who accepted them – only 4 per cent of choices were seen as rejections. However, they saw 9 per cent of rejections as acceptances. Rejection is not perceived accurately because it is often concealed, and misleading signals are sent. The correct attitude can be perceived only through study of the less obvious and less well-controlled cues, as in the case of negative emotions (p. 114). There may be mistakes in the recognition of dominance: Burns (1954) found that tactfully given instructions from superiors were interpreted as information or advice by the recipient. The persuasive–democratic style, for all its advantages, can be very misleading to those who are not used to it. Ingratiation is another interesting case. Ingratiation consists of the use of flattery, agreement, and other interpersonal rewards, verbal or non-verbal, in a misleading way, to induce another person to grant some favour. Luc Lefebvre in (1975), at Leuven, has found that bodily signals like smiling are used by ingratiators, but that target persons do not realize that these signals are deceptive and strategic. Experiments by E. E. Jones (1964) have shown that rather subtle verbal forms of ingratiation are used – otherwise the strategy would not work; probably NV signals are often used because verbal ones would be more definite and make others too aware of what was going on.

When two or more people meet, and are establishing a relationship, this is done by trial and error using bodily signals. This process is similar to a group discussion, except that suggestions are put into non-verbal equivalents of 'I suggest I should take charge', or 'I suggest we become friends'. Such NV suggestions are more tentative, scarcely noticed consciously, and easily withdrawn. One example is the man who elects himself foreman of the jury by placing himself in the centre of the table and adopting a foremanlike posture. Another is the gradual taking over of more and more talking time by means of the subtle synchronizing cues described later (p. 165f).

Just as some people are not very good at sending these interpersonal signals, so some people are not very good at decoding them. However, there appears to be little relation between the two abilities, a person may be good at encoding, but not at decoding. Schizophrenics are particularly poor at decoding NV signals. Ederyn Williams (1972), at Oxford, found that they were much more responsive to verbal signals, using the experimental procedure described on p. 127f. On the other hand some neurotic patients are extremely sensitive, but particularly to signals for rejection. T-groups, and similar training procedures are intended to increase sensitivity to social phenomena. Men are less sensitive than women, particularly men in technical, thing-oriented, jobs, which suggests that there is scope for improvement. On the other hand there is a possible danger of creating an overload of social information, which might hamper social performance.

We can now answer the question of why bodily signals are used, in preference to verbal, for interpersonal attitudes. These signals, and the associated bodily structures, were operating before language was developed, and language appears to have developed mainly for other purposes. While words *can* express attitudes to others, bodily signals have certain clear advantages: first, they are stronger, and have a more immediate impact; secondly, negative signals can be used outside full conscious awareness; thirdly, signals negotiating relationships can be used with subtlety, again outside awareness, and can be easily withdrawn.

Further reading

ARGYLE, M. (1969) *Social Interaction*. London: Methuen.

MEHRABIAN, A. (1972) *Nonverbal Communication*. Chicago: Aldine-Atherton.

References

ARGYLE, M. and DEAN, J. (1965) Eye-contact, distance and affiliation. *Sociometry* 28: 289–304.

ARGYLE, M., ALKEMA, F. and GILMOUR, R. (1972) The communication of friendly and hostile attitudes by verbal and non-verbal signals. *European Journal of Social Psychology* 1: 385–402.

BLURTON-JONES, N. G. (1972) Non-verbal communication in children. In R. Hinde (ed.) *Non-Verbal Communication*. Cambridge: Royal Society and Cambridge University Press.

BUGENTAL, D. E., KASWAN, J. W., and LOVE, L. R. (1970) Perception of contradictory meanings conveyed by verbal and nonverbal channels. *Journal of Personality and Social Psychology* 16: 647–55.

BURNS, T. (1954) The directions of activity and communication in a departmental executive group: a quantitative study in a British engineering factory with a self-recording technique. *Human Relations* 7: 73–97.

COOK, M. (1970) Experiments on orientation and proxemics. *Human Relations* 23: 61–76.

JONES, E. E. (1964) *Ingratiation*: *a Social Psychological Analysis*. New York: Appleton-Century-Crofts.

LEFEBVRE, L. (1975) Bystanders' evaluations of different sorts of illicit and attractive ingratiation overtures. *British Journal of Social and Clinical Psychology* 14: 33–42.

MEHRABIAN, A. (1968) The inference of attitudes from the posture, orientation, and distance of a communicator. *Journal of Consulting and Clinical Psychology* 32: 296–308.

SCHEFLEN, A. E. and SCHEFLEN, A. (1972) *Body Language and the Social Order*. Englewood Cliffs, N.J.: Prentice-Hall.

TAGIUIRI, R. (1958) Social preference and its perception. In R. Tagiuiri and L. Petrullo (eds.) *Person Perception and Interpersonal Behavior*. Stanford, Calif.: Stanford University Press.

WEITZ, S. (1972) Attitude, voice, and behavior. *Journal of Personality and Social Psychology* 24: 14–21.

WILLIAMS, E. (1972) *The Social Behaviour of Schizophrenic Patients*. Oxford D.Phil thesis.

7

Sending information about personality

Non-verbal signals indicating personality

Some aspects of animal communication are designed to convey information about the sender. Bird calls for example may contain information about the sender's species, his group may be indicated by his 'dialect' – the way the species song is performed, while he may be distinguished as an individual from several thousand other birds by his tone of voice. Animals may indicate their age, sex, and social status by vocalizations and other signals. It is obviously important to detect quickly some of the most important characteristics of another individual – in order to know how to behave towards him. While animals often send special signals which have this function, it cannot be said that individual animals intend to send such information – this is simply part of the communication system built up by evolution. Some information about individuals is provided without any special signals – information about species, age, sex, and size, for example, is provided visually with much use of special signals.

Information about human individuals is conveyed in a similar way – there information is given involuntarily about race, age, and sex. In addition there is also deliberate manipulation of cues, or 'self-presentation'; the ideas which the sender has about himself are converted into bodily signals,

which others have to decode. The manipulation of cues
extends to some degree of control over the apparently fixed
and involuntary cues for age, physique, and even race and
sex. Though this is difficult to achieve and there are
obviously limits to what can be done, nevertheless some
people do change their voice and appearance to a remarkable
degree by various methods including surgical operations.
Human beings need information about each other, just as
animals do. We have additional motives for sending it however; by creating a favourable impression on others we can
gain material advantages, sustain a satisfying positive self-
image, and – a 'self-fulfilling prophecy' – become more
effective in many social skills – teachers can teach their pupils
more, psychiatrists can make their patients recover faster, if
they are believed competent.

Personality can be interpreted in terms of the encoding
and decoding of mainly non-verbal signals. But what is the
message which is being sent? The involuntary cues convey
all kinds of information about the sender's body, roles, and
personality; these are then decoded by others in terms of
whatever cognitive dimensions or categories they use. In the
case of the manipulated cues, the information sent is how the
sender perceives himself, and how he wants others, in
general or particular, to see him. The situation is made more
complicated by the fact that people use quite different cognitive constructs in this sphere – people classify each other in
terms of a great variety of dimensions, partly derived from
the culture, partly individually developed. In Britain and the
U.S.A. three main kinds of construct are commonly used.
(1) Physical characteristics like height, skin colour, hair, and
so on; most important perhaps in this area is an inferential
dimension – physical attractiveness. (2) Roles played, and
social positions occupied – like age, sex, race, social class,
occupation, religion, and other group memberships. (3) Personality traits, like extraversion–introversion, neuroticism,
dominance. Here people vary a great deal in the dimensions

which are important to them, and in the number of dimensions used.

It must be admitted that there is a serious unsolved problem in this area at the present time. Psychologists have traditionally conceived of personality in terms of traits, like extraversion and dominance. However, it has become clear that in the field of social behaviour in particular, the same individual shows very different styles of behaviour in different situations, and that personality tests do not predict this behaviour very well (Mischel, 1969).

There is little doubt that the solution lies in discovering stable, underlying features of personalities from which behaviour in different kinds of situation can be predicted. Examples of such stable characteristics are abilities; attitudes and other cognitive structures; age, sex, and other demographic variables; motivations; mental health classification; physique and other physiological factors; the self-image. These interact with features of the situation to generate behaviour (Argyle, in press). For example, an underlying characteristic of 'anxiety' might interact with the 'stressfulness' of situations to produce actual anxiety.

A lot of research was done into finding out whether behaviour could best be predicted from 'personality', from situation, or from some combination of the two. However, it is now recognized that people choose the situations they like (Bower, 1973), and often succeed in changing them, by negotiation with the others present. So personality is partly encoded into the situations in which a person is found.

Personality attributes generate non-verbal signals directly and involuntarily without any intention to communicate, for example, a nervous person trembles and perspires, while people from different regions or social classes speak with special accents. However, these non-verbal signals are controlled and modified: people manipulate the same signals in order to emphasize certain attributes, or in order to present an improved version of themselves.

What signals are used in self-presentation? Physical appearance is greatly used – clothes, hair, face, physique, etc. Another specific cue is accent, a cue for group membership. General style of behaviour is used to indicate personality. Words may be used too, but in Britain and a number of other cultures, there is something of a taboo on verbal self-presentation, particularly of merits and achievements, except by very indirect methods, so that people are forced back to NVC.

If we are to study the encoding of personality, we must start with what is to be encoded. For the voluntary aspects of encoding this is the self-image. People categorize each other in various ways so that they know how to behave towards them; when a person finds himself consistently categorized and treated in a certain way he develops a self-image. Depending on how far others treat him with approval and respect he will acquire some degree of self-esteem.

The self-image, or 'ego-identity', refers to how a person perceives himself. He may only become aware of his self-image if he is asked special questions by psychologists, or if others react to him in a way which is sharply in conflict with his self-image, for example as if he belonged to a different social class. The central core usually consists of his name, his bodily feelings, body-image, sex, and age. For a man the job will be central – unless he is suffering from job alienation. For a woman, her family and her husband's job may also be important. The core will contain other qualities that may be particularly salient, such as social class, religion, particular achievements of note, or anything that makes a person different from others. The self-image thus contains a body image, a number of roles, and ideas about traits or individual personality qualities – the three spheres we distinguished earlier. A lot is known about the origins and structure of the self-image. One of the most interesting phases is the development of an ego-identity during late adolescence – as first described by Erikson (1956) and later confirmed by others. During this period there are heightened pressures to arrive at a consistent self-image, with the result that young people are very responsive to the reactions of others, become aware of their self-images, and probably more inclined to conceive them in verbal terms.

How does the self-image lead to self-presentation? As Goffman (1956) has pointed out, interactors need information about each other's attributes in order to know how to deal with one another. Direct evidence of, for instance, intelligence or social class is difficult to obtain, so one relies on 'gestures' – that is, on signals which are often associated with such attributes, as accent is with class. It is therefore possible for interactors to use such signals to send information about themselves which is not wholly accurate – to present an improved version of the self. Goffman maintains that interactors work out an agreed consensus, in which their perceptions of one another are agreed; self-presentation takes place by means of quasi-theatrical performances, in which there may be collusion between the members of a team, for example a family receiving guests, and this occurs in the 'front regions' of premises, e.g. the drawing room. This self-presentation includes expressing 'role-distance', indicating that the performer is a special kind of waiter or psychologist, that there is more to him than this role. If he is a spy or criminal he will create the illusion of 'normal appearance' by acting in accordance with his cover identity, and not creating a disturbance.

The self is not at work all the time, and people are not constantly sending signals about themselves. This only happens in those situations which Goffman called 'on-stage'. There are a number of such situations: literally appearing in front of an audience; putting on a professional performance as a doctor or salesman; being assessed by others, for example at an interview or oral examination; being a young woman in the company of a young man; being with older or more senior people; being differently dressed, or otherwise singled out. In all these situations people may feel self-conscious, that they are the 'observed' rather than the 'observer', and do their best to project certain aspects of their self-image. There are different motivations for self-presentation. Professional people like teachers want to appear competent, so that others will accept their influences. Candidates for jobs want to create the kind of impression which will get them the job. Those with insecure identities seek confirmation of their identity. Some want to project an image of physical attractiveness or high social status, because they enjoy the social relationship created.

The signals used to communicate personal qualities are these: (1) Appearance; we describe on page 333f an experiment in which people were found to choose clothes which communicated their self-images. (2) Style of social behaviour: this indicates the *preferred* style, as described above. (3) Verbal methods: Jones (1969) found that verbal methods of ingratiation are used strategically – such as describing positive attributes in unimportant areas, or being self-deprecating in some areas.

Individuals also communicate information about their intentions and the explanation of their behaviour, in order to make it intelligible to possible onlookers; Goffman (1971) has called this 'body gloss'. People are evidently aware of what their behaviour looks like to others, and they send additional NV signals to show that it has some acceptable and sensible purpose, or occasionally to mislead or deceive. In these latter cases there is much more conscious awareness than in relaxed, and spontaneous behaviour.

The perception of personality via non-verbal cues

Research on person perception is done by presenting samples of the performance of target persons and asking observers to rate, rank, group, or otherwise respond to them. The usual purpose of impression formation is to make some kind of prediction about another's behaviour. Under certain conditions these predictions are well above chance, and even quite accurate. Predictions can be made by personnel selection interviewers about which candidates will do a job most successfully; such interviewers can make substantially better predictions than can be made from the dossiers alone. *Post*-dictions can be made about actual past behaviour of individuals shown on films, and quite good predictions can be made about how people will fill in questionnaires about themselves. Some people make more accurate judgements than others – those who are similar in age and background to those being assessed, who have had more opportunity to see them, who are intelligent and not mentally disturbed.

When one person observes another's behaviour he will attribute it partly to that person's distinctive personality and intentions, partly to the normal requirements of the situation. Attribution theorists have shown that behaviour is attributed to the other's personality under the following conditions – when he deviates from situational norms (especially when his behaviour is socially undesirable), when there are no strong situational pressures and a number of alternatives are open to him, and when his behaviour is consistent over time (Kelley, 1967). Recent studies have shown that one's own or one's friends' behaviour is attributed to the situation; the behaviour of strangers is thought to be due primarily to their personalities. Since personality is partly encoded by the choice and manipulation of situations, it would be expected that if a person were repeatedly seen in a certain kind of situation, this would be decoded in terms of personality characteristics.

Everyone has his own favourite, or salient dimensions, in terms of which others are classified. If 'class' or 'intelligence' are salient to someone, he will focus first on the cues relevant to this dimension; he will categorize the other early in an encounter, and then adopt an interaction style adapted to the other's class or intelligence. People differ in the number of categories used on a dimension, e.g. two social classes or six. An alternative strategy is to allocate others to social types, rather than to points on dimensions; just as males and schizophrenics are types rather than points on dimensions, so are 'public school men', and 'skinheads'. Perceivers vary in the complexity of their classification systems; where some people use eight or more independent dimensions, others use very few. A cognitively complex person can recognize that another person is intelligent but lazy, nice but dishonest, a psychologist but insane, and so on. And the constructs a person uses to categorize others he also uses to direct his own presentation of self.

It is often assumed by investigators in this area that personality is coded verbally. In my opinion this is probably not true: if someone is asked to describe another, to give an opinion, or to write a reference, he has to think hard to find suitable words for the purpose. We have perfectly definite impressions of one another, but to put these into words is another matter. Asking subjects to rate people along seven point scales like

introvert — — — — — — — extravert

as is commonly done, may be an inappropriate method.

One way of studying non-verbal impressions of personality is the matching method, in which subjects are asked to allocate for example facial expressions to tone of voice. Another is the rep grid method, by which a person decides which two out of three people are most similar, and is *then* asked to put words to the way in which the third person is different. Unfortunately much of the research on which we are drawing in this chapter used verbal methods.

The way in which another is perceived depends also on the situation. A teacher is interested in a pupil's ability and how hard he works, rather than in his political or religious attitudes; the reverse might be the case for a social survey interviewer. In many situations – in public places, in a shop –

very little needs to be found out about another. Many professional people develop special kinds of expertise – barbers notice hair, tailors notice clothes. For purely social contacts the observer's salient dimensions are most important.

Observers form impressions of other people, see them as consistent and coherent, and label them as 'introvert', 'happy', 'unintelligent', and so on. Many psychologists now think that this is a widespread illusion, since everyone behaves in a wide variety of ways, sometimes introverted, sometimes extraverted, sometimes dominant, sometimes submissive. The illusory impression that others are consistent is based on, first, the fact that they are usually seen in the same role and situation, and secondly, the fact that the observer is usually present himself, and elicits a repeated pattern of interaction. The boss does not see his subordinates relaxing at home, and a wife does not see her husband alone with his boss.

How far can misleading self-presentation be decoded correctly by an observer? It is well known that people often try to present themselves in a favourable way – as being of higher social class, more intelligent, or virtuous, than they really are – and that they are liable to conceal such characteristics as homosexuality, drug-addiction, or mental disorder. Personnel selectors and superiors in organizations are usually well aware of all this, and will recognize ingratiation for what it is. Interviewers will ask persistent follow-up questions to get a more accurate picture. In everyday life people present a picture of themselves which is closer to what they would like to be than to what they really are. If this image is accepted by other people, the performer's self-image and in some cases his actual behaviour will be changed. He may undergo an actual change of social class for example, and some blacks may 'pass' as whites. Some professional performers like undertakers and doctors deliberately deceive clients in their own interest, and the latter are partly aware of this, but are glad to be deceived. There are two distinct processes in the perception of misleading self-presentation. The first is the immediate perception of the non-verbal signals, the second is cognitive reflection on whether they are genuine, or produced by other features of the situation. For example, flattering subordinates are more likely than flattering superiors to be seen as ingratiating. On the other hand it is hard to dispel the impact of the non-verbal signals; we have seen that in cases of conflict between verbal and non-verbal cues the non-verbal wins.

Communicating roles, and group membership

Bodily size, shape, and colour, and the condition of the hair and skin, are to a large extent due to age, sex, and race, the effects of innate properties, as well as of health and way of life. Clothes, voice, and other aspects of behaviour are affected by nationality, regional background, and social class. Many aspects of behaviour vary with occupational and other roles. These are not in the first instance examples of communication.

Three very important roles are conveyed primarily by involuntary bodily cues – age, sex, and race. These signals can, however, be modified by clothes and cosmetics up to a point, though it *is* possible to produce drastic changes in apparent age and sex, as on the stage.

Some roles need to be communicated in order to establish the appropriate interaction pattern: inside a hospital people need to indicate whether they are patients, visitors, nurses, or doctors, and they do this mainly by their uniforms. People also communicate role information because it is an important part of their self-image, and they want to be perceived and treated as occupants of a particular social class, or national group.

The roles which are often important in the self-image are:

age, sex, and race
social class, rank
occupation
school or college attended
nationality, regional origins
religious group
family connexions.

A number of signals are used to convey role information.
(1) Physical appearance is probably the most important –
clothes, badges, and hair. (2) In some situations, people actually play the role of teacher, doctor, or secretary. (3) Adopting
a style of behaviour can indicate role, as it can social status.
(4) Verbal communication may be used, like 'speaking as a
psychologist', or 'when I was at Cambridge'. (5) Accent is
also an important cue for social class, nationality, and region,
and some occupational roles.

Age, sex, and race are perceived at a glance, from a variety
of non-verbal cues. It is only on rare occasions, when the
main cues are absent, that more careful examination is
needed. For example, it may be difficult to tell the age of
Africans, since the normal cues of skin and hair condition
can't be used. It may be difficult to decide the sex of young
people with long hair and unisex clothes. The next stage of
decoding is to apply 'stereotypes' about the supposed typical
properties of different racial and other groups. Although
psychologists have traditionally decried the use of stereotypes, they often contain useful information. After all there
are real differences between children, teenagers, adults, and
old people, and experience leads people to discover what
these differences are. There are two ways in which stereotypes can be misleading; they may be wrong, as national
stereotypes often are; or particular individuals may not fit
them even though they are statistically accurate. The final
stage of decoding is the behavioural response to persons in
particular role categories. The social structure prescribes

certain patterns of relationship between people of different combinations of age and sex, and over and above this individuals develop their own distinctive pattern of behaviour to each category of others.

Another important role is occupation – other men particularly are classified primarily in terms of their jobs. Again there are definite stereotypes about the characteristics of doctors, clergymen, or miners, and these stereotypes contain a lot of information that is correct, as well as some that is not. The behavioural response may be directly related to the role, if the other is functioning in his role – as doctor, teacher, etc.

Social class is a very important role, though it is partly based on occupational status. Mary Sissons (1970) found that social class can be perceived quite accurately, and that the most useful cues in England are appearance, especially clothes, and accent. The behavioural response to another's social class depends on the general set of relationships in a society, and on an individual's degree of acceptance of the social hierarchy. An authoritarian, conservative person is deferential to those of higher class, and condescending to those below, while other kinds of personality vary their behaviour much less according to the other's class.

Personality characteristics

There are a number of different ways in which personality attributes affect NVC, and can therefore be regarded as sources of messages, even though there is no intention to communicate.

Bodily structures

Bodily size and shape, the structure of the face, and characteristic voice quality are not encoded signals. Nevertheless they may have meanings, since some sizes and shapes are preferred, or are thought to be associated with behaviour. Physique can, to a limited extent, be the product of a way of life, as in the case of fatness or muscularity, and this may be part of the meaning of physique. There are correlations between physique and personality (p. 336), so this may be part of its meaning too, both to its owner and to others.

Temperament

An individual's typical level of arousal, anxiety, depression, or other emotional states varies, unlike physique, from situation to situation, though people do show some consistency. Emotions affect facial expression, tone of voice, and other non-verbal signals, and they may also bring about structural changes – concerned anxiety affects the set of the face, as well as psychosomatic symptoms.

Personality traits

There are certain traits which are well-established in psychological research, and which affect behaviour in many situations – intelligence and other abilities, neuroticism and introversion–extraversion. However, the relation between these traits and social performance is a weak one – with correlations of the order of 0.2. Other investigators have thought up more specialized traits, which apply to social situations, such as dominance, affiliation, and social anxiety. Gough (1957) has found quite high correlations between personality questionnaire scales on the California Personality Inventory and corresponding forms of overt behaviour. Mehrabian (1972) predicts that affiliative people will show more 'immediacy' (proximity, gaze, etc.), while dominant people should be more relaxed, and anxious people less so. These are cases of intrinsic coding – the NV signals are simply part of a wider pattern of behaviour. All they stand for is other signals of the same kind. There is still the problem of situational variability however, and it is evident that persons interact with each other and with situations in complex ways, not yet understood.

Symbolic representation

Another approach to personality is through psychoanalytic and other depth methods, by clinical interviews and projective tests, in terms of identification with parents and others, or of basic attitudes towards people, and conflicts. Psychoanalysts interpret gestures and postures in terms of their symbolic representation of deep personal feelings, for example, fiddling with a wedding ring as discontent (p. 263f). However, there is little objective verification for this kind of interpretation. Another kind of clinical analysis has been made in terms of the structure of the identity (as opposed to its contents. Erikson (1956) distinguished several states of the ego-identity, and Marcia and Donovan (1974) have found that they produce characteristic social styles. In *identity foreclosure* for example, people accept the ideas of their parents; they are happy and optimistic, like to be praised, show little aggression or sexuality; they smile and laugh a lot, are polite, and are warm and submissive towards teachers. Those in *identity moratorium* on the other hand have rejected their parents and have not found a new commitment; they wear colourful clothes and long hair, have an active sex life and take drugs, they express a lot of hostility in class to peers and teachers, are very keen to lead, compete with the instructors. It can be seen how clinical analysis of this kind can provide an explanation of varied aspects of NVC.

However, a considerable amount of control is possible over the non-verbal signals which convey information about personality. A person who tends to be anxious will not deliberately indicate this – more often he will try to conceal it. But a person who regards himself as intellectual, colourful, widely travelled, or a rebel against society, may do his best to communicate this image to others. What he will communicate depends on the self-image he has formed, the constructs in which he thinks about it, and the insecurity of this image and consequent need for validation from others. An individual may be particularly keen to present a particular part of his self-image, because it is very important to him, because he thinks that others are mistaken about it, or because it is relevant to a particular group. He may want one group to know that he is a psychologist, another to know that he is not neurotic, another that he comes from Poland, and so on. This is all part of the very important business of sustaining a certain self-image which is sufficiently prestigeful, coherent, and accurate, and it requires some degree of confirmation from others.

The personal attributes which may be communicated are (1) abilities, intellectual or otherwise, (2) beliefs, values, (3) temperamental qualities and traits, like energy or stability, (4) past history. Styles of behaviour towards other people function rather differently. An individual may communicate his preferred relationships – like warm and dominant – and preferred tempo – fast and cheerful. However, he has to accommodate to the others present, and may end up by behaving in a quite different way.

We have seen that inferences about personality are derived from physical cues and roles. Information about personality is also obtained from the whole pattern of verbal and non-verbal behaviour, and is decoded in terms of personality traits like 'nice', 'honest', 'dominant', 'nervous', 'eccentric'. Since these judgements are partly mistaken, they do not describe the consistent behaviour of the other in all situations, but rather his behaviour in the specific range of situations in which he is encountered, and in the presence of the observer. Often they really describe a dyadic relationship, in which the other happens to be 'nice' or 'dominant', though this may be untypical of him. People have their own favourite categories, and use particular cues to allocate other people to them. Thus a person might distinguish between 'hippies', 'revolutionary students', and 'ordinary students', mainly on clothes and hair style. Our impressions of the personality of another are based particularly on his non-verbal behaviour, and we do not normally verbalize these impressions. Sanford (1942) describes the speech styles of two students: notice how difficult it was to describe them in words. The speech of one of them was 'complex, perseverative, thorough, unco-ordinated, cautious, static, highly definitive, and stimulus bound . . . we might conceive of his whole style as defensive and deferent . . . [it] seems to reflect a desire to avoid blame or disapproval'. The speech of the other was 'colourful, varied, emphatic, direct, active, progressing always in a for-ward direction. His speech is confident, definite, and in-dependent . . . to express his personality and to impress the auditor.' We recognize an individual by his appearance, his voice over the telephone, or his handwriting, just as birds recognize each other by their distinctive variation on the species song. Our impression of another's 'personality' are based on the particular patterns, not only of his speech, but of his entire social performance.

Some traits can be measured by psychologists, by direct observation of behaviour, or by questionnaires which have been validated against behaviour. Cook and Smith (1974) found that judges could rate introversion–extraversion fairly accurately, after interaction in a group, but not neuroticism. Intelligence cannot be assessed very accurately from non-verbal communication, though assessments can be made by a skilled interviewer. There are probably some involuntary cues for intelligence, but these can be simulated in order to create an impression of intelligence – talking very fast, taking a keen and critical interest in events, and so on.

Further Reading

ARGYLE, M. and LITTLE, B. R. (1972) Do personality traits apply to social behaviour? *Journal for the Theory of Social Behaviour* 2: 1–35.

150 The different uses of bodily communication

BANNISTER, D. and FRANSELLA, F. (1971) *Inquiring Man.* Harmondsworth: Penguin Books.

GERGEN, K. J. (1971) *The Concept of Self.* New York: Holt, Rinehart & Winston.

VERNON, P. E. (1964) *Personality Assessment.* London: Methuen.

References

ARGYLE, M. (in press) Personality and social behaviour. In R. Harré (ed.) *Personality.* Oxford: Blackwells.

BOWER, K. S. (1973) Situationism in psychology: an analysis and a critique. *Psychological Review* **80**: 307–36.

COOK, M. and SMITH, J. M. C. (1974). Group ranking techniques in the study of accuracy of person perception. *British Journal of Psychology* **65**: 427–35

ERIKSON, E. H. (1956) The problem of ego-identity. *American Journal of Psychoanalysis* **4**: 56–121.

GOFFMAN, E. (1956) *The Presentation of Self in Everyday Life.* Edinburgh: Edinburgh University Press.

GOUGH, H. G. (1957) *Manual for the California Personality Inventory.* Palo Alto: Consulting Psychologists Press.

JONES, E. (1969) *Ingratiation: a Social Psychological Analysis.* New York: Appleton-Century-Crofts.

KELLEY, H. H. (1967) Attribution theory in social psychology. *Nebraska Symposium on Motivation,* University of Nebraska Press.

MARCIA, J. E. (1974) *Studies in Ego-Identity.* Unpublished, Simon Fraser University.

MISCHEL, W. (1969) *Personality and Assessment.* New York: Wiley.

SANFORD, F. H. (1942) Speech and personality: a comparative case study. *Character and Personality* **10**: 169–98.

SISSONS, M. (1970) The psychology of social class. In *Money, Wealth and Class.* London: Open University Press.

8

Non-verbal communication & speech

Introduction

In the last three chapters we discussed the rather slow non-verbal signals which are used to manage social situations – to express attitudes to other people, emotions, and information about the self. However, while people are speaking they send another series of NV signals, which are more rapid and are closely connected with what is being said at the time. These signals affect the meaning of what is said, provide a simultaneous commentary by the listener, and manage the synchronizing of utterances. Some linguists now recognize that some of these signals are really part of language, not just an emotionally expressive 'paralanguage'. K. Abercrombie (1968) said, 'we speak with our vocal organs, but we converse with our whole body'. This is an unusual view however; many linguists accept NV signals in the vocal-auditory channel as part of language but do not accept those in the kinesic channel, and probably none of them accept the range of functions which will be documented in this chapter.

Research in this area is of more than theoretical importance. It has important practical applications for teaching foreign languages, and also the native language in schools. And it has important implications for all kinds of communication, in addition to other face-to-face interaction, where some of these NV cues are absent – like telephoning or writing.

We will start by listing the NV signals which are related to speech in this way.

Vocal-auditory

Prosodic signals: timing, pitch, and stress of utterances.
'Framing' signals: expressive commentary on a particular utterance by the speaker.

Kinesic

Hand-movements (and to a lesser extent other bodily movements) on the part of the speaker and listener which are related to the timing or contents of utterances.

Head-nods
Gaze-shifts
Facial expression

Our first concern in this chapter is to trace out the different ways in which these NV signals are related to speech. We shall find that they are linked to the on-going verbal messages in several different ways, and that all of these linkages are important in verbal communication.

However, while this empirical material is very interesting for its own sake, its theoretical implications may be more important. First, if all these signals are really part of language proper, should not linguists broaden their horizons to include these NV signals and look for broader principles of grammar and meaning? Secondly, a number of investigators have been treating these aspects of NVC as if they constituted a kind of language. However, are there a number of discrete signals, with standard meanings, with 'grammatical' rules of composition? Thirdly, are these aspects of NVC learnt at the same time that language is learnt, do they depend on the existence of similar neurological structures, and what light can they throw on the origins of language itself and the psychological processes involved in language?

Since many research workers in this area have regarded the NV signals as a kind of language, they have carried out research of the kind done by linguists. Linguists often work with 'idealized data', that is, they use good speakers or ask experts to eliminate the grammatical mistakes from their materials. They often work with quite small samples of linguistic material, believing that the rules they are looking for are all-or-none, so that no statistics are needed. There has been some criticism of this approach, since some of the laws appear to be a matter of probability, and grammaticality a matter of degree. When similar methods are applied to NVC, investigators have typically studied rather short samples of behaviour, in great detail, and tried to identify the basic elements (the equivalents of phonemes or words), and structure (the equivalent of grammar). No use has been made so far of expert social performers or of improved data. This research is criticized by more orthodox psychologists on the grounds that the samples of behaviour studied are too short (e.g. two minutes), the samples of persons studied too small (e.g. two), that no statistical tests are used, and no real empirical regularities established. In reply, A. E. Scheflen (1966) says 'In pattern and natural structure, co-occurrence is not probabilistic. We do not bother to assess the probabilities that human beings have hearts or that the word "heart" has an "a" in it.' It is also pointed out that it is no use trying to study empirical relationships until you know what the units are that need to be related, that linguists have been very successful in discovering the structure of languages by the non-statistical study of samples of 'correct' speech, and that units depend for their significance on their position in larger sequences of elements, like words in sentences.

The approaches and assumptions of psychologists and linguists are quite different. Psychologists are accustomed to looking for cause-effect relations of a probabilistic type. Linguists study systems of rules which are assumed to be independent of individuals, universally true, and are all-or-none, not a matter of degree. Indeed language behaviour can be studied from both points of view, dealing with either the grammatical structures used or the strengths of association between words. It looks as if human communicational behaviour may operate on two quite different principles, each requiring distinctive methods of research. Kenneth Pike (1967) assumed this in his distinction between 'etic' and 'emic', as did Chomsky (1957) in distinguishing between 'competence' and 'performance'; the first referring to the system of rules independent of persons, the second to the human ability to use language.

We shall make use in this chapter of those structural studies which took fairly large samples of behaviour. There are also a few studies which have used more acceptable research methods – testing hypotheses by statistical methods, or studying what happens when supposed rules are systematically broken.

One rather important issue is how small the elements are which need to be considered. There is certainly evidence that quite small elements can communicate; one example is the eye-brow flash lasting for one-sixth of a second. On the other hand larger units of behaviour are also important. Some interaction processes take place below the level of consciousness and depend on quite small signals such as shifts of gaze, while others consist of larger units, and have meanings as social acts.

Spatial and visual aspects of speech

The loudness of our voices and the sensitivity of our ears makes vocal-auditory communication possible over distances ranging from zero to, say, fifty yards. However, nearly all conversation takes place over a much more limited range

– of about two feet to fifteen feet. This is because of the gestural–visual communication that takes place at the same time, augmenting speech in a number of ways. If another person is too close only part of him can be seen; if he is too far away his facial expression cannot be seen. Orientation also affects how much can be seen; however, if he adopts the best orientation for seeing – head-on – the looker is also fully exposed himself, perhaps more than he wants to be.

Conversation involves the simultaneous use of audition and vision. We shall come across a number of examples of the linking of these two channels: facial and gestural signals are used to augment and qualify the words spoken; a listener provides visual feedback at the same time as the other person is sending him auditory information; gestural synchronizing signals are used to control the use of the vocal channel.

The visual–gestural channel may also play a more fundamental part in the process of communication. Some linguists think that language developed out of gesture, for example, in the first place from two people pointing at the same object. Communication depends on 'intersubjective' experience, that is, on two people being aware they are both thinking about the same thing. This can be brought about by their both pointing, or both looking at the same objects, and by their looking at one another.

Non-verbal aspects of speech itself

It is familiar that people do not speak to each other like the toneless computers and robots in science-fiction films. Anyone who did so would probably be locked up. There is an appropriate 'speech melody' for different kinds of utterance, and variations in certain non-verbal aspects of NVC affect the meanings of the sentence spoken. There are three aspects of vocal NVC which are closely integrated with the verbal message in this way: *timing, pitch,* and *loudness* – the so-called 'prosodic' features. Linguists accept the prosodic elements as part of language; methods of transcribing them have been developed, and the rules governing their use in particular languages have been worked out.

We shall discuss these non-verbal vocalizations in Chapter 18. The three prosodic signals of timing, pitch, and loudness are generally used together. Crystal (1969) found that when a high pitch range is used, speakers often speak more loudly, as well as using crescendo, falsetto, and tremulousness. Speed is often associated with a high pitch. Prosodic signals are also associated with other NV signals: for example gaze and different kinds of pause. Linguists disagree on the status of prosodic signals, for example whether they are quite separate from language, or whether they act only as modifiers of language. The position can be clarified by considering the different ways in which they work.

(1) Regular links with verbal structures. There are rules about timing and punctuation, and the pitch and stress patterns for questions and other kinds of utterance. However, these rules are obeyed only as a matter of degree – e.g. in the length of pause for a comma – and may not be obeyed at all. The minimum degree of intonation has not been established, though there are considerable cultural variations in this respect.

(2) Completing the meaning of sentences. Many sentences are ambiguous without the prosodic signals indicating which meaning is intended. This may be done by signals for emphasis (pitch or loudness), or for linkage (timing, common pitch or loudness). Linguists like to give examples of sentences whose surface structure is ambiguous, like 'they are hunting dogs'. Such sentences have a perfectly clear meaning when spoken, if certain words are stressed, like 'they are hunting *dogs*'.

(3) Framing or qualifying sentences. The attitude of the speaker can be communicated by the prosodic patterns we

mentioned for friendly or suspicious questions. Crystal found quite distinct prosodic patterns when speakers were asked to speak the same sentence in an excited, haughty, puzzled, angry, amused, matter-of-fact, or precise manner. However, such framing partly depends on sheer tone of voice as well. These signals also communicate attitudes towards listeners, emotional states, and the identity of the speaker – they are examples of the paralinguistic and similar signals discussed in Chapter 5. If the verbal contents are the 'message', the non-verbal framing signals are a message about the message; but it is really the combination of the two that constitutes the complete message. Some psychologists have maintained that the message and the frame belong to completely different communication systems; but it is perfectly possible for the 'real' message to be carried by the non-verbal signals, as when two people agree about the contents but not about their relationship. These are really 'messages about the relationship'. However, from the point of view of the message proper it may be argued that the two channels combine to produce a total act of verbal communication, for example, a question asked in a spirit of polite inquiry, a piece of information given as a devastating rebuttal, or an order given as a mild suggestion.

(4) Individual variations. Individuals vary in their 'expressiveness', i.e. the range of timing, pitch, and loudness which they use. They may also vary to some extent in the particular prosodic patterns which they use. This is partly a function of personality, partly of occupational role, cultural background, and the nature of the situation.

Fonagy (1971) has drawn attention to the way that utterances are 'double-coded' – by the grammar and by the non-verbal structure. Similar effects can be produced by either medium: for example, emotions can be aroused by emotive words or emotive expressions, tension can be created by leaving crucial words to the end, or by the manner of delivery. Extra messages can be added by using accents or special intonations, using question intonation for statements, and in other ways.

Recent studies of language acquisition by children show that the prosodic aspects are acquired very early. For example, at about eighteen months children use the rising tone to indicate questions, and are able to stress one word in a two-word sentence.

It looks as if prosodic signals are an integral part of verbal utterances, since they clearly add to the meaning of what is said, and since there are rules about how different kinds of utterances should be spoken. If prosodic signals are cut out by using writing, the words have to be supplemented by punctuation and underlining, and some of the message is still lost. The NV signals here are definitely subordinate to the verbal message, and do not send an independent message. The NV signals follow rules, but these are only obeyed as a matter of degree, and the signals are continuous rather than discrete. The NV signals here resemble language to different degrees. The signalling of grammar and stress is most like language, the framing of sentences is less so, and the paralinguistic expression of emotion less still.

Bodily movements made while speaking

While people speak they move their hands, head, eyes, feet, and body. The analysis of these movements is known as 'kinesics' and will be discussed in more detail later. Most linguists do not regard these movements as a part of language like prosodic signals, though kinesic signals are if anything more closely connected with the meanings of utterances. We shall consider here just those bodily movements which are co-ordinated with speech; those which express emotions and interpersonal attitudes (the equivalent of paralinguistics) were discussed in Chapters 5 and 6. The bodily movements which are co-ordinated with speech are: (1) hand movements, and to a lesser extent movements of the body and legs, (2) head-nods and other head movements, (3) shifts of gaze, and (4) facial expressions.

Direct accompaniments of speaking

Some facial movements are the direct result of the act of speaking (opening the mouth, for example). Different languages use different sounds, needing special facial expressions (e.g. *'schön'*, *'être'*) so that it is possible to tell what language someone is speaking without hearing him. Lip readers can of course decode the whole message, and it seems likely that other people besides the deaf derive a certain amount of information about the verbal contents of a message by watching the lips. It is possible that hand movements are also linked to speech production in some way. It is alleged that Neapolitans could not speak if handcuffed though I am not aware that this experiment has been carried out. Englishmen often gesticulate while telephoning or broadcasting. Part of the explanation in the case of broadcasting may be that gestures are a product of general arousal, and perhaps help to reduce it; as we have seen (p. 110f) gestures are related to emotional state.

Detailed studies of sound films have shown that there is a very close co-ordination between body movements and speech, at the level of individual syllables. Scheflen (1965) has found that different parts of the body start to move, and change direction at the same time ('self-synchrony'): these changes of direction take place at the beginning of syllables and larger verbal units; the larger and slower bodily movements are related to the larger units of speech. Kendon (1972) has confirmed these findings; and he also finds a hierarchical structure in which smaller bodily movements are linked to smaller verbal units; he finds that there are 'speech preparatory movements' just before each speech unit, these being earlier for larger speech units.

The hierarchies are related like this:

Verbal	Non-verbal
Paragraph, longer period of speech	Postural position
Utterance	Head or arm position
Words, phrases	Hand movements, facial expressions, gaze shifts, etc.

Dittmann and Llewellyn (1969) studied the links between bodily movement and speech, using mechanical recording of body movements. They found that movements of hands and feet coincided with the first word of a fluent phonemic clause, and with nonfluent hesitations; there was a tendency for vocally stressed words to be accompanied by movements; and there were enormous individual differences – from 40 to 1,934 movements in 30 minutes. Lindenfeld (1971) did a careful examination of conversation during psychotherapy, and found that 30 per cent of kinesic units did not fit syntax units. However, most of the 'violations' were minor – most kinesic units fell within sentences, though they crossed phrase boundaries; he also found that the kinesic pattern fitted the surface structure of speech better than the deep structure. Both these studies used mechanical methods of recording, which show amount of body movement but may fail to show changes of pattern or direction.

We must now consider what these bodily movements communicate to listeners.

Providing punctuation and displaying structure

This is done partly by shifts of gaze: a speaker looks up briefly at grammatical pauses (though he looks away during unintended pauses) and he gives a more prolonged gaze at the end of his utterance. We have seen that a question can be indicated by a rising pitch; it can also be signalled by an eyebrow raise and an upward head movement; usually prosodic and kinesic signals are used together.

Sometimes speakers enumerate with their fingers a number of points that they are making. This is unusual, but speakers commonly display the structure of their utterances by their bodily behaviour. The hierarchically structured bodily movements described above probably convey information about the verbal structure to listeners.

Emphasis

Emphasis can be provided by hand or head movements just as by changes of pitch or loudness. Mehrabian found that speakers who were trying to be persuasive looked more at their listeners, used more gestures and head-nods, more facial activity, and spoke faster, louder, and with less hesitation. Again the vocal and gestural signals are normally used together. Kinesic signals are used to send a message about the message.

Framing utterances

Vocal signals can be used to indicate whether a sentence is meant to be funny, sarcastic, matter-of-fact, suspicious, and so on, but this also can be done by facial expression and other bodily movements; again both are commonly used together. In an extreme case the sentence is actually negated by the frame, so that the precise opposite is communicated, for instance sarcastically. This is signalled by a special tone of voice and facial expression. Gestural signals are also used to indicate that a person wants to speak, and to give advance warning of what sort of thing will be said. Kinesic signals also reveal, unwittingly, whether a speaker is telling the truth or not. Studies by Exline et al. (1970) and Mehrabian (1972) found that when not telling the truth a speaker looked less at a listener, used less gestural and bodily movements, talked less and smiled more.

Illustrations

Bodily movements, and particularly hand movements, can communicate in a quite different way from the voice; they can provide spatial illustrations of what is being talked about. These gestural illustrations take a number of different forms, e.g. making pictures of acts and objects being referred to, gestures with agreed arbitrary meanings in a particular culture, and gestures which represent paths or directions of thoughts. This is discussed further on p. 254f. We also show there how the kinds of gesture used vary greatly between cultures.

The pattern of verbal and NV communication depends on the physical features of the setting, and on what is going on in that setting. The communications, verbal and non-verbal, made by people engaged in a game of water-polo, climbing a mountain, making a TV programme, or holding a religious service, would be completely unintelligible without reference to the physical setting, the nature of the social activity, and the rules and conventions of this activity.

Kinesic signals appear to play a very similar role to prosodic signals in communicating the structure of utterances, indicating questions and other kinds of framing, and giving emphasis. Illustrations are an additional set of NV messages which add to the verbal contents, though there is great individual variation in their use.

Vocalization and bodily movement on the part of listeners

So far in this chapter we have been concerned with the NVC of people speaking. However, verbal communication requires a listener as well as a speaker, and the NVC of the listener is important to the speaker in various ways. Several linguists have recognized that it is possible to study more than single utterances, and consider the structure of sequences of utterances. NVC plays a number of important roles in managing such sequences. We will start by considering what a listener does while someone else is speaking.

Condon and Ogston (1966) found that while the speaker is moving the listener is moving as well; that when the speaker changes the direction of his bodily movements the listener changes direction too; there is 'interactional synchrony' between them. Kendon (1970) took this further and distinguished three kinds of NV responsiveness by listeners. We will follow his three divisions.

Speech analogous movement, and feedback

Listeners provide a continuous commentary on what is being said, particularly by their facial expressions. Sometimes they may make mouth movements, or help the speaker by providing missing words or ending sentences for him. Listeners also indicate their own reactions and comments on what is being said; they may show understanding, puzzlement, pleasure, sadness, amusement, or surprise by the positions of eyebrows and mouth. They may nod or shake their heads.

Verbal interaction involves the simultaneous use of two channels of communication – the auditory–vocal and the visual–gestural. The visual channel is linked to the auditory one carrying feedback in the opposite direction, and closely co-ordinated in time. As we said, the main signals are rapid movements of eyebrows and mouth. They are picked up by speakers at crucial points in their utterances, they look up at grammatical pauses and at the ends of utterances partly for this purpose. When other people are invisible, as on the telephone, interaction with them is found to be more difficult.

One kind of feedback is particularly important in social interaction – reinforcement. If one person nods his head every time another speaks, the latter's speaking will be reinforced and he will talk more. A number of non-verbal signals can act as reinforcers – nodding, smiling, looking, leaning forward, and making encouraging noises; verbal signals can act as reinforcers too – saying 'yes', 'very interesting', and agreeing with what has just been said. Quite specific aspects of speech can be reinforced – the amount of speech, the topic of speech, long and short utterances, asking questions or giving opinions, and so on. As far as can be seen from the extensive research in this area neither the person being reinforced or the person rewarding him is aware of what is happening.

Movement mirroring, and imitation

Listeners often produce a sequence of bodily movements which imitate closely those of the speaker. Kendon (1970) found that this happened particularly at the beginning and end of utterances. For example, if A turns slightly towards B, B will turn slightly towards A. If A nods his head, B will nod his, if A smiles, B will smile. This matching of responses is a common feature of human social interaction, and affects both verbal as well as NV components. For example, if A makes long utterances, asks questions, or tells jokes, B is likely to do the same. This process is probably the result of unthinking imitation in most cases.

Listening behaviour

While A is talking, B emits a number of NV signals indicating that he is attending to A and is still interested in what he is saying. This is done partly by maintaining an appropriate proximity and orientation (as will be described on p. 306f), and an attentive posture. Other attention signals are head-nods which are given mainly at the ends of clauses, intermittent gaze, smiles and other responsive facial expressions, and bodily movements which are co-ordinated with those of the speaker in a 'gestural dance'. Listeners make attention noises at the ends of clauses. These noises may be just grunts, or expressions such as 'yes', 'I see', 'really', 'how interesting', or 'you don't say'.

Controlling the synchronizing of utterances

When two or more people are conversing, they take it in turns to speak, and usually manage to achieve a fairly smooth 'synchronized' sequence of utterances, without too many interruptions or silences. When two or more people meet, it is unlikely that their spontaneous styles of speaking will fit together, and there is a period during which adjustments are made – one person has to speak less, another has to speak faster, and so on. Study of the NV signals accompanying the starting and stopping of speech has shown that synchronizing is controlled by a wide range of NV signals. Since some of these signals are visual, it follows that synchronizing should deteriorate in telephone-type conversations; it is found that utterances are shorter, there are more pauses, but *fewer* interruptions when vision is experimentally restricted (Argyle and Cook, 1975).

The following figure gives examples of the timing of utterances.

A's speech ——————————————   ——————————
                              ←y→
B's speech   —————————————————   —————

        ←x→

B interrupts successfully   B interrupts
                                   unsuccessfully
x = the time for B to stop A talking
y = the pause before A replies

Experiments by Kendon (1970), Meltzer (1971), and Duncan (1972) have led to the discovery of the signals which are used to govern synchronizing.

(1) If a listener wants to *take the floor* he can use the following signals:
    (*a*) actually interrupting; he is more likely to win if he speaks louder than the other; most of these battles last less than a second, suggesting that volume is the main signal being used

(b) making triple head-nods or other impatient NV signals, often accompanied by verbal signals like 'yes', 'but', or 'well'

(2) If a speaker wants to keep the floor he should:
 (a) raise the volume of his voice when another interrupts *and* speak louder than the other, if the interruption continues
 (b) keep a hand in mid-gesture at the ends of sentences

(3) If a speaker wants to *yield the floor*, he should:
 (a) come to the end of a sentence
 (b) end by trailing off, or saying 'you know', etc.
 (c) drawl the final syllable
 (d) end on a prolonged rising or falling pitch
 (e) come to the end of some of the hand-movements accompanying speech
 (f) gaze at the other

(4) If a listener wants to decline an offer of the floor he can use the following signals:
 (a) nod
 (b) grunt or make 'uh-huh' noises
 (c) complete the sentence
 (d) briefly request clarification
 (e) briefly restate what the speaker has said

These signals play a role similar to the prosodic signals for punctuation and grammar, except that they are part of a two-person communication system. Like the other NV signals considered in this chapter, they appear to be related to speech in a regular way, though the rules in question are followed only as a matter of degree.

We have seen that longer units of conversation are marked by larger bodily shifts, for example in posture, or spatial position. Angela Steer (1972) has studied these 'transition points' in two experiments. She found that they have three phases – pre-transition, point of change, and adjustment to a new steady state; in this they are similar to greetings and farewells, which are also transition points (p. 179f). She also found that there was an increase in amount of gaze with a peak at the point of change; she suggests that this has the function of increasing intimacy at a point of social stress; it could also be due to a greater need for feedback at these points.

Interaction sequences containing both verbal and non-verbal acts

We turn now to some more complex sequences of inter-action, consisting of a series of acts, some verbal and others non-verbal. Very often there are verbal and non-verbal events going on together, making up a complex sequence of social behaviour.

The common patterns of behaviour in specific situations (buying something in a shop, eating a meal, playing a game, and so on) are governed by social conventions, which direct both the verbal and the non-verbal aspects of behaviour. One such sequence which has been studied, and which appears to have a standard sequential structure is the greeting. We shall discuss greetings as an example of ritual later; here we are interested in the detailed structure. Field studies by Goffman (1971), Kendon and Farber (1973), suggest that greetings have the following components: (1) *Distant salutation* (non-verbal only). Two people sight each other, a distant salutation like a wave or smile may be made, one or both approach. (2) *Approach and preparation* (non-verbal only) gaze is averted, they groom themselves, and an arm may be brought across the front of the body; in the final approach there is mutual gaze, smiling, the head is set in a special position, and the palm of a hand is presented. (3) *Close phase* (verbal and non-verbal). Stereotyped utterances are exchanged ('Hello', 'How nice to see you'), usually with bodily contact – hand-shake, embrace, or kiss. (4) *Attachment phase* (mainly verbal). There is less stereotyped conversation, establishing the identity and status of the other if necessary, inquiring after his recent activities, inquiring purpose of visit, looking after his immediate needs, for example providing him with seat or drink.

In complex rule-governed and ritualistic social situations, both verbal and non-verbal signals play prescribed parts. At an auction sale for example the auctioneer conducts the bidding verbally, but most of the bids are made non-verbally; the conclusion of the sale is announced by the auctioneer striking the table with his hammer. In games most of the action consists of NV bodily acts. However, the decisions of the umpire or referee consist of a NV signal (e.g. blowing a whistle) sometimes combined with a verbally stated decision (e.g. 'out'). The captain of a team often uses words to direct his team, though NV signs are often used as well. In rituals and ceremonials both verbal and NV signals are used. Often the verbal part consists of standardized verbal formulae, so that any variations introduced must be on the NV side, that is, in the manner in which the ritual is performed.

The social behaviour involved in these sequences can be interpreted in terms of three basic principles.

(1) All social behaviour can be regarded as the performance of a motor skill, in which each interactor is pursuing certain goals (usually responses from the other), and takes corrective action as the result of feedback, that is, by perceiving of the effect of his behaviour on the other. The skilled responses emitted can be either verbal or non-verbal. A fuller account of the social skill model can be found in Argyle (1972).

(2) An individual's performance consists of a sequence of social acts, each of which has verbal and non-verbal components. A social act has a hierarchical structure, in which a central plan or intention generates a meaningful sequence of words, and an accompanying NV pattern.

(3) The string of utterances or social acts between two or more people often follows a standard sequence. Greetings and rituals are highly standardized; interviews and meals are intermediate. Just as there are grammatical rules governing the sequence of words in an utterance, so there appear to be rules governing the sequences of social acts.

There can also be various kinds of interaction between verbal and NV acts. First, verbal messages can influence NV behaviour, for example one person may ask the other to speak louder or move nearer. Secondly, the NV can affect the verbal, as we have seen, in cases of reinforcement (p. 163f). Thirdly, verbal labelling of NV signals, as in social skills training, may make the other person self-conscious and aware of his NV signals. Last, a person may provide a verbal explanation of his own NVC, explaining for instance that he has to sit close because he is deaf. Or he may also provide NV explanations of his behaviour, in this case by cupping a hand round his ear, and other cases of 'body-gloss' (p. 56).

Further Reading

BIRDWHISTELL, R. L. (1970) *Kinesics and Context*. Philadelphia: University of Pennsylvania Press.

CRYSTAL, D. (1969) *Prosodic Systems and Intonation in English*. Cambridge: Cambridge University Press.

EKMAN, P. and FRIESEN, W. V. (1969) Categories, origins, usage, and coding: the basis for five categories of non-verbal behavior. *Semiotica* 1: 49–98.

KENDON, A. (1970) Some relationships between body motion and speech: an analysis of an example. In A. Siegman and B. Pope (eds.) *Studies in Dyadic Communication*. Elmsford, N.Y.: Pergamon.

References

ABERCROMBIE, K. (1968) Paralanguage. *British Journal of Communication* 3: 55-9.

ARGYLE, M. (1972) *The Psychology of Interpersonal Behaviour.* 2nd edition. Harmondsworth: Penguin Books.

ARGYLE, M. and COOK, M. (1975) *Gaze and Mutual Gaze.* Cambridge: Cambridge University Press.

CHOMSKY, N. (1957) *Syntactic Structure,* The Hague: Mouton.

CONDON, W. S. and OGSTON, W. D. (1966) Sound film analysis of normal and pathological behaviour patterns. *Journal of Nervous and Mental Diseases* 143: 338-47.

DIEBOLD, A. R. (1967) Anthropology and the comparative psychology of communcative behaviour. In T. A. Sebeok (ed.) *Animal Communication – Techniques of Study and Results of Research.* Bloomington: Indiana University Press.

DITTMANN, A. T. and LLEWELLYN, L. G. (1969) Body movement and speech rhythm in social conversation. *Journal of Personality and Social Psychology* 11: 98-106.

DUNCAN, S. (1972) Some signals and rules for taking speaking turns in conversations. *Journal of Personality and Social Psychology* 23: 283-92.

EXLINE, R. V. et al. (1970) Visual interaction in relation to Machiavellianism and an unethical act. In R. Christie and F. L. Geis, *Studies in Machiavellianism.* New York: Academic Press.

FONAGY, I. (1971) Double coding in speech. *Semiotica* 3: 189-222.

GOFFMAN, E. (1971) *Relations in Public.* London: Allen Lane.

KENDON, A. (1970) Movement co-ordination in social interaction: some examples considered. *Acta Psychologica* 32: 1-25.

KENDON, A. (1972) Some relationships between body motion and speech. In A. Siegman and B. Pope (eds.) *Studies in Dyadic Interaction.* Elmsford, N.Y.: Pergamon.

KENDON, A. and FARBER, A. (1973) A description of some human greetings. In R. P. Michael and J. H. Crook (eds.) *Comparative Ecology and Behaviour of Primates.* London: Academic Press.

LINDENFELD, J. (1971) Verbal and non-verbal elements in discourse. *Semiotica* 3: 223–33.

MEHRABIAN, A. (1972) *Nonverbal Communication.* New York: Aldine Atherton.

MELTZER, L., MORRIS, W. N. and HAYES, D. P. (1971) Interruption outcomes and vocal amplitude: explorations in social psychophysics. *Journal of Personality and Social Psychology* 18: 392–402.

PIKE, K. L. (1967) *Language in Relation to a Unified Theory of Human Behavior.* 2nd revised edition. The Hague: Mouton.

SCHEFLEN, A. E. (1965) *Stream and Structure of Communicational Behavior.* Commonwealth of Pennsylvania: Eastern Pennsylvania Psychiatric Institute.

SCHEFLEN, A. E. (1966) Natural history method in psychotherapy: communication research. In L. A. Gottshalk and A. H. Auerbach (eds.) *Methods of Research in Psychotherapy.* New York: Appleton-Century-Crofts.

STEER, A. (1972) Transition points in social encounters. Paper to British Psychological Society.

9

NVC in society - ritual & ceremony

By rituals are meant standardized patterns of social behaviour which are mainly symbolic rather than instrumental, and concerned with religious or occult ideas. Marriage services and religious healing are examples: they produce changes of social relationships or states of mind rather than physical effects. By ceremonies are meant standardized symbolic patterns of social behaviour not concerned with religion. Greetings and graduations are examples. The distinction between rituals and ceremonies is difficult to draw in primitive societies; it is also difficult to decide whether an act is primarily symbolic if the performers believe it will have material consequences. 'Ritual' is often used to refer to both kinds of event. Bodily communication always plays an important part in rituals and ceremonies, though verbal communication is often used as well. Both kinds of communication stem typically from the priest, elder, or whoever is in charge, and are directed towards those being processed – married, healed, or admitted – though these have to make verbal and non-verbal responses. The NVC here is of a rather different kind from the forms of communication that have been considered so far, and it raises a number of new issues.

We shall consider three main kinds of ritual. First, those which confirm, change, or restore social relationships – the best-known cases are what are known as 'rites of passage'; secondly, those intended to heal bodily and psychological complaints; and thirdly, religious services of various kinds, which express beliefs, ask for guidance, or seek to influence events. However, these rituals are similar to a number of more everyday events, which have a standardized and symbolic character, and which have similar consequences, such as affirming social relationships, or expressing beliefs. Examples are greetings and farewells, and formal meals which bring people together at fixed times.

How can the meanings of these ritual NV signals be discovered?

(1) *Decoding by the participants.* There may be written texts giving the official interpretation, there may be more or less widely shared ideas about what is going on, and there may be mythical or other theoretical ideas closely associated with a ritual. Or one may ask for associations or metaphorical meanings of the acts or objects used. In an elaborate African ritual for helping barren women to have children (p. 181f) a red clay is used which is regarded by ethnologists as symbolic of menstrual blood. However, the meanings produced by participants are often rather varied, or may only be known by the priests.

(2) *Inference by observers.* Since asking the participants has not been found to provide satisfactory meanings for ritual acts and objects, anthropologists have resorted to inference and interpretation, based on studies of rituals in their social settings. These interpretations are in some ways similar to those made by psychoanalysts, except that they are concerned with social institutions, rather than individual behaviour. The trouble with these interpretations is that different observers make different kinds of interpretation – some in terms of analysis of the social structure, others in terms of bodily symbolism. And there appears to be no clear way of deciding which of them, if any, is right.

(3) *Behavioural consequences.* We have seen that some NV signals have little or no phenomenological meaning, but do have behavioural consequences – like the head-nods used as synchronizing and reinforcement signals. It is an entirely objective matter to study the behavioural consequences of a ritual, though almost no research has done this. The meaning of a healing ritual could then be said to be the healing that takes place. Experiments could be done to see what difference it would make *not* to have greetings or farewells – though it might prove very difficult to omit them.

We discussed ritualization in animals in Chapter 2. Briefly this is of three main kinds: (1) clear social signals or displays evolved from originally non-social acts (for example bodily intention movements); (2) patterns of behaviour which prevent aggression (such as appeasement signals and re-direction of aggression); (3) rituals which bring about social bonding, such as courtship ceremonies. There are some interesting similarities between human and animal rituals: both consist of highly stereotyped sequences of social behaviour; both consist of social signals rather than instrumental acts; both control aggression and bring about social cohesion; both consist of exaggerated, repeated, and simplified signals. However, human and animal rituals are clearly produced by different mechanisms: animal ritual is the result of biological evolution, human ritual is the result of cultural development; the first is passed on genetically, the second is passed on by tradition and learning – though there may be universal structures underlying human rituals. Human rituals develop much faster than animal rituals. There is also greater individual variation between humans, and innovators and leaders play an important role in changing the tradition. Humans are influenced by ideas, and acts and objects acquire symbolic meanings.

Some neurotic patients adopt individual rituals, of which repeated hand-washing is a familiar example. This is usually interpreted as the symbolic cleansing of guilt. Such rituals are thought to reduce the anxiety which would otherwise be experienced – though they incapacitate the patient in other ways. Experiments on rats and cats have shown that if they are placed in intense approach-avoidance conflicts (for instance given electric shocks while eating), or given impossible discriminations at a jumping stand, they will adopt stereotyped patterns of behaviour which are quite unresponsive to any changes in the environment. Ritualized behaviour is apparently a response to anxiety, and ritual is able to reduce the anxiety. Malinowski concluded that the rituals associated with deep sea fishing in the Trobriand islands served to reduce the anxiety produced by this occupation. The rituals which we are considering in this chapter may be in part a response to anxiety; certainly if they succeed in healing individuals and promoting social cohesion they will reduce anxiety. However, the rituals which we shall be considering are social events, in which one person communicates to others, or a number of people express the same ideas or feelings together; these are socially shared rituals which are passed on from generation to generation. Although individual rituals may employ similar kinds of symbolism, no communication is involved, because there are no shared signals.

While we may usefully distinguish ritual behaviour from animal behaviour, and neurotic behaviour, we can also contrast human rituals with 'rational everyday behaviour', in which ordinary cognitive processes are operating, and when people can give a straightforward explanation of what they are doing. As we have seen, in much human ritual people have no clear idea of what they are doing, or why they are doing it. Ritual can be regarded as a kind of language which expresses things that cannot easily be put into words.

Rituals which change, confirm, or restore social relationships

Changing social relationships – rites of passage

There are a large variety of these – rituals of birth, naming, birthdays, greetings and farewells, puberty, menstruation, graduation, engagement, marriage, promotion, decoration, admission to office, coronation, and death. In primitive society these rites are very numerous; among the Todas in India for example a woman who becomes pregnant must go through twelve separate rites before she can return to normal life after the birth of her child. As Van Gennep observed, there are rituals to mark all the main stages of life, and transitions from one state to another are an essential part of life. Van Gennep (1908) showed that rites of passage all have a three-step structure: separation, transition, and incorporation, though different phases are emphasized in different rituals. When a person moves from one group or role to another, social relationships are ruptured and a new set must be established. Rites of passage carry out the necessary ritual work. The ritual is performed primarily by priests or senior members of the group. They also use spoken words which have the character of 'performative influences'; that is, the act of saying 'I marry you' accomplishes this change in social state. The emotive power of the ritual is needed to bring about the changed attitudes, cognitions and pattern of behaviour, and public affirmation is given to the change of state.

Van Gennep's second, transitional, stage is of particular interest. During this, the initiate is outside society – he belongs to neither the previous nor the subsequent group, he occupies neither role. He may have to live apart physically, as do boys undergoing puberty rites, and women at certain stages of pregnancy in some tribal societies. Since he is outside society he may be allowed special licence. Alternatively the initiations he receives and the myths he is taught may give him a wider perspective of the whole society, while he is in a position to see it from outside. Another interesting feature of these rites of passage is that they are usually associated with territorial changes – for instance where initiates in transition move to huts outside the village.

Confirming social relationships

There are some rituals whose main purpose appears to be maintaining social cohesion and role relationships. These rituals are very common in primitive societies, but less so in modern societies. Army drill parades, school daily assemblies, family gatherings at Christmas or Sunday lunch, marches, reunions, and seasonal celebrations at New Year, Thanksgiving, and Harvest Festival, are examples of such ceremonies in our own society. We can distinguish different aspects of such ceremonies. (*a*) Producing cohesion, reducing conflicts between groups. In all societies or large groups there are a number of smaller groups, and there is often a certain amount of conflict between them. Ceremonies at which all groups are present or represented suppress and control these conflicts, and emphasize the unity and common purpose of the society. One thing all groups have in common is their history, and the ceremony may take the form of re-enacting or recapitulating the history of the society. The senior leaders of a society, sometimes kings, are the objects of reverence and religious awe; it has been suggested that this is because they embody the values of the society. (*b*) Expressing role differentiation. As Bernstein (1966) has observed, school meetings of various kinds serve to strengthen cohesion but also to differentiate roles. Distinctions are made between different ages, sexes, houses, and in some schools between pupils of different ability. Rituals of all kinds are much more common in primitive societies; Gluckman (1965) suggests that this is because the same people are related in several overlapping role systems, so that ritual is needed to clarify the roles. (*c*) Strengthening authority relations. This is also a function of school assemblies, where the headmaster, the assistant masters, and the prefects all play different parts. The same is true of Army drill parades, and in these the relations are demonstrated and expressed by parade ground orders.

In primitive societies much use is made of sacred objects, such as the animal figures or 'totems' of the Australian aborigines. Durkheim and others observed that these objects stand for parts of the society, or society as a whole, and that they are regarded as sacred because they symbolize the moral force of the community, a force which maintains social cohesion. However, this does not explain how particular objects are selected, or why they should be regarded as sacred.

Restoring social relationships

This can be done in a number of ways – apology, restitution, reinstatement, and so on. Goffman (1972) has drawn attention to a common ritual sequence which does this in the case of minor transgressions. When a person has deviated or offended in some way, thus upsetting the social scene, the following ritual is enacted: the offender gives an excuse, explanation, or apology, the others present accept this, the offender thanks them, and the others minimize the thanks ('That's all right'). There are variations in this ritual sequence, for example, the initial apology may not be accepted, in which case the offender has to do more explanatory or expiatory work before he is forgiven and the *status quo* is restored.

Greetings and farewells

These are perhaps the commonest rituals in modern society, since they occur at the beginning and end of every social encounter. Goffman describes them as 'ritual brackets' surrounding periods of heightened access. The longer the separation before the encounter, the more elaborate, intense, and effusive are the greetings; a more elaborate farewell is given when a long separation is anticipated; a certain amount of 'ritual work' has to be performed, and once done it cannot be done again immediately, when, for instance, a guest comes back for a forgotten item. The rituals used vary greatly; they include hand-shaking, kissing, or other physical contact, exchanges of gifts, polite verbal formulae (which often sound like questions but require no answer), inquiring after the health of the other and his relations, eating and drinking together, smoking a pipe together, and so on. What is communicated is something like this: each party is now prepared to attend to the other, in a spirit of trust and co-operation, for a period of heightened access and intimacy. Other information may be exchanged, such as a clarification of the identity, status, and purpose of the visitor. Greetings may involve a number of stages. In primitive society visitors may first have to wait outside the village for an initial period of palaver; then there may be a period of gift exchange, etc., and then finally a ceremony of admission consisting of a hand shake or formal meal. We discuss the ways of greeting in modern society on p. 78f. It is possible to detect Van Gennep's three stages in such primitive greetings. However, most greetings can more readily be divided into phases in a quite different way: (1) distant salutation, (2) approach and preparation, (3) bodily contact and words of greeting, (4) leading into group, or activity (see p. 167f). The central point in this sequence is the *climax* rather than a *withdrawal*, and other rituals usually have a similar climax.

What are the conditions under which rites of passage are

needed? We would expect that they would occur when there was some doubt over a person's status, or where he underwent a sudden change of status or relationships with others. Whiting, Kluckhorn, and Anthony (1958) found that initiation of adolescent males at puberty was much more common in those societies in which infant boys sleep with the mother during the first year of life. Young (1965), however, found that such initiation depended on the existence of male organizations for hunting or war. In either case there may be doubts about boys adopting the male sex role.

Are rites of passage effective in bringing about the changes they are intended to produce? There is little satisfactory evidence on this point. Aronson and Mills (1959) found that an embarrassing initiation made girls keener to join a mythical discussion group. People who are married in church are more happily married and less likely to get divorced, but there could be other reasons for this (Argyle and Beit-Hallahmi 1975).

Healing rituals

Some rituals are primarily concerned with healing either bodily or mental conditions – usually no distinction is made between them. These rituals differ from the activities of doctors in that the action is symbolic, though the difference is a matter of degree, since doctors also use placebos and persuasion. There is no sharp distinction between healing rituals and those just discussed which deal with social relationships: often a person is disturbed in mind or body because of disturbed social relationships.

Healing

In most primitive societies there are rituals for curing barrenness, frigidity, or illnesses in general. These have of course been replaced by medicine in modern societies, but even here prayers and other rituals for the sick are common. The Pentecostal and similar churches emphasize spiritual healing, the Church of England has special services, one of them involving annointing with oil. At Lourdes about 3 per cent of visitors are cured; in primitive healing the recovery rate may well be much higher, since more powerful rituals are used, and Lourdes patients include many who were previously incurable. I witnessed healing at an Africanized Christian church in Ghana. Several hours of singing and dancing in a very crowded hall resulted in seventy-five conversions. The converts were then treated by the casting out of devils each representing one bodily ailment; elders pressed their hands on the converts' heads and shouted at the devils to come out. I think that important factors here were the emotional excitement and exhaustion, and the very high level of social pressure. Turner describes a much more complex ritual for treating barrenness, in Zambia. This ritual is of interest because of the elaborate symbolism involved.

'Essentially what happens is this: a young *mukula* tree is first consecrated and then cut down by a male religious practitioner or doctor. This doctor and others then cut it into short sections which they proceed to carve into crude figurines, representing infants. Next they cut small round calabashes in half, sacrifice a red cock, and prepare with its blood as lubricant a glutinous paste from a number of red ingredients, each of which has symbolic value. Some of this paste they insert in a hole made in the figurine's heads. The rest is pressed into one half of each cut calabash. The figurines or dolls are then placed in the empty halves, which are then worked over the other halves to reunite the divided sections. Holes had previously been pierced in the now overlapping circumferences and a piece of bark string had been threaded through them. The calabashes are then placed in closely woven baskets. Meanwhile, the subjects of the ritual, the "patients", young married women, had been obliged to sit some fifty yards or so away with legs extended before them, hands in laps and bowed heads

– the traditional posture of modesty or shame.' (Turner, 1967: 295–6.)

This includes a number of symbols, for example, the calabashes represent wombs, the death of the cock represents the end of the patient's being troubled by a spirit, red clay is used representing menstrual blood, and in another part of the ritual castor oil is used – which is also used to anoint couples before marriage and to massage new-born infants. Each of these objects has powerful emotional associations or metaphorical meanings.

The ritual is also bolstered cognitively by a set of religious or mythical ideas, which make the effects of the ritual credible – for example, shouting at devils to come out. In addition, however, there is a very interesting form of non-verbal communication, in which a number of acts and objects are used which have symbolic value, either by association (castor-oil and babies), or metaphorically (red gum and menstrual blood). These symbols communicate at a deeper, more emotive, less cognitive, non-verbal level, and are able to influence the biological condition of the patient.

Psychological healing

In primitive society no distinction may be made between bodily and mental ailments. Some primitive priests, however, probably have some intuitive understanding of mental disorder, for example, tracing it to guilt or damaged social relationships. Catholic priests have a considerable understanding of mental problems. In these cases the ritual is combined with sound psychological guidance.

In every society there are characteristic forms of mental disorder. Francis Huxley (1966) has described the rituals which have been developed in Haiti to deal with the local mental problems. In Haiti it is common for adolescents to have nervous breakdowns, probably due to harsh and strict treatment by their parents; the breakdowns take the form of seizures, and these are cured by ritual washing of the head in water containing crushed vine leaves. When novices are initiated into voodoo they undergo a symbolic illness and cure – they are put into a condition of hysterical arousal or dissociation, becoming unconscious through intense singing, dancing, and drumming. Both patients and novices experience characteristic images of the God (thought to be possessing them), seen as a fig-tree with a goat eating its leaves, and snakes caring for it. These rituals can be interpreted in various ways, in terms of catharsis of repressed feelings, in terms of a Freudian view – e.g. of the snake, or as symbolic death and re-birth. The specific symbols are of interest, for instance, washing the head with water and fig-leaves. Water symbolizes cleanliness, and fig-leaves are associated for Haitians with the holy tree, whose leaves are full of magical virtue. These symbolic rituals have a curative effect, and also produce images, which Francis Huxley regards as the direct apprehension of bodily states.

In our society confession, followed by some symbolic means of making amends, is a common means of psychological healing. It is much used by Catholics. The relief of guilt also plays an important part in Protestant religion, and it finds ritual expression in the Communion service, which may or may not be accompanied by beliefs about atonement.

Funerals

Funerals have two different purposes. We consider them in this section since they are partly concerned with the emotional and social readjustment of the bereaved. However, they can also be seen as rites of passage for the deceased. The treatment of the body depends on the beliefs held about the next world. The deceased is separated from his previous life and possessions, goes through a transitional stage of preparation, and is then incorporated into the world of the dead. He may be elaborately equipped for the journey, as were the ancient Egyptians, or there may be symbolic rites to prevent his return, such as pointing his feet away from the house. The contributions to society made by the deceased are reviewed and praised – these will live after him.

However, funerals are even more important for those left behind. Bereavement is one of the most distressing human experiences, since close social bonds are of great importance to the personality. It may do permanent damage to the personalities of the bereaved. This inability to cope with bereavement can almost be regarded as a 'biological flaw' in our constitution – but one which is shared by all, unlike barrenness or other failings. The period of mourning accomplishes some degree of readjustment, by rituals of family meals creating social support for the bereaved, and publicly licensed grief which is cathartic. During this period some readjustment both of emotions and social relationships can take place. At the end of the period of withdrawal and transition the bereaved return to normal life.

Religious rituals

The rituals which have been discussed so far often have a religious component, but we turn now to other rituals of a primarily religious character – seeking to influence a deity, and to express religious beliefs and attitudes. There is most overlap in two areas – relief of guilt and reassurance of immortality. We described rituals which relieve guilt as healing rituals, but they may play an important part in the main religious ceremonies, as they do in the Christian church. Reassurance of immortality is an important motivational root of religion, and occurs particularly in funerals but also in other kinds of service.

Influencing the deity

In most religions attempts are made to influence the god or gods by petitions, offerings, and sacrifices – of objects, animals, or people. At root this may be a case of reciprocity –

it is felt that something must be done in exchange. It is not understood why sacrifices are often used for this purpose – perhaps for primitive people the animals were their most valued possessions. As Edmund Leach (1968) points out the meanings given to sacrifice by those performing it may vary considerably – that the victim is a gift or a bribe to the gods, that the victim is a substitute for the giver of the sacrifice, that the victim is a symbolic representation of sin, or that the victim is identified with God. Furthermore, none of these explanations seem entirely satisfactory, since they do not explain why killing an animal should have any religious power at all.

When things go well – the harvest is good, a war is won, the rains come – then there may be ceremonies of thanksgiving.

Magical practices also use non-verbal symbolism in order to influence events. The difference from religion is that instead of appealing to a deity, direct suggestion is used, at a distance. Again the two different kinds of symbolism are used – analogical in sympathetic magic, and arbitrary in contagious magic. In sympathetic magic a model may be made of the person to be influenced, in contagious magic some object associated with him, or previously belonging to him is used.

Expressing religious beliefs and attitudes

Religious beliefs have the function of providing a cognitive system which interprets the experience of life in a satisfactory way, and of linking this explanation to life goals. To express such beliefs requires more than words, it requires action, and it can be done by NVC in religious ceremonies. Just as children dramatize their most interesting experiences, so in religious rituals there are dramatizations of the most basic and important aspects of experience – birth and death, relations with parents, eating and drinking, love and sex, the sun, moon, and seasons, and so on. Concern with these matters is expressed by non-verbal symbols, which are metaphorically related to these objects and which express and partly arouse the emotions felt towards them. Attitudes of humility and repentance can be expressed by bodily postures such as bowing the head, kneeling, or lying flat on the floor. Attitudes of joy can be expressed by singing and dancing, attitudes of aspiration by looking and reaching upwards.

Religious ceremonies take place in a sacred place, which is marked out for the purpose; inside this sacred place objects and actions acquire special symbolic power. People can here participate in the ritual, and feel that something special is taking place and being accomplished. Why are particular objects – animals, trees, or stones – endowed with religious power? Some anthropologists maintain that it is because they are connected with factors important for the survival of the society – so there are sacred turtles in the Andaman Islands. Lévi-Strauss (1962) suggested that sets of objects are selected which can act as conceptual models of society, for instance kinship systems; by thinking in terms of these objects other ideas can be grasped more easily. In some cases the importance of ritual objects is, however, due to association, as is the case with Catholic relics, or similarity, as with the Cross. In primitive religions it is believed that these objects themselves have magical powers to heal, or exert other powers. We would now regard this as a mistake – these sacred objects *do* have powers, but only because they affect the beholder through their capacity to express basic and important emotional attitudes.

'Sacredness' appears to be communicated by special NV signals; in the main world religions these are – silence, darkness, incense, candles, special music and bells, special clothes, washing before entering, particular symbols such as the crucifix, special shape of building, e.g. cross-shaped and pointing up to heaven.

The nature of ritual communication

Ritual has come to be regarded as a form of communication, primarily non-verbal, and we may inquire about its structural properties.

The way ritual has meaning

As we have already seen, the meaning of ritual cannot wholly be discovered by interviewing those involved. Field workers have inferred from careful studies of primitive rituals that they seem to acquire meaning in two different ways. (*a*) Similarity, metaphor, or analogy. Examples are the cross, and wine for blood. In healing rituals they symbolize parts of the body or physiological processes. Other religious rituals symbolize basic emotional experiences relating to birth, love, death, and so on. (*b*) Contiguity, association or other arbitrary associations. Examples are Catholic relics, and animals or flags representing social groups. In rituals which are concerned with social relationships, they symbolize social groups, or relations between people. As we have seen there is no objective means of deciding on the meaning of these rituals. It seems most probable that a ritual can have a number of different meanings at the same time – the same act or object can have a large number of metaphorical links. Turner (1966) suggests that symbols can 'condense' several meanings simultaneously, both analogical bodily meanings, and arbitrary reference to social groups. In this way group values become charged with emotion, while basic emotions become ennobled through being linked with social values. Ritual is often closely connected with myth and the myth provides an interpretation for the ritual.

The NV signals used in ritual are quite different from verbal communications. They arouse images and feelings metaphorically, and this is what gives them their power. We shall discuss later the idea that ritual or artistic messages function quite differently from verbal communication (p. 383f).

Ritual signals often stand for social relationships, and as Edmund Leach (1968) has pointed out there are a number of common ways of symbolizing these. Social status is represented by a person being on a higher level for example. More abstract ideas and feelings about life are expressed metaphorically in terms of everyday social behaviour: washing represents purification or removal of guilt, eating an animal suggest the acquisition of its properties, changes of status suggest death and rebirth, which in turn may be linked with the sun, moon, and seasons.

Why NVC is used in ritual

There are three reasons why NVC rather than language is used here. In the first place language is not well adapted to describing subjective emotional experiences and the niceties of social relations, especially for primitive people. Language is designed to communicate about events in the external world, rather than those of the inner world. Secondly, verbal expression does not evoke powerful emotional feelings, produce bodily or psychological healing, or effect changes in social relationships. What we have called 'ritual work' can be accomplished by NVC, but not by language alone. The power of NV signals here is derived from the emotive associations which they have. Some NV signals are probably used simply to increase the impact of other signals, or to communicate social influence – bodily contact, mutual gaze, and the impressive costume of the priest, for example. Thirdly, some personal and interpersonal problems can evidently be handled better if they do not come fully into consciousness, where their contradictions and difficulties would be disturbing or embarrassing. As Meyer Fortes (1966) puts it: 'It is not surprising that there is some ritual in most human societies aimed at grasping, binding, and incorporating, into the overt customs and practices of life, the ambivalences of love and hate, dependence and self-assertion which underlie the relations of parents and children, but cannot be understood in causal terms and dare not be admitted as motives of action.' Turner (1966) gives examples of the symbolic expression of suppressed feelings which it would be distressing to verbalize. In some Ndembo rites the hostility of daughters to mothers is expressed indirectly by certain rituals and beliefs, for instance that the mother would die if the daughter got parts of the ritual wrong.

However, words are used in ritual, and rituals derive meanings partly through verbalized sets of ideas, such as Christian theology. Rituals can be described in words and initiated in words, but as Raymond Firth (1970) said, gestures 'have a significance, a propriety, a restorative effect, a kind of creative force which words alone cannot give'. Words add to the meanings of NV signals, and religious ritual thus consists typically of a combination of verbal and non-verbal, where the two kinds of meaning are combined. This adds the precision of words to the emotive power of bodily signals.

Are there structural relations between symbols?

Lévi-Strauss (1962) and other structuralists maintain that ritual forms a system of communication, like a language. If so, there should be sets of interchangeable signs, which can be used at the same point of a ritual. There should be rules whereby sequences can be constructed out of different selections from these sets. And the total sequence should constitute a message, like a sentence or a piece of music. Leach (1972) points out that the same piece of music can be represented by notes on a page, grooves on a record, waves in the air, or sounds in the head – what they have in common is the tune, or the structure. Lévi-Strauss maintains similarly that sexual behaviour, eating, and behaviour in other spheres of life have underlying common structures, so that there can be metaphorical cross reference from one to another, as Freud had noted earlier. Rituals can have metaphorical reference to different spheres of life: several binary pairs function in this way, for example, round/straight refers to female/male, raw/cooked to nature/culture, left/right to evil/good, and so on. Lévi-Strauss maintains that ritual messages can be expressed by means of all kinds of common objects which are ready to hand (bric-à-brac), but which are classified by the culture in a symbolic manner. The reason that similar structures appear in diverse areas of life is that they are all generated by the human brain.

There is one aspect of ritual which clearly functions in this way – the three stage sequence identified by Van Gennep. The three stages correspond to dying and rebirth (in another role), and comprise a universal structure which is used for many rites of passage. The 'climax' sequence which we identified in greetings and other ceremonies is another such structure.

Do other rituals have an underlying structural meaning in the same way, for example, in the case of rituals which express religious beliefs? Since the communication is mainly non-verbal, we would not expect that there would be a simple verbal translation. The elements are non-verbal symbols, just as the elements of a tune are the notes. Although the construction of religious rituals is left to experts, most people are able to design birthday celebrations and other simple rituals, and these have a clear impact on those involved. While the rules for constructing rituals are not generally understood, the meaning of the message seems to be clear enough.

Another feature of structuralism is the discovery of relationships between different members of sets, especially of opposition and inclusion. Rituals do contain symbols related by binary opposition, especially life–death, male–female, right–left, sacred–profane, higher and lower status. There is another way in which ritual can usefully be seen as a communication system. In order to interpret particular rituals, it is often necessary to refer to the proper form, of which one is seeing a shortened and distorted example. As in the case of language, the structure can be seen in the actions of competent performers.

However, the anthropological theories discussed so far do not really explain why non-verbal signals are used in rituals, or how the ritual work is accomplished. Here is the basis of a social psychological explanation of ritual. It may be suggested that rituals develop in groups, when there are situations in which individual identities or social relationships need to be strengthened or changed. The sequence of behaviour constituting the ritual develops, by trial and error, in much the same way as norms and rules develop. Use is made of non-verbal signals which define identity (e.g. clothes), or relationships (e.g. postures). Ritualized signals, like the eye-brow flash, are incorporated in longer series of signals. Bodily contact and mutual gaze are used to heighten the influence of the person officiating.

Further Reading

HUXLEY, J. S. (ed.) (1966) *A Discussion of Ritualization of Behaviour in Animals and Men*. Philosophical Transactions of the Royal Society of London. Series B. **251**, p. 247–524.

LEACH, E. R. (1972) The influence of cultural context on non-verbal communication in man. In R. Hinde (ed.) *Non-Verbal Communication*. Cambridge: Royal Society and Cambridge University Press.

TURNER, V. W. (1967) *The Forest of Symbols*. Ithaca and London: Cornell University Press.

VAN GENNEP, A. (1908) *The Rites of Passage*. Chicago: University of Chicago Press, 1960.

References

ARGYLE, M. and BEIT-HALLAHMI, B. (1975) *The Social Psychology of Religion*. London: Routledge & Kegan Paul.

192 The different uses of bodily communication

ARONSON, E. and MILLS, J. (1959) The effects of severity of initiation on liking for a group. *Journal of Abnormal and Social Psychology* **59**, 177–81.

BERNSTEIN, B., ELVIN, H. L., and PETERS, R. S. (1966) Ritual in education. In J. S. Huxley (ed.) *A Discussion of Ritualization of Behaviour in Animals and Men*. Philosophical Transactions of the Royal Society of London.

DURKHEIM, E. (1915) *The Elementary Forms of the Religious Life*. London: Allen & Unwin.

FIRTH, R. (1970) Postures and gestures of respect. In J. Pouillon and P. Marande (eds.) *Échanges et Communications*. The Hague: Mouton.

FORTES, M. (1966) Religious promises and logical techniques in divinatory ritual. In J. S. Huxley (ed.) *A Discussion of Ritualization of Behaviour in Animals and Men*. Philosophical Transactions of the Royal Society of London.

GLUCKMAN, M. (1965) *Politics, Law and Ritual in Tribal Society*. Oxford: Blackwell.

GOFFMAN, E. (1972) *Relations in Public*. London: Allen Lane.

HUXLEY, F. (1966) The ritual of voodoo and the symbolism of the body. In J. S. Huxley (ed.) *A Discussion of Ritualization of Behaviour in Animals and Men*. Philosophical Transactions of the Royal Society of London.

LEACH, E. R. (1968) Ritual. *International Encyclopaedia of the Social Sciences* **13**: 520–6.

LÉVI-STRAUSS, C. (1962) *The Savage Mind*. London: Weidenfeld & Nicolson.

TURNER, V. W. (1966) *The syntax of symbolism in an African religion*. In J. S. Huxley (ed.) *A Discussion of Ritualization of Behaviour in Animals and Men*. Philosophical Transactions of the Royal Society of London.

WHITING, J. W. M., KLUCKHORN, R. and ANTHONY, A. (1958) The functions of male initiation ceremonies at puberty. In E. E. Maccoby et al. *Readings in Social Psychology* (3rd ed.). New York: Holt, Rinehart and Winston.

YOUNG, F. W. (1965) *Initiation Ceremonies: a Cross-Cultural Study of Status Dramatization*. New York: Bobbs-Merrill.

10

NVC in society – politics & persuasion

In large groups of animals social order is maintained and leadership exercised by non-verbal encounters, mainly between the older and stronger males. In primitive human societies things are similar, except that words are used – though words have little effect unless backed up by the appearance or reality of power. In modern societies our affairs appear to be conducted rationally, democratically, and verbally. In fact non-verbal signals are extremely important. In recent years NVC has come to assume an additional importance, since many young people and disaffiliated groups have come to distrust the use of language in politics. They do not trust smooth-talking politicians, who can make anything sound reasonable, and they find that they cannot influence events by using the usual verbal channels. So they have resorted to the various political uses of NVC.

Symbolic action in politics

Bosmajian (1971) describes an hour in the life an imaginary American student:

'At 8.00 a.m. a college student gets ready for his morning classes. He puts on his work levi's, a psychedelic shirt, and a pair of boots; he hangs a peace medallion around his neck and pins a clenched-fist button to his shirt. He leaves his apartment, sees an acquaintance across the street, and holds up his hand in the V symbol. On reaching the campus, the student enters the Union for a cup of coffee, and there he witnesses a demonstration against racial discrimination and sees protestors wearing black armbands in a silent vigil against the war. He moves on into the cafeteria, which is filled with a folk-rock sound coming from a juke box. Among the many posters on the walls he notices a civil-rights placard which consists mainly of a depiction of a teen-age black being attacked by a snarling police dog loosed upon him by a law officer. Later, on his way out of the cafeteria, the student again passes the demonstrators and observes that they are now standing side by side, holding hands, singing and swaying to the rhythm of "We Shall Overcome." ' (p.viii)

This gives examples of some of the non-verbal signals used for political purposes. We can distinguish five different kinds of political activity, each of which makes use of non-verbal signals.

Direct political action

Industrial workers are able to bargain for better wages by striking, supported by non-violent picketing, both of which are now legal in most countries. This can turn into violent, and illegal picketing. Revolutionary groups engage in other forms of illegal activity, such as kidnapping and hijacking. While these actions are partly, indeed primarily, intended to coerce, they are also communications. Picketers are communicating (with or without words) their view that people should stay away from work, and their intense disapproval of those who do go to work. Hijackers and kidnappers get a great deal of publicity, even though it is unfavourable for their cause. Political kidnappings are quite different from private ones from this point of view.

Civil disobedience

Civil disobedience consists of unaggressive law breaking and passive resistance, in a way which is socially disruptive and which communicates clearly what is felt to be wrong. It was started in the modern world by Gandhi who organized an illegal march in 1913 by Indian workers in South Africa, in protest against taxes on Indians and a law against non-Christian marriages. This was followed by hunger strikes and various forms of civil disobedience against the British authorities in India. Gandhi taught non-violent resistance and inculcated feelings of high morale among his followers, who felt that their behaviour was right. Since then there have been numerous campaigns of civil disobedience on the part of racial and other oppressed groups. The American Negroes between 1942 and 1965 had an extensive campaign of protests, led latterly by Martin Luther King.

Non-violent resistance in the face of brutality by the police and others can be a very powerful non-verbal signal. The theory is that the aggressors will be sickened and guilty at their actions, and give up. In practice the authorities usually respond with firm but non-violent means of control.

The segregation laws were broken in the U.S.A. by eating in segregated restaurants, travelling in segregated buses, and so on. (This phase came to an end in 1964 with a series of Negro riots, and the rise of more violent leaders.) Demonstrations against the Viet Nam war and other student protests set off a further wave of civil disobedience on the part of American students. Sit-ins became popular in the 1960s, together with teach-ins and the burning of draft cards. Attacks on politicians and embassies, disruption of sport, and confrontation with the local police took place all over the world from the mid-sixties.

While it might seem pointless to wrestle with the local police over events in distant lands, this gets into the news with the message that a lot of people feel strongly about something. This in turn creates problems of non-verbal behaviour for the police. They know that the demonstrators will have won a moral victory if the police are seen on TV behaving badly, and that the demonstrators may become more violent if the police are too tough. In Britain the strategy has been adopted of keeping the police horses and water cannon in reserve and using a lot of restraint.

Some of this political behaviour is aggressive, as a result of pent-up frustration often unconnected with the particular issue. Most disobedient behaviour, however, is symbolic. Occupying a building doesn't usually do much real harm, but it communicates the depth of feelings, and the number of people who share them. These feelings may be expressed more strongly – by occupying the Vice-Chancellor's office and defecating in his waste-paper basket, or by driving a herd of cows into the Senior Common Room. The solidarity of those involved is further displayed by wearing similar clothes, badges, and carrying placards.

Peaceful demonstrations

Minority and low status groups have difficulty in gaining access to the mass media. However, they can do so by manufacturing news themselves by means of peaceful or violent demonstrations of various kinds. An individual can create news and support for his cause by going on hunger strike or setting himself on fire.

The sheer size of a demonstration can be news. The Aldermaston marches against the nuclear bomb were impressive by virtue of the length of the procession – several miles. John Breaux, at Oxford, has found that leaders of demonstrations often exaggerate greatly the number present, and that these astronomical figures give great confidence to those present; they can't see for themselves how many people are really there. The Washington protest against the Viet Nam war was impressive because of the enormous numbers involved, because of their quiet dignity, and the symbolic value of the coffin paraded.

A number of non-verbal signals are particularly associated with demonstrations. These include:

(a) the presense of large numbers
(b) marching in procession, with linked arms
(c) the use of raised fists or other special salutes
(d) chanting slogans, singing hymns, and so forth
(e) holding torches or candles, during meetings after dark

Other non-verbal signals are used under particular social conditions. For example, in Japan the 'zigzag' dragon protest march is used as a result of laws about the width of processions; in South American countries 'ténèbres' is used – standing round lamp posts, banging them with metal rods, because of fear of reprisals against large demonstrations. At American revivals a 'sea of green' is created by waving dollar bills which are being donated. (I am indebted to John Breaux for these examples.)

The effects of these non-verbal signals are likely to be (1) to communicate to observers the strength of the movement and the commitment of its members, as well as perhaps fear of them, and (2) to create shared enthusiasm, and militant or other emotions, among those who participate.

Demonstrations of power by the authorities

How can those in authorities reply to the non-verbal signals of civil disobedience, and the other communications which we have discussed? Clearly a verbal reply will have little effect. However, there are special ways of communicating symbolically the power of the government. As Charles Merriam (1965) suggests these include:

Memorial days and periods

Public places and monumental apparatus

Music and songs

Artistic designs, in flags, decorations, statuary, uniforms

Story and history

Ceremonials of an elaborate nature

Mass demonstrations, with parades, oratory, music

Parades of soldiers, policemen, marching bands, tanks, etc. have been familiar in Red Square, the streets of Belfast, Nazi Germany, and elsewhere. Such parades have two different effects – on those who see them, and on those who take part. Observers are impressed by the large numbers of men and the military equipment in the parade. A Nazi parade might consist of 50,000 men and take seven or eight hours to pass. They are also impressed by the demeanour of the men – the smartness of their uniforms, the precision of their discipline, their keenness and common purpose, their acceptance of the leaders' will. Observers may also note the aggressive superiority displayed for example by the Nazi goose-step. The participants are also affected by all this; they develop a strong feeling of dependence and togetherness, they share collective enthusiasm for the goals of the movement, they feel a sense of superiority to those who do not belong. This is enhanced by stirring martial music, and parade orders and saluting, which reinforce obedience to the hierarchy.

Attempts to change the social position of a group

Racial and other minority groups, members of lower social classes, and young people occupy underprivileged positions in society. In addition to their material frustrations there are also those of being treated as social inferiors in everyday social contacts: the style of non-verbal behaviour of members of superior groups constitutes the main source of frustration. For a long time it was common for low-status people to accept their position, and behave in a humble manner towards their superiors and to adopt their fashions. In recent years the blacks, some of the young, and others, have abandoned this strategy in favour of an aggressive assertiveness. From 1964 onwards American blacks changed their appearance, adopting the Afro-Asian hair-cut and treating whites with hostility and contempt. Many students gave up behaving nicely and trying to be approved of by their elders: by their clothes and hair and manner of behaviour they communicated the message that they were totally rejecting the way of life of polite, middle-class society, and that they constituted a new social group with ideas of its own about how life should be lived.

It is interesting that attempts to change an established relationship between two groups led in both cases to violence and a breakdown of communication. Younger teenagers often have a similar problem: before settling down into a relation of equality with parents and other adults they often go through a period of rejecting them entirely. It should be possible, however, for an individual or group of lower status simply to change the relationship by gradual modification of the non-verbal signals, replacing deferential signals by equality signals. The violence strategy does not improve the status of a low status group in the eyes of the others, and it also leads to a rift in society.

Persuasion and propaganda

In previous historical periods influence was exerted by leaders, politicians, and prophets by word of mouth at public meetings. A number of studies have shown that emotive messages have more effect than rational ones; 'emotive' messages involve a combination of verbal and non-verbal signals. The leader's performance on these occasions is very important in building up the right image. He must look right, and he must sound right – left-wing leaders often cultivate regional accents. Religious leaders often develop a very intense and dramatic manner, with the result that they are seen as specially holy, 'charismatic' characters. This probably explains why a number of severely disturbed persons have become successful religious leaders for a time.

Roosevelt made much use of the radio and later political leaders have used TV. The Kennedy–Nixon debates influenced many of those who saw them to vote for Kennedy, partly because of his evident persuasiveness and charm, partly because of the less favourable impression created by Nixon's face. New media demand new kinds of image-making. We shall discuss later McLuhan's ideas about the effects of media of communication on society (p. 370f).

We shall discuss persuasion and propaganda in terms of the changing of images. Commercial products, political parties, and public figures all have images, as a result of the way they are presented to the public. The information conveyed is partly verbal, partly non-verbal. By an 'image' is meant the ideas a person has about an object or person, usually the socially shared, or stereotyped views held by the public. A 'brand image' is the image of a particular brand of car or soap.

A variety of methods are used for assessing images. Often purely verbal methods are used. For example Mark Abrims and Rose (1959) found that Macmillan and Gaitskell had different images.

Quality	Macmillan	Gaitskell
Strong leader	50	12
Some qualities of greatness	40	7
In touch with ordinary people	17	38

Later workers used a set of seven-point rating scales designed to assess reactions along a number of relevant dimensions. However, the problem is how to discover the dimensions which are most relevant for distinguishing between different politicians or brands of margarine. This is often done by depth interviews or group interviews, to see what verbal concepts emerge. Market research people want to know whether the relevant components for soaps are price, hygiene, cosmetic power, soothing rather than irritating the skin, smell, or what. Another way of finding the concepts which discriminate between brands is the repertory grid in which stimuli (e.g. brands) are presented three at a time and the subject is asked to say which is different from the other two; this is a means of discovering the concepts (dimensions) which are actually used by people in the domain in question (Bannister and Fransella, 1971). When the likely verbal concepts have been identified in these ways they can then be incorporated into seven-point scales, which in turn can be factor analysed to discover the main dimensions.

An alternative approach is to use indirect methods, which we may regard as semi-verbal. In a famous study of the image of instant coffee, Mason Haire (1950) asked house-wives to imagine themselves as having bought one of two lists of groceries, of which one included instant coffee: about 50 per cent regarded the person visualized as 'lazy'. Sentence-completion methods ask respondents to complete sentences like:

'Powdered coffee is . . .'

'She was ashamed of the coffee she had just served be-cause . . .' Or respondents can simply be asked what sort of person they think would use certain brands.

Not much use has been made of non-verbal methods in studying brand images. However, in studying the impact of advertisements, verbal methods have proved inadequate. Research with the eye-marker camera showed that people did not always look where they said they looked, especially if they found part of an advertisement embarrassing or unpleasant. It was also found that people claimed to recog-nize control advertisements which had not been shown at all, claiming perhaps that this was the kind of advertisement they would have noted. Other studies have found that people can recall the contents of advertisements without any attitude change taking place, and that it may have no effect on their buying habits. So advertising research has to some extent turned to non-verbal measures of response – pupil dilation, skin resistance changes, and manipulation of knobs to indicate degree of interest or liking–dislike of successive parts of a presentation. The ultimate measure of success of a commercial is of course the buying, voting, etc. that results: this can be studied by using different commercials in a number of different but carefully matched areas.

Having established the image of a product, advertisers and propagandists then want to change it, in a way that will result in buying or voting. Advertisements are not used only by commercial firms and political parties, but also by governments, for example, to encourage people to drive more carefully, or go into schoolteaching. There are several basic methods.

Changing the image of the product itself

When the image of a product is known, it can be examined to see which features of it are negative in some way. For example, Mason Haire's study of instant coffee found that coffee was associated with tiredness and strain, and with exhausted office workers. Subsequent advertisements tried to associate coffee with gay and gracious living, on the part of vivacious and attractively dressed young women. Another example derives from the British Conservative Party's campaign in the 1959 election – the first time an advertising agency was used in British politics. It was found that 27 per cent saw the Conservative Party as the party of the privileged minority. Posters were then designed with the verbal message 'The Conservatives are the party of the whole country', others carried a primarily non-verbal message: photographs of a cloth-capped worker peering through a hole in a boiler, saying 'You are looking at a Conservative' (Butler, 1960).

In this campaign the person shown in the posters was skilfully varied between different newspapers: the cloth-capped worker was shown in the *News of the World*, a clerical worker in the *Sunday Express*, a young scientist in the *Observer*, and a working woman in the *Sunday Pictorial*. By the end of the campaign only 17 per cent of the population associated the Conservative Party with privilege.

The Conservative campaign was of course carefully planned with an eye to the appeals of the rival party. Commercial advertisement campaigns are conducted like minor wars, in which each of the main brand manufacturers in each field is constantly changing the images offered, and in some cases the product itself, in order to woo the public away from his competitors. Different images are offered to different sections of the public, to different social classes, ages, sexes, regions, and so on.

The Conservative Party posters consisted of both verbal and non-verbal messages. The coffee advertisements were purely non-verbal. No arguments or evidence were produced; there was simply a flat non-verbal assertion that coffee is associated with a certain kind of person and mood. This is completely non-rational: no doubt there are gay coffee drinkers, and no doubt coffee is also drunk by spies, lunatics, and criminals. The recipient will not wonder whether the message is true or not; the counter argument might consist of a different image, but this would probably not spring to mind.

Linking the product to need-satisfaction

Motivation research discovers what needs a product appeals to in different sections of the population; advertisements are designed to persuade people that these needs will indeed be met and in a satisfying way. Thus motivation research on toilet soap found that it is bought by women, that women establish their brand preference when young, and that young women are more interested in the glamour and cosmetic powers of soap, than in hygiene or other functions. Consequently soap advertisements focus on the glamorous consequences of using soap. Posters inviting young men to join the Army show soldiers water-skiing in romantic and exotic parts of the world. Advertisements for the teaching profession show teachers behind big desks, directing lesser teachers, or surrounded by admiring pupils, or signing cheques for new cars. In such still photographs or cartoons, a clear cause-effect relation is asserted: join the Army and you can travel and go water-skiing. In TV or film commercials little sketches show the cause-effect sequence very vividly, for example, the effect of a powder on dirty sinks, or of dog food on unhappy dogs. Again, a non-rational assertion is made, this time of a causal kind

A certain amount of use is made of sex in advertising. In some cases this is a plausible motivational appeal, as in the case of cosmetics and clothes. Sex is also used in less plausible cases: topless models sit on cars at the Motor Show. This may be partly to attract attention (which it does), partly perhaps to create a basic positive attitude towards the product. At one time some use was made of Freudian symbolism in advertisements, for example, of pictures of phallus-like pipes at petrol stations to advertise petrol. However, there is no evidence that such methods are effective.

Suggesting changes in the self-image

Another kind of advertisement holds out the promise that your self-image will be changed in some way if you adopt the product. The suggestion of increased social status is one of the most ancient advertising methods – 'Use this brand of car, shirt, or china, and you too will be as upper class as the people in the advert.' The advertisement may associate the object with other objects – a make of whisky is shown on an antique table, with old silver, or riding equipment. Or the object is associated with a mythical person, an actor wearing expensive clothes, expensively groomed, and looking very upper class, or it is associated with a real person – The Countess of X who always eats such and such. Advertising men find that they have to be careful not to pitch these real or imaginary persons too far above the social status of the target audience. This approach is used to appeal to upwardly mobile people, and for highly visible possessions like clothes, cars, and household equipment used for entertaining.

Advertisements may offer other kinds of self-image, in addition to social class. Young people may be offered the vivacious, fascinating, and attractive 'getaway people' image. Mothers may be offered the 'good mother – happy home' image. These self-images are offered for products like petrol where the different brands are in fact identical – only the image is different.

The non-verbal message here is again a causal one, except that the supposed effect is a change in how people see themselves and how they are seen by others. It is done by offering the product as a new symbol, e.g. a brand of shirt as a status symbol. The message tries to change the meaning of the product by associating it with other symbols. There is indeed a constant change in status symbols in particular, as lower status people adopt them and high status people find new ones (p. 341f). Advertising men say in defence of their activities that people really do buy the self-image with the product, and after all there is more to a car than just getting about.

Enhancing the public image of political leaders

Whether or not a political leader is elected to high office depends partly on his personal public image, quite apart from the policies he and his party stand for. This public image is derived partly from real events in his career, partly from the impression he gives on TV and in person, and it is partly the result of impression-management by public relations experts. An early operator in this field, Ivy Lee, is reported to have changed the image of John D. Rockefeller from robber baron to philanthropic old gentlemen who loved to play golf and hand out shiny coins to children. This was done by widely publicized donations to charity, and ingeniously drafted press releases. The art of impression management has developed, particularly in the U.S.A., so that it is impossible to tell how much is real and how much is bogus.

Eugene Burdick (1964) describes in a novel *The 480* how real and bogus events affect a politician's public image. The hero of this novel takes part in various real events. One is highly symbolic: he prevents a war between India and Pakistan by hanging perilously from a crane on a girder between the ends of an unfinished bridge between the two countries, and making a speech reminding the two sides of when they had suffered together, with the result that the bridge was completed and the war averted. There were also a series of completely managed events – a man is paid to throw a tomato at the hero's part-Filipino wife, a crowd of students create what appears to be a spontaneous riot on behalf of the candidate outside the convention hall.

The syntax of persuasive NVC

Why is NVC used in these spheres? The main reason is simply that it is more effective. Although man is partly rational, he is greatly swayed by NV messages in this area. If a large crowd is seen shouting in support of something this has some influence – one does not necessarily think of the much larger crowd who think otherwise. If two images are presented together – such as gay young women and coffee – this constitutes a persuasive argument and one does not necessarily think of all the gloomy, elderly, male coffee drinkers. Just as a smiling face has more impact than friendly words, so NV signals in politics have more impact than speeches. There is another advantage, that persuasion can be used without it being too obvious, not only in symbolic and sub-threshold commercials. Things can be said which it would be embarrassing or absurd to put into words – such as the alleged effect of adopting a commercial product on one's social status or sex life.

What is the structure of these persuasive messages? The signals used are very carefully designed to convey certain images – of social class, sexual attractiveness, and personality attributes, for example. They are also designed to avoid sending certain images, when a public image is being modified. Some use is also made of symbolism – like the Viet Nam coffin, and similar symbols, which are able to evoke a powerful (and non-rational) emotive response. The message is usually a simple one, that two images are in fact associated, or that one thing leads to another. The Viet Nam coffin said that a lot of people have been killed in Viet Nam; no attempt was made to deal with complex political, moral, or military arguments on this topic. Another kind of message consists simply of indicating that a lot of people feel strongly about something.

Further reading

BOSMAJIAN, H. A. (1971) *The Rhetoric of Nonverbal Communication*. London: Scott Foresman.

BROWN, J. M. *et al.* (1966) *Applied Psychology*. London: Collier-Macmillan.

SAMPSON, E. E. (1971) *Social Psychology and Contemporary Society*. New York: Wiley.

References

ABRAMS, M. and ROSE, R. (1959) *Must Labour Lose?* Harmondsworth: Penguin Books.

BANNISTER, D. and FRANSELLA, F. (1971) *Inquiring Man*. Harmondsworth: Penguin Books.

BURDICK, E. (1964) *The 480*. London: Glencoe.

BUTLER, D. (1960) *The British General Election of 1959.* London: Macmillan.

HAIRE, M. (1950) Projective techniques in marketing research. *Journal of Marketing* 14: 649–56.

MERRIAM, C. (1965) *Political Power and the Governmental Process.* London: Collier-Macmillan.

The different bodily signals

Part 3

The different bodily
signals

11

Facial expression

The face is the most important area for non-verbal signalling. It is a highly expressive region, able to send a lot of information, and therefore most attended to. The eyes are an important part of the face, but these will be discussed separately in the following chapter.

How did the face come to be so important for NV signalling? Biologically the face consists of the mouth, eyes, and nose, and the earliest facial expressions to evolve were intention movements (like showing the teeth), or attempts to see better (like opening the eyes wide and raising the eyebrows). These biologically useful expressions became ritualized as social signals in the course of evolution, so that a number of standard social signals became part of the innate repertoire, and the face itself evolved as a communication area. Visual discrimination has also developed in higher animals so that they are able to perceive facial expressions at the distances at which social interaction takes place.

Rather little use is made of facial expression in animals below the primates, though some of them use biting movements, and direction of gaze. Some frogs, snakes, and fish produce a swelling in the face or neck, as a threat display. Lower animals make more use of posture and less of facial expression. A number of species of birds erect a crest or comb, as an invitation to grooming, as a sexual display, or threat. Many species have not been studied very carefully from this point of view, but it has been found that wolves have a quite extensive range of facial expressions, and this is most likely due to their hunting in packs.

Primates live in groups and have a complex social life, and probably for this reason have an elaborate set of facial expressions. They have not taken over all of the signals used by lower animals, but we have taken over some of theirs. The number of facial expressions varies between species; several species have about thirteen distinctive patterns of expression, each occurring in a particular situation, and accompanied by other signals. The evolutionary origins of some human facial expressions such as smiling and laughing have been traced back through our primate ancestors (p. 41f). Primates have facial expressions for each of the main interpersonal relationships – dominant, submissive, threatening, sexual, parental, playful, etc. The face is a very efficient means of communication at close quarters, where it is important to be clear who is communicating to whom, and where social relationships are rather intricate. What is communicated is primarily interpersonal attitudes and emotions, together with status and identity.

In man facial expressions are used in three rather different ways.

(1) *Personality characteristics*: by the structural features of the face and the typical expression, and perhaps by some faster reaction patterns which are characteristic. The control of facial expression is taught by parents as part of cultural socialization.

The reason that impressions of personality are formed from the face is probably that the face is the area which is attended to most; hence people are recognized most readily from their face, and their facial behaviour stands for their personality. This can be controlled to a certain extent, so that what is seen is partly the result of self-presentation.

(2) *Emotions*: by slow-moving patterns of expression; *interpersonal attitudes* are expressed in a similar way. In man expressions of emotion and interpersonal attitudes are modified and controlled by cultural rules, and partly directed by cognitive factors.

(3) *Interaction signals*, and signals linked to speech, are sent by rather fast movements of parts of the face, for instance, eyebrow raises. With the development of speech, facial expression has been taken over for a quite new purpose – the supplementation and support of speech, for example by feedback and synchronizing signals. These are quite different from emotional expression, they involve only parts of the face, and have an intricate syntactic structure. The development of speech has included the development of an elaborate system of communication, consisting of the vocal-audio channel linked with the facial/gestural visual channel.

There is a general difference of speed, in that the first is static, the second slow, and the third fast, except that personality can also be expressed by repeated fast reactions, e.g. a constant tendency to laugh, or show sudden anger or surprise. It is tempting to suggest that the first depends on bodily structures, the second on the autonomic system, and the third on the central nervous system; however, emotions depend on cognitive as well as autonomic factors, and personality is expressed by all three levels.

The face has a number of different parts which can act independently:

Mouth: turned up or down, with different degrees of opening, showing teeth or tongue
Eyebrows: raised or frowning
Skin: coloured white or red, perspiring or not
Nose: sneering, flared nostrils

There are configurations of the face as a whole, as in the main emotional states. Facial movements can be distinguished from static positions, e.g. startle, laugh, and micro-momentary expressions.

Facial expressions for emotions and interpersonal attitudes in man

As we saw, the main facial expressions in animals signal attitudes to other animals – invitations to play, sexual attraction, dominance, etc. Research on humans has, however, concentrated on emotions; the face has been found to signal emotions like happiness, surprise, fear, or anger. Some of these can be regarded as interpersonal attitudes, since it is usually clear which individual is the object of fear or anger. However, there are several other interpersonal attitudes – especially liking/dislike, inferiority/superiority, and sexual attraction. We shall discuss these later in the section.

What are the different facial expressions for emotion which can be distinguished by observers? A number of studies have been done, in which many posed or real-life photographs are judged by observers in relation to lists of provided emotions. This method is open to criticism on grounds of artificiality, through use of posed expressions, static photographs, lack of context, and provided categories. Early research with posed photographs by Woodworth and Schlosberg suggested various sets of categories. One of the most sophisticated studies of this kind was carried out by Osgood (1966) who asked judges to identify forty different facial expressions. Cluster analyses showed that seven main groups of expressions were clearly distinguished. From this and other studies it looks as if the main facial expressions for emotion are as follows:

happiness	anger
surprise	disgust, contempt
fear	interest
sadness	

1 Fear grimace by chimpanzee (from Reynolds, 1967)

The silent bared-teeth face by chimpanzee (from Morris, 1967)

3 Mother chimpanzee
tickling infant who
shows the typical
play-face (from
Morris, 1967)

4 A specialized
threat gesture, the
baboon yawn (from
Jolly, 1972)

8 Female baboon presents to male while directing her gaze towards him (from Altmann, 1967)

9 Demonstration against the war in Vietnam (from a circular distributed by Initiative Internationale Vietnam-Solidarität)

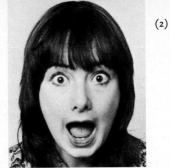

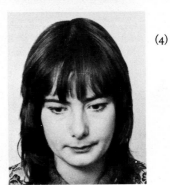

(2)

(4)

(6)

10 The main facial expressions: (1) happiness, (2) surprise, (3) fear, (4) sadness, (5) anger, (6) disgust, (7) interest

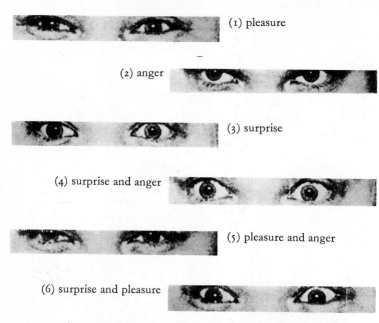

(1) pleasure

(2) anger

(3) surprise

(4) surprise and anger

(5) pleasure and anger

(6) surprise and pleasure

11 Emotions perceived from the eyes alone (from Nummenmaa, 1964)

12 Two photographs, identical but for pupil size, elicited very different responses from male subjects (from Hess, 1965)

14 A married Nuer girl
(photograph B. H. MacDermot)

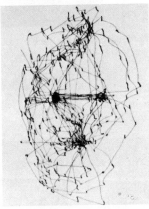

13 Record of the eye movements during free examination
of a photograph with both
eyes for three minutes
(photograph S. Fridyland,
from Yarbus, 1967)

15 A Guinea man whose
costume includes a pig's
tusk and cassowary quills
(from Severin, 1973)

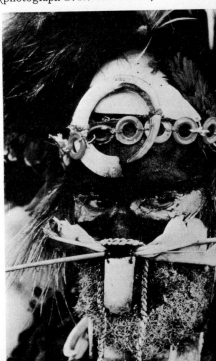

16 A mild degree of courting tonus: head erect, eyes bright with lids slightly narrowed (from Scheflen and Scheflen, 1972)

17 High tonus shown quite visibly; accentuated by pressing upper calf against lower knee and flexing foot (from Scheflen and Scheflen, 1972)

18 A man's courting behaviour may resemble that used in dominance: he draws up to full height, protrudes jaw, stands close, and displaying what is generally regarded as a masculine stance (from Scheflen and Scheflen, 1972

19 & 20 An actor on Paddington station drew different responses to requests for information depending on his apparent social class

Examples of these expressions are given in Figure 11.1.

Osgood and others also used the method of asking sub-jects to rate photographs on a number of verbally labelled rating scales: these ratings were then analysed statistically to show the dimensions being used by the judges. These experiments produce the following main dimensions:

Pleasant – unpleasant
Emotional intensity – control
Interest – lack of interest

The seven expressions can be plotted against the three factors as Osgood has done, but it is not clear which mode of analysis best represents the encoding and decoding of emotions. Dimensions have the advantage that they consist of opposite poles – which fits Darwin's idea that some emo-tional expressions are simply the opposite of others; it also fits the Lévi-Strauss idea that non-verbal signals are ulti-mately based on binary oppositions. On the other hand the seven categories correspond better with known and familiar states.

These studies all suffer from the limitation of using stills rather than moving pictures. But it has been found that although emotions can usually be recognized better from sequences of film, the difference is not great, which shows that the static position of the face conveys most of the information about emotions. Another limitation is that in most of this research observers were asked to respond in terms of verbal categories; perhaps there are no adequate words for some emotions.

However, the methods discussed so far have depended entirely on *verbal* methods of responding to the non-verbal stimuli. Peter Stringer (1967) used a method which avoids this problem: he asked judges to sort photographs into groups based on similarity, and carried out a statistical analysis of those groupings. He found three dimensions, which he labelled as follows:

Happy – worried
Thoughtful – surprised
Thoughtful – disgusted, in pain.

The explanation for this discrepancy may be that the observers went beyond the range of emotions, and included expressions used in connexion with verbal communication (e.g. thoughtful, puzzled).

Are different emotions communicated by different facial displays? There have been a number of encoding studies, in which it has been found that arousing different emotions does produce measurably different facial expressions. And there have been decoding studies in which measurably different photographs have been judged differently by observers. At one time it was thought that different emotions were expressed in different areas of the face, for instance, happiness in the mouth and surprise in the brows, but there is little agreement between later investigators, and it looks as if each emotion is expressed by a pattern involving the whole face. Frois-Wittman (1930), for example, found that pictures judged as *angry* contained frowning, raised upper lid, wrinkled lower lid, dilated nostrils, open lips, lower teeth exposed, and depressed lower lips. Pictures judged as *happy* contained depressed upper lid, wrinkled lower lid, dilated nostrils, open lips, raised and retracted corners of the mouth. Thayer and Schiff (1969), however, found that emotions could be recognized quite easily from schematic diagrams of faces, in which only mouth and eyebrows were varied (Fig. 11.1).

Ekman and colleagues (1972) developed a scoring system for facial expression, in which photographic examples were shown of each of six emotions in (1) brows/forehead, (2) eyes/lids, and (3) lower face. A particular photograph could be scored by matching each area to the sample photographs. They scored 51 photographs in this way and found that in 44 cases the majority of 82 observers agreed with these scores.

Figure 11.1. Emotions perceived in schematic faces (from Thayer and Schiff, 1969: 76)

PERCENT (ROUNDED) RESPONSES TO FACES IN EACH DESCRIPTIVE RESPONSE CATEGORY
AND MODAL INTENSITY RATING OF PREDOMINANT JUDGEMENT (IN PARENTHESES)

Descriptions	Blank	Control	Neutral	Happy	Sad1	Angry1	Fiendish	Angry2	Sad2	Happy Sheepish	Sad3
1 Elated				03						03	
2 Happy		11	33 (2)	81 (4)			03			36 (3)	
3 Neutral	89 (5)	38 (4)	39 (3)	08				06	50 (3)		61 (5)
4 Sad		22 (2)	08		42 (3)	13					
5 Angry						58 (4)	03	53 (5)	03		
6 Furious						17		33 (4)			
7 Amused			03	08			03		03	19 (3)	
8 Sheepish		06	03							25 (3)	
9 Mischievous		06		03		11	16			06	
10 Fiendish						03	75 (5)	11			
11 Depressed					17	03		03	08		24
12 Apprehensive		06	06		19	03		03	22 (3)	12	06
13 Afraid			03		03	03			03		06
14 Horrified	03								06		
15 Other	06	11	03			03					03

How accurately can emotions be recognized from facial expressions? This depends on a number of factors.

First, if a small number of alternative categories are used the judge's task is easier – they get about 66 per cent correct with seven alternatives, and 13 per cent right with forty; evidently judges can't go far beyond the seven main expressions. Secondly, an emotion can be distinguished more easily from emotions that are expressed most differently. Woodworth arranged emotions in a series, where judgements of facial expressions were rarely more than one step out. However, this turns out to be a more than one-dimensional problem, i.e. faces vary along three dimensions, not one. Thirdly, it depends on how much information the judge has about the situation (p. 115).

Most of these studies used posed expressions; it can be objected that these may be different in some way from natural expression. Ekman points out that posed expressions are probably more extreme and less inhibited versions of natural ones. While the early studies used rather exaggerated expressions, this is not true of the later ones. A number of experiments elicited actual emotions by such devices as firing a revolver behind the subject, releasing disgusting smells and hypnotizing subjects and giving them bad news. Other studies used news photographs of spontaneous behaviour. The accuracy of identification was 66–70 per cent – much the same as with posed photographs.

Part of the difficulty of judging emotions from facial expressions is due to concealment of negative affect. The face is more carefully controlled than any other source of non-verbal signals. This is particularly true in Japan, but is an important factor in many other cultures. However, concealed emotions can be seen in the face on closer inspection. Anxiety may be shown by small beads of perspiration on the temples. Sexual arousal or intense interest can be seen from pupil expansion. Concealed emotions may be revealed by 'micromomentary expressions', for example, when an angry expression suddenly crosses the face of someone who is talking about a friend. These expressions last about one-fifth second, and can be seen on slow motion film, and by mental nurses, but may be missed by many others.

There is evidence that the subjective experience of emotions is partly due to awareness of one's facial expression. Kimiko Shimoda, at Oxford, has found that if a person adopts a facial expression during a period of interaction his mood changes towards that of the emotion expressed. This supports the idea that a person discovers his own emotional state by using cues such as his own facial expression.

Are emotions expressed in a similar way in different cultures? Some have maintained that emotional expression is innate and much the same in all cultures, others that it is highly culture specific. There have been a number of studies, which make it clear that there are both similarities and differences. There seems little doubt that some emotions are expressed in much the same way everywhere – the startle pattern, and expressions for disgust and grief may be more biologically primitive and hence universal. The startle pattern, with its rapid eyebrow raise, is probably the basis for the slower expressions of surprise and disbelief. Ekman (1972) found that people from Borneo and New Guinea could select the correct photograph, out of three, for the emotion appropriate to a story in about 80 per cent of cases. The subjects were also asked to pose the emotions indicated in the stories; videotapes of their expressions were correctly judged by American subjects in 47 per cent of cases on average. Ekman concludes that basic facial expressions for emotions are innate, but that there are 'display rules' which control the amount of expression displayed, or mark one emotion by the expression for another. The author and Kimiko Shimoda have found that English and Italian subjects can judge videotapes of emotional expression nearly as well for the other culture as for their own; however, Japanese expressions were judged much less accurately and were evidently expressed differently (p. 77). Ekman and Friesen found that Japanese subjects showed stress responses in the face when they thought they were alone, but not if they thought they were being observed. It seems likely that Japanese facial expressions are difficult to recognize partly because of this control, but also because some emotions are simply expressed differently.

As we said at the beginning, while certain interpersonal attitudes are almost identical with emotions (e.g. fear, contempt, anger), other attitudes fall outside the list of emotions commonly expressed in the face. These are liking, dislike, sexual attraction, dominance, and submission/appeasement. In some of the research on emotions, categories of expression corresponding to these attitudes have appeared – if appropriate photographs and verbal categories or dimensions have been included. Probably like/dislike is expressed by the dimensions pleasant/unpleasant and interest/rejection. If there is a difference it lies in other cues, such as gaze and orientation, which indicate that the signal is directed towards a particular person. Dominance/submission has occasionally appeared in photograph rating studies. There may be special facial expressions for these two attitudes; other cues may be more important, for example head tilt, posture, and tone of voice. We might expect that sexual attraction would have some universal features. One such element has been found – the rapid eyebrow flash. Another is expansion of the pupils of the eyes. Facial expression is otherwise much the same as for liking.

Facial signals during interaction

During social interaction the face goes through a rapid and complex sequence of displays, which play a central part in the conduct of verbal communication, and are essential in the maintenance of social relationships. Izard (1973) carried out an experiment in which the facial muscles of a young monkey were severed, with the result that the monkey failed to establish a relationship with its mother. During human verbal interaction, facial movements of speakers, and listeners are essential. These facial signals are not connected with emotional states or personality – though photographs of them might be interpreted in these ways. We are concerned now with movements rather than static or slow-moving expressions, and with parts of the face rather than total patterns. A scheme for classifying these movements has been provided by Birdwhistell (1970), on the basis of the detailed examination of a great deal of filmed behaviour (Fig. 11.2). We discuss Birdwhistell's kinesic vocabulary later (p. 251f).

As we showed earlier, facial and other NV signals are used in close combination with speech to complete the meanings of utterances in various ways, provide feedback from listeners, and give evidence of continous attention (p. 162f). There are a number of other signals with conventional meanings, which may be made by the face, such as winks, grimaces, sticking out the tongue, pretending to scream, imitating a gorilla, etc. These signals are different from emotional expressions in being faster, involving only part of the face, in having referential meanings, and in being syntactically structured. The signals refer primarily to other signals, either those being sent or those just received; there is, therefore, a peculiar kind of referential meaning. This is of a basically digital character – agree/disagree, understand/don't understand – though this can also be a matter of degree. The syntactic structure is of several kinds.

(1) During conversation there is a rapid sequence of facial and other signals, which are dependent on the verbal messages for their organization. There is a total system of communication, but the non-verbal is subsidiary to the verbal.

(2) These facial signals have definite meanings as reward or punishment, approval or disapproval, and therefore have a

Figure 11.2. A code for the face (from Birdwhistell, 1970: 260)

Symbol	Description	Symbol	Description
−◌−	Blank faced	◠	Out of the side of the mouth (left)
−◠	Single raised brow ◠ indicates brow raised	◡	Out of the side of the mouth (right)
−◡	Lowered brow	◠	Set jaw
∨	Medial brow contraction	◡	Smile tight — loose o
⋰⋰	Medial brow nods	⊢⊣	Mouth in repose lax ortense —
◠◠	Raised brows	⌢	Droopy mouth
◦◡	Wide eyed	Ɔ	Tongue in cheek
−◦	Wink	⌢	Pout
> <	Lateral squint	⁂	Clenched teeth
>< ><	Full squint	☻	Toothy smile
	Shut eyes (with	⊞	Square smile
A	A-closed pause 2 count	◎	Open mouth
⋌ ⋋ or	Blink⊣	s◎ʟ	Slow lick—lips
B	B-closed pause 5 plus count	Q◎ʟ	Quick lick—lips
◉◉	Sidewise look	∞	Moistening lips
⋖ ⋗	Focus on auditor	⌷	Lip biting
◉ ◉	Stare	⩗	Whistle
◉◉	Rolled eyes	⋋◦⋌	Pursed lips
⅁ ⅁	Slitted eyes	⬦	Retreating lips
◉ ◉	Eyes upward	⋋◦⋌⊣	Peck
−◉ ◉−	Shifty eyes	⋋◦⋌ !	Smack
⬩◉ ◉″	Clare	⊞	Lax mouth
◉ ◔	Inferior lateral orbit contraction	⩁	Chin protruding
Δs	Curled nostril	⩁	"Dropped" jaw
sΔs	Flaring nostrils	⊢××	Chewing
⸜Δ⸌	Pinched nostrils	⋋ ⋌	Temples tightened
⬠	Bunny nose	ε з	Ear "wiggle"
⬠	Nose wrinkle	⁓⁓	Total scalp movement
∿	Left sneer		
∼	Right sneer		

direct effect on the behaviour that follows. If an act of A's is clearly approved of by B, then A will repeat the act, or move on to another stage in a sequence, for example, of love-making or salesmanship. A signal of puzzlement or incomprehension will lead to attempts to clarify. Signals of dominance may lead to complementary signals of submission/appeasement, or to competing dominance signals. Very often signals of a particular kind elicit similar signals from another, either through sheer imitation, or as an exchange of rewards. (3) In particular social settings there are rules governing the 'rituals' involved – as in greetings, church services, banquets, or sporting occasions. These rules often prescribe what is the correct facial expression at each stage of the ritual – one must look cheerful during greetings, solemn during church services, including weddings, and miserable at funerals; victors at sporting occasions should appear modestly pleased, and so on.

These facial expressions are not controlled by the autonomic system in the way that emotions are. They are closely linked with language, so they are probably controlled by the part of the brain governing language. And while the signals have to be learnt, the capacity for this kind of facial signalling is innate.

The face and personality

People are known by their faces, and photographs and paintings concentrate on the face in representing them. One person can clearly be distinguished from another by his face, but what further information is conveyed? Animals categorize one another by species, sub-group, as individuals, and by age, sex, and status. We do all this, and we also categorize one another in terms of 'personality'.

There are many different features of the face which affect impressions of personality. We will divide them into different

types, according to how far they are under the control of the
subject.

FEATURES	JUDGED AS
Structural aspects	
thin lips	conscientious
thick lips (female)	sexy
high forehead	intelligent
protruding eyes	excitable
dull eyes	not alert
Persistant emotional expressions and their effects	
mouth curvature	friendly, cheerful, easy-going, kind, likeable, with a sense of humour, intelligent, well-adjusted
facial tension	determined, aggressive, quick-tempered, not easy-going, friendly, carefree, patient
Grooming	
much make-up (females)	feminine, sexy, frivolous
dark or coarse skin (males)	hostile
Spectacles	intelligent, dependable, industrious

These results were obtained in investigations by Secord
and others (1959) in which photographs were judged for
personality. Secord and his colleagues also found in a study
of photographs of twenty-four white males that they fell
into a number of clusters, where similar personality characteristics were ascribed to photos in each cluster. Each cluster
also contained certain *combinations* of facial features, as
follows:

FEATURES	JUDGED AS
shallow-set eyes light eyebrows bright eyes widened eyes neatly groomed	carefree, easy-going, cheerful, with a sense of humour, honest, warm-hearted
younger face few horizontal wrinkles slicked-down hair	energetic, conscientious, patient, honest, warm-hearted, friendly, intelligent, responsible, kind, trustful, easy-going
older face averagely thick lips (average-looking people)	meek, studious
thin lips neatly groomed	moral/social respectability
older face thin lips wrinkles at eye corners	distinguished, intelligent, refined
dark complexion oily, coarse skin	hostile, boorish, sly, quick-tempered, conceited
younger face low eyebrows narrowed eyes	carefree, excitable sly, conceited

In addition judges have a definite preference for average, as opposed to unusual, features. Secord gave descriptions of very nice and very nasty persons and asked subjects to imagine their physiques. They imagined the bad person as having eyes close or wide apart, lips thick or thin, nose wide or narrow, and so on.

Some of these results were obtained from perception of photographs, and it is possible that they do not apply when more information is available. The author and Robert Mc-Henry (1970) found that target persons are judged to be more intelligent by fourteen points of IQ when wearing spectacles, if they are seen doing nothing for fifteen seconds.

However, if they were seen in conversation for five minutes the effect of the spectacles vanished.

Is there any real relation between the cues above and personality characteristics? There is a definite, though small, correlation between physique and temperament. Muscular people tend to be out-going and aggressive, thin people are more intelligent and neurotic, fat people are relaxed and placid (p. 336). Persistent expression presumably indicates the mood a person is most often in, and this can lead to permanent changes in the face, such as wrinkles. Grooming is a piece of self-presentation, i.e. is an item of deliberate communication. Spectacles are mainly for seeing with, but curiously enough there is a small correlation between intelligence and short-sightedness. Can judges form accurate impressions of people just by looking at them? Judgements based on photographs are found to have very low validity, typically about 0.10.

However, judgements of age, sex, race, and to a lesser extent social class, can be made from the face. This categorization leads to the application of social stereotypes. For example, Secord found that target persons were classified as 'Negro', if they had curly hair, dark skin, and thick lips; they were then thought to be religious, superstitious, happy-go-lucky, and stubborn.

Facial features can lead to impressions of personality in several other ways, as Secord has pointed out. A person's face is similar to that of other people one has known, and creates the anticipation that he will be similar in personality too. If he smiles or looks anxious one may assume that this is his normal condition, and not in this situation only. There may be inference from the function of parts of the face – high foreheads are thought to contain large brains, thick lips to be good at kissing, spectacles are used for reading and intellectual work. And there may be metaphorical associations, people with coarse skins and dishevelled hair are thought to be coarse and aggressive. Empathy may also be involved:

by imagining what we would feel like if we adopted that facial expression, we imagine what it would feel like to be the other person.

To the extent that facial features can be manipulated, communication is involved, but the code used depends on the kinds of judgement commonly made, as described above. Probably the main way in which people manipulate their facial features is by adopting certain expressions – suggesting that they are happy, keen, thoughtful, or superior. The grooming code varies with class and culture, and changes rapidly with time, as has the significance of beards, side-whiskers, and long hair. While women spend more time and trouble on grooming, length of hair is very important to men.

There are some peculiarities about the perception of personality. One is that everyone has his own set of categories or dimensions; this is rather different from the perception of emotions, where we all use the same ones. Secondly we do not always give verbal labels to other people, as psychologists do. It is partly a matter of memories of similar people, functional and metaphorical impressions, not in the form of words but as images, anticipated behaviour, anticipated reaction to them, and empathized imagination of what it would feel like to be they.

Further reading

EKMAN, P., FRIESEN, W. V., and ELLSWORTH, P. (1972) *Emotions in the Human Face*. Elmsford, N.Y.: Pergamon.

VINE, I. (1970) Communication by facial–visual signals. In J. H. Crook (ed.) *Social Behaviour in Birds and Mammals*. London: Academic Press.

References

ARGYLE, M., and MCHENRY, R. (1970) Do spectacles really affect judgements of intelligence? *British Journal of Social and Clinical Psychology* 10: 27–9.

228 The different bodily signals

BIRDWHISTELL, R. L. (1970) *Kinesics and Context*. Philadelphia: University of Pennsylvania Press.

EKMAN, P. (1972) Universals and cultural differences in facial expressions of emotion. *Nebraska Symposium on Motivation*. Lincoln, Nebr.: University of Nebraska Press.

FROIS-WITTMAN, J. (1930) The judgement of facial expression. *Journal of Experimental Psychology* 13: 113–51.

IZARD, C. E. (1973) Reported in B.B.C. 2 *Horizon* programme on The Human Face.

OSGOOD, C. E. (1966) Dimensionality of the semantic space for communication via facial expression. *Scandinavian Journal of Psychology* 7: 1–30.

SECORD, P. F., DUKES, W. F., and BEVAN, W. (1959) Personalities in faces, 1: An experiment in social perceiving. *Genetic Psychology Monographs* 49: 231–79.

STRINGER, P. (1967) Cluster analysis of non-verbal judgements of facial expressions. *British Journal of Mathematical and Statistical Psychology* 20: 71–9.

THAYER, S. and SCHIFF, W. (1969) Stimulus factors in observer judgement of social interaction. *American Journal of Psychology* 82: 73–85.

12

Gaze

People look at each other primarily to collect information rather than to send it; the eyes are receptors, a means of receiving another's NV signals. Nevertheless when a person looks at another, this can be decoded by the other person in a number of ways, so opening the channel becomes a signal. It is curious that this very familiar aspect of social behaviour should have evaded the attentions of research workers until so recently. Although gaze is a familiar phenomenon when attention is drawn to it, people are normally unaware or barely aware of the gaze patterns of themselves or others.

There are a number of different variables. Here are the basic statistics for two people in conversation, on an emotionally neutral topic, at a distance of six feet. This will also serve to introduce some of these variables.

Individual gaze	60 per cent
while listening	75 per cent
while talking	40 per cent
length of glance	3 seconds
Eye-contact (mutual gaze)	30 per cent
length of mutual glance	1½ seconds

These figures are averages, and there is wide variation, according to the personalities of those involved, their attitudes towards each other, and the topic of conversation, as will be described below. In groups of three, for example, each person divides his gaze between the other two, and each person spends only about 5 per cent of his time in mutual gaze with each of the others. When there is a physical task to attend to, interactors look at it most of the time, and much less at each other, as we found in a study of selling in a department store. Interactors may look to see the direction of the other's gaze and then follow his line of regard.

In addition to *amount* of gaze, there are a number of closely associated variables to do with the *quality* of gaze, though these have been less extensively studied so far:

Pupil dilation (from 2–8 mm in diameter)
Blink rate (typically every 3–10 seconds)
Direction of breaking gaze, to the left or right
Opening of eyes, wide-open to lowered lids
Facial expression in area of eyes, described as 'looking daggers', 'making eyes', etc.

The pattern of looking between two or more people can be analysed to find if the amount of mutual gaze is more or less than would be expected from the amount of individual gaze. If each person looks 50 per cent of the time, there should be 25 per cent mutual gaze by chance. The expected gaze is equal to the percentage of A's gaze multiplied by the percentage of B's gaze. However, since people look nearly twice as much while listening as while talking there is a certain amount of alternation.

Gaze is studied in the laboratory by observing the behaviour of two or more subjects, or of one subject interacting with a trained stooge – whose gaze pattern has been standardized in some way. The actual recording can be done by observers from behind a one-way screen, or from video-tape recordings. Observers press buttons, which either activate a pen-recorder or an electronic counter.

Research has found that gaze functions in several distinctive ways, and that these different aspects of looking are intricately combined. The author and his colleagues (1973) carried out an experiment which separated the different aspects of looking. Pairs of subjects talked to one another across a one-way screen, via microphones and loudspeakers as shown below:

Figure 12.1. Laboratory arrangements for one-way screen experiment

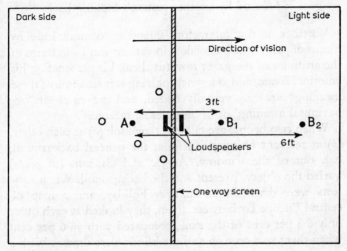

O = Observer

The amount of gaze by each subject was recorded, under different conditions. Some of the findings were:

(1) A (who could see) looked 65 per cent of the time, while B (who could not) looked only 23 per cent of the time. Presumably A was looking in order to collect information, and he did so both while talking and while listening.

(2) B (who could see nothing) still looked 23 per cent of the time; his gaze was accompanied by the usual series of facial expressions and head nods; presumably he was *sending* information, though this may have been partly habit.

(3) Proper conversations were compared with monologues. During monologues A's gaze fell from 65 per cent to 47 per cent, presumably because there was no need to send synchronizing (and possible feedback) signals.

(4) There was more gaze under these conditions than when there was no one-way screen between the subjects – especially at close proximities. Evidently the amount of gaze is reduced by another person's looking back.

Whether or not interactors intend to communicate by means of gaze, others decode it in various ways – in terms of the attitudes of the gazer towards them, his personality, his emotional state, and as a synchronizing signal. Some of these meanings are not verbally coded, and are cases of 'behavioural meaning' or of 'non-verbal meaning'.

When two people are talking, they look (*a*) at each other, (*b*) at relevant objects, and (*c*) at the general background, e.g. out of the window. Argyle and Graham (in press) varied the objects present and the background. When subjects were discussing a summer holiday, and a map of central Europe lay between them, they looked at each other only 6·4 per cent of the time, compared with 76·6 per cent when there was no map and the blinds were drawn. With a very vague, outline map of Europe, they still looked at each other only 27 per cent. It is interesting, and surprising, that people choose to manage with very little looking at the other under these circumstances.

Interpersonal attitudes

Patterns of gaze play an important role in establishing relations between people. Gaze functions as an efficient signal here in that there is a match between encoding and decoding – people interpret gaze patterns correctly.

People look more at those they like. Exline and Winters

(1966) arranged for subjects to talk with two confederates; as expected each subject preferred one stooge to the other; they were asked to say which one they preferred, thus making their preferences more salient. It was found that subjects looked 2·7 times as much at one stooge than at the other. Males behaved somewhat differently in this experiment, and looked less *while listening* to the non-preferred interviewer. Similar results have been found in other experiments: Rubin (1970) devised a questionnaire for measuring how much in love couples were. He found that for couples who were most in love a higher proportion of their gaze was mutual. Gaze is almost certainly used as a courtship signal, especially by females, who take a lot of trouble to decorate their eyes, and have recently taken to wearing decorative dark glasses.

There have been a number of decoding experiments showing that gaze is perceived as a signal for liking. Mehrabian (1972) found that if an experimenter interviewed two subjects, the subject who was looked at most inferred that she was preferred. Direction of gaze was found to be a more effective signal than bodily orientation in this experiment. Other experiments have shown that if A looks at B, not only does B perceive A as liking him, but he in turn likes A more.

Pupil size also acts as a signal for interpersonal attraction. At one time ladies enlarged their pupils by belladonna to make themselves attractive, and it is reported that Arab salesmen study the pupils of their customers to see which goods they are most interested in. Ekhard Hess (1972) carried out a series of laboratory experiments in which he found that the pupils of males dilated when they were shown photographs of attractive females, the pupils of females dilated with photographs of males and of babies, and the pupils of homosexuals dilated for nude male but not for nude female photographs. However, this is not only a sexual response: the pupils dilate to works of art and silver-

234 The different bodily signals

ware patterns – not always in accordance with the verbally expressed views of subjects; for example, not all who claimed to like modern art produced pupil reactions to it. Hess showed two photographs of a girl to male students, where one had been touched up to enlarge the pupils – they preferred the girl with larger pupils and their own pupils dilated, though they had no conscious awareness of the cue to which they were responding (Pl. 12). But do people react to pupils under normal conditions of social interaction? Stass and Willis (1967) experimentally manipulated both the amount of gaze and the size of pupils (using a drug), and found that subjects chose as partner the person who looked more, but that pupil dilation also had some effect. Pupil dilation is a difficult cue to use – it can only be seen at close quarters, and in a good light, and pupils respond in any case to changes in the illumination, by enlarging when it gets darker. To sum up so far, interpersonal attraction is both encoded and decoded by amount of gaze, amount of eye-contact, and pupil size.

Why do people look more at those they like? It has been found that subjects look more at those who reward them in some way, for example by making approving remarks. Since approval is partly expressed in the face, it is likely that the gaze itself has been rewarded; the eyes have seen rewarding signals.

However, the amount of gaze is restrained, and is usually well below 100 per cent. Argyle and Dean (1965) suggested that an equilibrium level of gaze is used, which is the product of a conflict, between forces to look and forces to avoid looking; if one person likes another, the balance is shifted and he looks more. We also suggested that there are a number of different signals for intimacy which can substitute for one another. We found that at greater distances there is more gaze (p. 305f), and Exline (1965) found that with more intimate topics there is less gaze, and with less intimate topics more. Experiments on deceit have found that if one person is deceiving another (a less intimate relationship) he normally looks less (p. 245).

A variety of studies have been carried out to test different predictions from the model, with generally positive results (Patterson 1973): it works best when there is an established relationship which is then disturbed by altering one variable, e.g. distance.

Differences of dominance or status also affect gaze. In groups of animals it has been found by Michael Chance (1967) that there is an 'attention structure', whereby the dominant animals are the focus of attention for their subordinates; the dominant animals influence the others, who make way for them, stop their activity as the leader approaches, or follow the leader's behaviour. In humans too, the individuals who are looked at most see themselves and are seen by others as the most powerful members of the group. Exline and Long (1971) created differences in dyads by allowing one member to divide up the payment money in his own favour. Where this was legitimated by using OTC members of different ranks, the low status person looked 25 per cent more than the other. This may be partly due to a basic and perhaps innate attention-structure process. It is partly because dominant people usually speak more, and therefore look *less*, since people look about half as much while speaking as when listening. Strongman and Champness (1968) found that a group of people formed a consistent dominance hierarchy in terms of which person in each pair broke mutual gaze first more often; the pattern of gaze-breaking was established at the very first mutual glance. Thus the more dominant person looks less, though he breaks gaze last. Similarly Thayer (1969) found that senders of long glances were seen as more dominant than senders of short glances. It seems very likely that a high level of gaze is used to establish a dominant relationship, but that the dominant person then reduces his amount of gaze.

The decoding of gaze in terms of liking and dominance is

shown in an experiment by Argyle, Lefebvre, and Cook (1974). Each confederate used each of five patterns of gaze with different subjects. Statistical analysis of seven-point rating scales filled in by the subjects produced two main factors (1) liking *versus* dislike, and (2) active, dominant, self-confident, friendly, and fast, *versus* passive, submissive, anxious, reserved, and slow – which can be called 'activity' or 'potency'. The five patterns of gaze were perceived as shown in Figure 12.3.

Figure 12.2. The meanings of five patterns of gaze

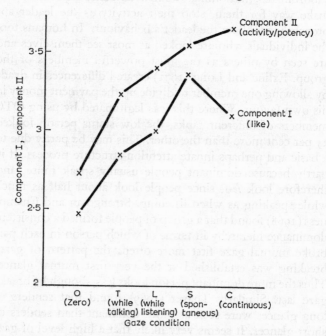

It can be seen that the more a person looked the more active (i.e. active, dominant, self-confident, etc.) he is seen to be. And the more he looks the more he is liked, up to the normal level, after which he is liked less. This last result can be explained on the affiliative balance model; too much gaze creates too much intimacy, which is uncomfortable, so the other is liked less.

In addition to liking and dominance, a third dimension of interpersonal attitudes – threat – is also signalled by gaze. In animals a direct gaze very often signals threat, and its opposite – 'cut-off' or aversion of gaze – signals appeasement. Exline (1971) found that humans can communicate with monkeys in this way. If the experimenter gave a downcast, deferent look, or 'cut-off', the monkey did not respond aggressively.

The act of cutting off gaze is probably performed in order to reduce arousal, or anxiety. However, this act has become ritualized for animals in the course of evolution so that it is decoded as appeasement. Some experiments suggest that a stare can act as a threat signal for humans too. Phoebe Ellsworth et al. (1972) found that if an experimenter stared at a motorist or a pedestrian who was waiting for a stop light to change, the person stared at would move off more immediately after the lights changed. However, experiments like this can also be interpreted in terms of invasion of privacy, or as disturbing pieces of rule-breaking; it could be the meaningless character of the act of staring that makes those stared at want to leave the situation.

Co-operation and competition are also signalled by gaze, but the signals sent vary with the sender. Exline (1963) found that female subjects with strong affiliative motivation looked a lot in a co-operative situation; females low in affiliative motivation looked a lot in a competitive situation; males showed a similar pattern but much less strongly. A high level of gaze is used in a variety of interpersonal relationships; the common meaning is that the gazer is interested in and attending to another person, and his gaze is perceived in this way. The specific interpersonal attitude being expressed is decoded with the help of facial expression and other cues.

The gaze signals used for communicating interpersonal attitudes probably contain more than gaze. Affiliative looks are usually accompanied by smiles, threat signals are not; appeasement signals involve looking away, usually downwards. Sexual attraction as we have seen, includes other signs of arousal such as pupil dilation.

Being looked at by another can be interpreted as 'being observed' by that person. The author and Marylin Williams (1969) found that people felt observed in certain role relations, such as being interviewed, being younger, or being a young female with a young male. This leads to self-consciousness and concern with self-presentation. Some mental patients find it deeply disturbing.

Personality

We know that the amount a person looks depends on the situation he is in – whether he likes the person he is with for example. However, level of gaze is also a fairly consistent characteristic of persons across situations – talking to different people.

A number of personality dimensions are related to gaze. These are not the result of self-presentation, but a product of other personality structures.

Extraversion

The results are not very consistent, but all studies have found *some* relationship between extraversion and gaze; the clearest result is that extraverts look more frequently expecially when talking. There is also evidence that their percentage of gaze is greater and their glances longer. One explanation is that extraverts are at a lower level of arousal, and therefore are less aroused by a given level of gaze or length of arousal, and can tolerate more before cutting off.

However, it is also found that those high in affiliative motivation look more, in co-operative and sociable situations. The explanation of this could be that gaze, or mutual gaze, is one of the goals that provides affiliative satisfaction. This could explain the extraversion finding also. There have been occasional findings to the effect that dominance and aggression are also correlated with a high level of gaze; this probably occurs only in special situations, in competition, or while staring down.

Schizophrenia and depression

Psychotic mental patients have often been reported to show peculiarities of gaze, and in particular aversion of gaze. Rutter and Stephenson (1972) carried out a carefully controlled study of twenty acute schizophrenics, twenty depressives and forty matched controls from a non-psychiatric hospital; they found that the schizophrenics looked, on average 65 per cent as much, the depressives 73 per cent as much as normals, and that the schizophrenics used shorter glances – 2·1 seconds, compared with 3·4 for the depressives and 3·9 for the controls. But why do schizophrenics look less, is it to avoid people or to avoid stimulation in general? Ederyn Williams (1974), using a waiting room situation, found that schizophrenics spent more time looking at a television programme of fish, than at a person, especially when the person tried to engage the patient in conversation. The patients were clearly avoiding social contact rather than stimulation. Less well-controlled observations of chronic schizophrenics who have been in hospital for some years show that they have an almost complete aversion of gaze.

Autistic children

Aversion of gaze is so great in autistic children that it is one of the defining criteria: one study (Coss, 1972) found that they looked 4 per cent of the time (65 per cent for normal controls), in glances of 0·5 secs (3·5 for controls); they actively avoid mutual gaze – by pulling hats over their eyes or looking through their fingers. On the other hand social contact of other kinds is not avoided; autistic children will sit on adult laps or lead by the hand – while looking in the opposite direction. Clearly autistic children have a strong and specific aversion to eyes or faces; it is generally supposed that these stimuli are very arousing for them, but it is not known why.

Sex differences

Sex differences have appeared in many studies of gaze. Females look more, pairs of females show a high level of mutual gaze, and they are more disturbed by the absence of visual cues in experiments where vision is reduced. Other people are more aware of the gaze behaviour of females than of males; and of course females in many cultures put more effort into making up their eyes. Exline found that females looked more in co-operative situations and when high in affiliative motivation.

Personality differences

There are personality differences in the direction of breaking gaze when asked a question. Most males break consistently to the left or the right, typically 75–85 per cent of their shifts being in the same direction; females are less consistent. Experiments by Bakan (1971) and others have found that left-movers are more sociable, musical and religious, tend to be studying classics or humanities, are more easily hypnotized, and have strong alpha-rhythms. Electrical stimulation of parts of the right frontal cortex produces a gaze-shift to the left; it is argued that left-shifters have a dominant right hemisphere, and vice-versa. This research is consistent with clinical studies of patients with split brains in suggesting that the left hemisphere is verbal, rational, and propositional, while the right hemi-sphere is non-verbal, analogical, subjective, and emotional.

Later experiments have generally confirmed these results, for right-handed males at least. Kinsbourne (1972) found that right-handed males looked to the right when given verbal problems, left for spatial ones. Recent research suggests that the effect is weak in social situations and stronger when the subject is facing a wall; it has also been found that questions about words produce a shift downwards as well as to the right, while spatial questions produce a shift upwards, as well as to the left (Galin and Ornstein 1974). This line of research is extremely interesting, in suggesting a neurological basis for verbal and non-verbal styles of thinking, reason, and intuition, which we shall discuss later (p. 383f).

A number of experiments have investigated how different patterns of gaze are decoded. Kleck and Nuessle (1968) made films in which interactors looked either 15 per cent or 80 per cent of the time; judges who saw the films rated them as follows:

15 per cent	80 per cent
Cold	Friendly
Pessimistic	Self-confident
Cautious	Natural
Defensive	Mature
Immature	Sincere
Evasive	
Submissive	
Indifferent	
Sensitive	

But are the same results obtained in real interaction situations? In a study in which subjects met programmed confederates, Cook and Smith (1975) found very little effect of gaze on impressions of personality. There was no effect on ratings, but for subjects who noticed the target persons' gaze patterns, free descriptions revealed that the low gaze target persons were seen as nervous and lacking in confidence. It can be seen that the more a person looks, the more active (i.e. active, dominant, self-confident, etc.) he is

seen to be. And the more he looks the more he is liked, up
to the normal level, beyond which he is liked less. This last
result can be explained on the affiliative balance model;
too much gaze creates too much intimacy, which is uncomfortable.

Gaze accompanying speech

Gaze is used in the initiation of interaction. According to
Kendon's observations, there are two periods of mutual
gaze. The first is before two people have moved together,
and it conveys a joint agreement to begin the encounter.
Other signals, such as a smile or nod, are probably needed as
well. As two people approach they nearly always avert their
gaze, then glance at each other again at the 'close phase' of
the greeting. Angela Steer (1972) found an increase in gaze
at 'transition points', where there is a change of activity. Gaze
is also used at the ending of an encounter. Angela Steer
found that when one person was asked to leave another,
while doing a laboratory task, the period of closure lasted
36 seconds on average, with a glance of 5·7 seconds, which
was longer for friends (8·5 seconds) than for strangers (3
seconds). Mary Sissons (1970) found a strong class difference
in the use of terminal gaze. Working-class people who were
asked the way simply stopped speaking, turned, and walked
away at the end of the encounter; middle-class people gave a
terminal look together with a smile and farewell gesture.

During social interaction there are constant eye-move-
ments, as in other situations. Yarbus (1967) studied the eye-
movements of people looking at still photographs, using an
eye-movement recorder. He found that the eyes go through a
repeated cycle of fixation of points of interest, such as the
eyes and mouth. The fixations last about one-third of a
second, and are linked by saccades – very rapid rotations of
the eyes. An example of this pattern of gaze is shown in
Plate 12. Records of gaze in social interaction studies show
much longer fixations than one third of a second. Other

research by Yarbus and others shows that if the eye looks at exactly the same field for between one and three seconds the subjective field goes blank – since the optic nerve records changes in light intensity. It seems very likely that there are a series of fixations in the same area, for example, the area of the eyes; research on interaction with an eye-movement recorder is needed to trace this out in detail.

During conversation there is a regular connexion between talking and looking. Looking is used to collect feedback, at strategic points; it is used as a synchronizing signal, and as a signal to accompany or comment on speech. As we have seen, people look twice as much while listening as while talking; the reason is probably that speakers do not want to be distracted continually, so look to collect feedback only at certain strategic points in their utterances. Kendon (1967) made a detailed study of these relationships. He found that interactors look up at the ends of utterances; this both provides them with feedback and gives the other person warning that they are about to stop. Kendon found that interactors look away at the beginnings of utterances. While this has not been found in all studies, it occurs when questions are being answered. They look up more briefly at grammatical breaks; at these points the other person gives accompaniment signals, such as head-nods, indicating willingness to listen further. They look away at hesitations and when talking unfluently – presumably to avoid input of distracting information. They look up when asking short questions, when giving attention signals, and when laughing. There is mutual gaze during attempted interruptions.

The pattern of gaze linked with speech forms a closely integrated system. For example, the terminal gaze both acts as a full-stop signal to the other and enables collection of feedback. Gaze plays a central role in social performance: it opens the channel for receiving visual non-verbal signals from others, which are the main sources of feedback during interaction. While gaze is a channel, it is also a piece of behaviour which is governed by reinforcement and other factors – so that under certain conditions the channel will be mostly closed, fewer non-verbal signals will be received, and social performance will deteriorate.

Gaze functions in other ways too during conversation:

Signal	Effects
gazes at end of another's utterance	reinforcement; he will talk more on same topic
gazes during parts of own utterance	gives emphasis
gazes more while speaking	is more persuasive
gazes more while asking questions about the other	other talks more about himself

While these variations are permissible and meaningful, there are definite rules about the pattern of gaze during interaction. It would be quite unacceptable, for example, to look on and off every half-second, or to stare at the other's genitals, or not to look at him at all. If terminal gazes are not given at the ends of utterances the other fails to reply, and the synchronizing system breaks down. Though the sequence of gaze is rule-governed and intricate, it does not produce very complex information. Perhaps the most important message communicated is that the person gazing is attending, that the channel is open. When there is mutual gaze both people know that the channel is open for two-way communication. Simmel (1921) described it as 'a wholly new and unique union between two people . . . it represents the most perfect reciprocity in the entire field of human relationships'.

Emotional state

Avoidance of gaze accompanies negative emotions like anxiety, shame, and embarrassment; the reverse is probably true of other emotions. Exline and his colleagues (1970) found that when subjects were experimentally implicated in an unethical act of deception they looked less – unless they were 'machiavellian personalities', in which case they gave a frank and open look while lying. Emotions affect other aspects of eye behaviour; for example, in fear the eyes are frozen open, in anger they are narrowed, in joy there are wrinkles around the eyes. Pupil dilation can act as a cue for changes in emotional arousal, but it is affected by other variables too, such as the light intensity. Blink rate also varies with arousal; it is increased during states of anxiety or tension, but decreased during concentrated thinking or visual attention. It is not known whether any use is made of this signal by decoders. Nummenmaa (1964) showed subjects parts of photographs of faces of target persons displaying different emotions. Most accurate recognition of emotions was found for the area round the eyes; this was particularly true of complex emotions like 'pleasure and anger'. (See Pl. 11.)

The biological and cultural basis of gaze

Gaze is widely used by animals, as a threat signal, and as a means of collecting visual information in social situations. Moths and fish have fake 'eye-spots', birds have 'eye-rings', which have evidently developed as social signals to repel predators. It has been found that if the eye-spots are removed from butterflies, birds will eat them, whereas when the eye-spots are present birds will retreat. While it has been suggested that eye-spots are the product of evolutionary 'mimicry' of the eyes of predators, Scaife (1974) argues that this is not so – often they are quite different from, e.g. the eyes of owls, and their power may simply be due to their being strong stimuli with good black and white contrast.

Animals also use gaze as an affiliative signal, and in primate hierarchies, as described above; however, there is a definite shift in humans, for whom gaze is more often affiliative than threatening. Human infants, in the first hour of life, will follow a moving object with their eyes; by three or four weeks they respond particularly to a pair of eyes, or to masks including this design. It is not known whether this early interest in eyes is innate, or, as Fantz (1971) suggests, there is an innate preference for stimuli of a certain degree of complexity, brightness, and rate of movement. The mother's eyes would be the most arresting object in sight, and there may then be early learning of and attachment to the mother's eyes and face. Gaze, mutual gaze, and cut-off play a central role in early peek-a-boo and similar games (Bruner: lecture at Oxford). Gaze and mutual gaze play a central role in the development of attachments and sociability. Longitudinal studies show that looking at others is established early in life, declines in early adolescence, when children are self-conscious, and reaches a higher level in early adulthood (see Argyle and Cook, 1975).

Coss (1970) found that the eye-pattern produced greater pupillary dilation in adults than a number of similar patterns, though this does not prove anything about innateness (Fig. 12.3). It has also been argued that this early visual contact with the other is biologically useful in reinforcing the mother.

While the main gaze phenomena appear to be much the same in all human cultures, there is some variation. The

Figure 12.3. Pupillary reactions to eye-spot patterns (from Coss, 1970)

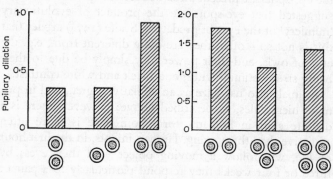

most striking difference found so far is that Arabs have a higher level of gaze than Americans or Europeans, despite also standing closer. The Japanese look at the neck rather than the eyes, though these must come into peripheral vision except at very close proximities. Greeks look more than British or Americans, both during encounters and at strangers in public places. Some American and South American Indians on the other hand look much less than we do. Since Roman times it has been believed that witches and others have the 'evil eye'. This is still believed in Naples, where it is ascribed to some priests, and monks, though formerly to old ladies with squints or deep-set eyes. It is believed that those who are looked at by the evil eye are cursed.

Gaze is not a signal in the way that facial expression and gestures are signals. People look primarily in order to see, not to send messages. They are, however, unwittingly sending two signals, first that the communication channel is open and visual signals can be received, secondly that they have some interest in the person being gazed at. The meaning of gaze for others is no doubt derived from this. Cut-off is used by animals to reduce arousal, but becomes a ritualized signal for appeasement during evolution. The end-of-utterance gaze in humans is used to collect feedback, but acquires meaning as a full-stop signal, via learning. The way gaze is interpreted depends on the facial expression and the situation, which enables the person gazed at to distinguish between love and threat for example. For some of the cues we have discussed the decoding goes beyond what is encoded; in the case of gaze it does not go far enough. If a person averts his gaze others may not be able to decide whether this is because he is too close, is discussing a very intimate or difficult topic, has other interesting things to look at, dislikes his companion, is of higher status, is an introvert, schizophrenic or depressive, is embarrassed or depressed or is a member of certain American Indian tribes, to list some of the main possibilities.

248 The different bodily signals

Further Reading

ARGYLE M. and COOK, M. (1975) *Gaze and Mutual Gaze*. Cambridge: Cambridge University Press.

EXLINE, R. V. (1971) Visual interaction: the glances of power and preferences. *Nebraska Symposium on Motivation*, 163–206.

References

ARGYLE, M. and DEAN, J. (1965) Eye contact, distance, and affiliation. *Sociometry* 28: 289–304.

ARGYLE, M. and GRAHAM, J. A. (in press) The Central Europe experiment – looking at persons and looking at objects. *Environmental Psychology and Nonverbal Behavior*.

ARGYLE, M. and INGHAM, R. (1972) Gaze, mutual gaze, and distance. *Semiotica* 1: 32–49.

ARGYLE, M., INGHAM, R., ALKEMA, F. and MCCALLIN, M. (1973) The different functions of gaze. *Semiotica* (in press).

ARGYLE, M., LEFEBVRE, L. and COOK, M. (1974) The meaning of five patterns of gaze. *European Journal of Social Psychology* 4: 125–36.

ARGYLE, M. and WILLIAMS, M. (1969) Observer or observed? A reversible perspective in person perception. *Sociometry* 32: 396–412.

BAKAN, P. (1971) The eyes have it. *Psychology Today* 4: 64–7.

CHANCE, M. R. A. (1967) Attention structure as the basis of primate rank orders. *Man* 2: 503–18.

COOK, M. and SMITH, J. M. C. (1975) The role of gaze in impression formation. *British Journal of Social and Clinical Psychology* 14: 19–25.

COSS, R. G. (1970) The perceptual aspects of eye-spot patterns and their relevance to gaze behaviour. In C. Hutt and S. J. Hutt *Behaviour Studies in Psychiatry*. Oxford: Pergamon.

COSS, R. G. (1972) Eye-like schemata: their effect on behaviour. Ph.D. thesis, University of Reading.

ELLSWORTH, P. C., CARLSMITH, J. M. and HENSON, A. (1972) The stare as a stimulus to flight in human subjects. *Journal of Personality and Social Psychology* 21: 203–11.

ELWORTHY, F. T. (1895) *The Evil Eye: an Account of this Ancient and Widespread Superstition*. London: John Murray.

EXLINE, R. V. (1963) Explorations in the process of person perception: visual interaction in relation to competition, sex and need for affiliation. *Journal of Personality* **31**: 1–20.

EXLINE, R. V., GRAY, D. and SCHUETTE, D. (1965) Visual behavior in a dyad as affected by interview content and sex of respondent. *Journal of Personality and Social Psychology* **1**: 201–9.

EXLINE, R. V. and LONG, B. (1971) unpublished study reported in R. V. Exline (1971).

EXLINE, R. V., THIBAUT, J., HICKEY, C. B. and GUMPERT, P. (1970) Visual interaction in relation to Machiavellianism and an unethical act. In R. Christie and F. L. Geis (eds.) *Studies in Machiavellianism*. New York: Academic Press.

EXLINE, R. V. and WINTERS, L. C. (1965) Affective relations and mutual gaze in dyads. In S. Tomkins and C. Izzard (eds.) *Affect, Cognition and Personality*. New York: Springer.

FANTZ, R. L. (1961) The origin of form perception. *Scientific American* **204**: 66–72.

GALIN, D. and ORNSTEIN, R. (1974) Individual differences in cognitive style. I. Reflective eye movements. *Neuropsychologia* **12**: 367–76.

HESS, E. H. (1972) Pupilometrics. In N. S. Greenfield and R. A. Sternback (eds.) *Handbook of Psychophysiology*. New York: Holt, Rinehart & Winston.

KENDON, A. (1967) Some functions of gaze-direction in social interaction. *Acta Psychologica* **26**: 22–47.

KINSBOURNE, M. (1972) Eye and head turning indicates cerebral thought processes. *Science* **176**: 539–41.

KLECK, R. E. and NUESSLE, W. (1968) Congruence between the indicative and communicative functions of eye contact in interpersonal relations. *British Journal of Social and Clinical Psychology* **7**: 241–6.

MEHRABIAN, A. (1972) *Nonverbal Communication*. Chicago: Aldine-Atherton.

NUMMANMAA, T. (1964) *The Language of the Face*. University of Jyvaskyla. Studies in Education, Psychology and Social Research, 9.

PATTERSON, M. L. (1973) Compensation in non-verbal immediacy behaviors: a review. *Sociometry* **36**: 237–52.

RUBIN, Z. (1970) Measurement of romantic love. *Journal of Personal and Social Psychology* **16**: 265–73.

RUTTER, D. R. and STEPHENSON, G. W. (1972) Visual interaction in a group of schizophrenic and depressive patients. *British Journal of Social and Clinical Psychology* **11**: 57–65.

SCAIFE, M. (1974) The responses of animals to eyes and eye-like patterns. Oxford D.Phil. thesis.

SIMMEL, G. (1921) Sociology of the senses: visual interaction. In R. E. Park and E. W. Burgess (eds.) *Introduction to the Science of Sociology*. University of Chicago Press.

SISSONS, M. (1970) The psychology of social class. In *Money, Wealth and Class*. London: Oxford University Press.

STASS, J. W. and WILLIS, F. N. Jnr. (1967) Eye contact, pupil dilation and personal preference. *Psychon. Sci.* **7**: 375–6.

STEER, A. (1972) Nonverbal cues in the termination of encounters. Paper to British Psychological Society.

STRONGMAN, K. T. and CHAMPNESS, B. G. (1968) Dominance hierarchies and conflict in eye contact. *Acta Psychologica* **28**: 376–86.

THAYER, S. (1969) The effect of interpersonal looking duration on dominance judgements. *Journal of Social Psychology* **79**: 285–6.

WILLIAMS, E. (1974) An analysis of gaze in schizophrenics. *British Journal of Social and Clinical Psychology* **13**: 1–8.

YARBUS, A. L. (1967) *Eye Movement and Vision*, translated by Basil Haigh. New York: Plenum Press.

13

Gestures & bodily movements

The hands and to a lesser extent the head and feet can produce a wide range of gestures, which are used for a number of different purposes. Biologically the hands have evolved for grasping and manipulating objects, including other animals. However, the hands can also communicate, particularly by illustrating objects and movements. In higher mammals and men a large area of the brain is associated with them. We have seen that primates use gestures (1) to express attitudes to others, for instance, by banging and stamping (truncated intention movements), (2) as 'displacement activities' such as scratching, in states of conflict or frustration, (3) for pointing, indicating direction of attention. Primates can also be taught gesture languages, but apparently do not use them spontaneously.

Gestural communication in human societies is rather different; it involves the development of signs with agreed meanings. Some bodily movements are similar to those used by animals; others develop because of the natural similarity of gestures to movements and objects; others acquire complex arbitrary meanings.

One of the most important contributors to the study of bodily movements has been Ray Birdwhistell (1970; and see review by Kendon, 1973). He has been concerned with the total communication process, both verbal and non-verbal, and he has assumed that bodily movements function as a kind of language – using a limited vocabulary of common signs in any particular culture. He has accordingly used a linguistic rather than an experimental approach. Bird-whistell's method is to study short sequences of film in great detail, in order to find the units of behaviour and how they function. At one time he spent 100 hours on each second of film, taken at 48 frames per second. However, there are now systematic research methods for tackling these problems: standard elements can be found by cluster analysis, as has been done for facial expression (p. 214f), and rules of com-bination and sequence can be found by rule-breaking experi-ments (p. 63f). Birdwhistell looked for elements of behaviour such that, although they might vary in detail, they would be reacted to in the same way. He called these 'kinemes', an analogy with phonemes, and drew up a vocabulary of 60 kinemes which he found in American subjects. Part of this list is reproduced on p. 222. Others have objected to this scheme on the grounds that some bodily movements func-tion as continuous variables, and not as a series of discrete categories. Birdwhistell maintains that these kinemes com-bine to form larger units (kinemorphs), on the analogy of morphemes (or words). One example would be shaking a fist combined with a smiling or angry face. Similarly facial expressions consist of different combinations of eyebrow position, mouth curvatures, etc. (p. 216). Birdwhistell also stresses that the meaning of bodily signals varies in different social settings: a smile can mean a number of different things; as we have seen some gestures have special meanings in cricket matches and auction sales. However, Birdwhistell goes further and thinks that bodily signals have no standard meanings of their own (as words have) but acquire them in particular situations; however facial expressions for emo-tions and gestural illustrations appear to be exceptions to this. A number of other people have followed Birdwhistell in looking for a linguistic structure in non-verbal behaviour, and we shall discuss this approach later (p. 374).

A further criticism of this approach is that it is not clear how far these combinations of kinemes, and combinations of kinemes and situations, have shared social meanings. The main facial expressions have been shown to have shared meanings, but this has not been established for the subtler combinations of small facial and gestural movements which Birdwhistell describes.

It should be said that one of Birdwhistell's main contributions has been in drawing attention to bodily movements at a microscopic level. He has provided a number of detailed descriptions of short sequences of behaviour. For example:

'Just west of Albuquerque on Highway 66 two soldiers stood astride their duffle bags thumbing a ride. A large car sped by them and the driver jerked his head back, signifying refusal. The two soldiers wheeled and one Italian-saluted him while the other thumbed his nose after the retreating car.'

A complete kinesic analysis is given of this event; part of it is translated as follows:

'The driver of the car focused momentarily on the boys, raised both brows, flared his nostrils, lifted his upper lip, revealed his upper teeth, and with his head cocked, moved it in a posterior-anterior inverted nod which in its backward aspect had about twice the velocity of the movement which returned the head and face to the midline and, thus, to driving focus.'

However, kinesic phenomena have been studied experimentally as well as structurally. Rosenfeld, for example, found that subjects who were seeking the approval of another person engaged in more head-nods, smiles, and gestural activity. Other experiments have shown that there is often response matching, i.e. if one person nods his head or produces some other bodily movement, another person is likely to do the same, by a kind of imitation. There is a further complication that head-nods and smiles also act as reinforcers for behaviour on the part of another person.

Although Birdwhistell has been concerned with the total process of communication, in fact he has not dealt with gestural illustrations or with conventional signs. In our view communication by bodily movements can be understood better by considering separately the different ways in which they function. There appear to be several quite different kinds of signalling here:

illustrations and other signals, linked to speech
conventional signs, and sign languages
movements expressing emotional states
movements expressing personality
movements used in ritual (these were discussed
in Chapter 9)

Gestures are very difficult to understand, since all these kinds of communication, functioning in entirely different ways, may be operating simultaneously, all of them through the hands.

Gestures and bodily movements linked with speech

We discussed in Chapter 8 the different ways in which bodily movements support verbal communication:

punctuating and displaying the structure of utterances
emphasizing
framing, i.e. providing further information about
utterances
illustrating
providing feedback from listeners
signalling continued attention
controlling synchronization

Bodily movements provide a second channel, in addition to the vocal channel, which is very useful, for example for synchronization and feedback. Gestures are also very useful for illustrating objects or actions which are difficult to verbalize.

We have carried out experiments on encounters where two people cannot see each other. They find this situation difficult since without visual signals they can't discern the reactions of the other. There are also difficulties about synchronization. The telephone requires special social skills, since all this material must be put into the auditory channel. For example there is more 'listening behaviour', of the form 'I see', 'good', or 'go on'. As Ekman and Friesen (1969) have shown, there are several different ways in which hand movements can illustrate speech: (*a*) pointing to people (including oneself), or to objects, or turning and facing them, (*b*) showing a spatial relationship (under, inside), (*c*) showing spatial movements (through, round), (*d*) showing tempo or rhythm, beating time, showing slow movements ('batons'), (*e*) showing a bodily action ('kine-tographs'), (*f*) drawing a picture, for instance, of a spiral staircase ('pictographs'), (*g*) showing a direction of thought ('ideographs'). These illustrations are 'iconic' in that they are examples of, or physically represent, the objects referred to. Although most people make some bodily movements while speaking, there are very wide variations in how they do it, and it appears that the rules which may exist here are very flexible. One of the most standardized illustrations in English is perhaps the indication of 'I' and 'you' which is done by movements of the hand towards self and others: 'we' and 'you' are shown by short sweeps of the hand. Other common signals are those for 'yes' and 'no', 'up' and 'down' and so on. In some countries, there is a more elaborate gesture language and in ordinary conversation some of the words are replaced by symbolic hand signals.

There are cultural differences in the gestures used to

accompany speech. Efron (1941) observed that Italian and Jewish immigrants to America were different in their use of illustrations; some of the main differences he found are shown below:

	Eastern Jews	Southern Italians
Area of gestures	confined	wide radius
Shape	angular, zig-zag, sinuous	round, elliptical
Axis	from waist to elbow	from shoulder
Plane	towards other person	at side of body
Parts of body	one hand, head	two hands
Tempo	jerky transitions	smooth flow
Touching	pokes or grasps other, close proximity	no touching
Type of gesture	ideographs (showing direction of thought), batons (showing tempo), pointing.	emblems (i.e. with fixed arbitrary, meaning), illustrations

Examples of these gestures are shown in Figure 13.1. This is a historically important study, since it led to the distinctions between illustrations, emblems, and other kinds of gesture.

Finally we should mention a very interesting theory about the gestural accompaniments of speech. Hewes (1973), among others, has suggested that language originated in gestural communication among primitive men. This gestural communication somehow became transferred to vocalizations, but we still retain the residue of an iconic gesture language, which accompanies our speech. Primates make some use of gesture, and can learn gesture language (p. 27); in the tool-using stage further gestures could have developed, the actions for making or using a tool representing the tool, just as imitations of another animal represents that animal. One theory of the possible transfer of communication from hands to mouth is that mouth movements were used which copied the hand movements.

It is not entirely clear why or when people use gestural

Figure 13.1. Ghetto Jews: *a* head gestures, *b* gesturing with lapel of interlocutor, *c* gesturing with object, *d* thumb-digging movement, digging out an idea, *e* palm on cheek or behind ear, astonishment, bewilderment, rejection, *f* plucking beard or stroking chin in thoughtfulness, deliberation, or doubt. (from Efron, 1941)

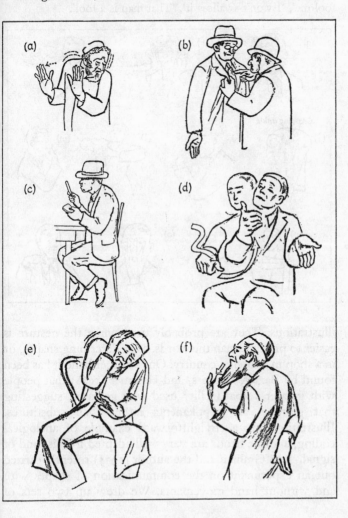

Figure 13.1. *contd.*— South Italians: *g* 'Look out', 'You won't fool me', derisive attention, *h* derisive attention, 'I cannot hear', *i* good, delicious, beautiful, *j* jail, chain gang, slave, *k* imposing silence, 'I'll sew your lips together', *l* braggadocio, arrogance, *m* bad odour, no good, *n* finished, through, *o* jail, *p* 'You can't fool me', 'I won't swallow it', 'That man is a fool'.

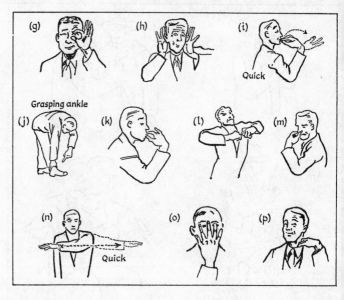

illustrations. They are probably used when the gesture is easier to produce than the words, as in describing shapes, or in a shop in a foreign country. On the other hand it has been found by Baxter, Winters, and Hammer (1968) that people with greater verbal facility used *more* gestures, suggesting that gestures are supplements rather than substitutes. Illustrations are a straightforward example of analogical coding, and the hands are very well adapted to this kind of signal. Jean Graham and the author (1975) recently carried out an experiment on the communication of shapes with and without hand movements. We drew up two sets of

Figure 13.2. The high and low codability material. Figures shown represent mean percentage improvement when gesture is allowed for each individual picture.

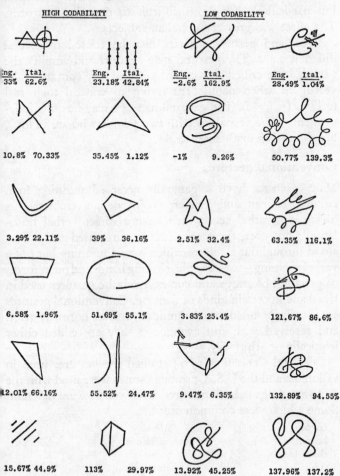

shapes, one easily codable in words (e.g. triangle or circle), and the others more difficult. We found that hand movements improved the communication of both sets of shapes, but particularly for those difficult to describe in words. The effect was greater for Italian subjects.

Vocal and gestural activity may be related in several different ways. The gestural may support and amplify the verbal, as described above. The gestural may contradict the verbal, as when people are trying to conceal their real feelings (p. 128f). The gestural message may be quite independent of the verbal, as with two people who are in love, but discussing mathematics.

Conventional gestures

Many gestures have a generally accepted meaning in a culture. Ekman and Friesen (1969) define 'emblems' as 'those non-verbal acts which have a direct verbal translation'; however, there are many gestures used and understood throughout a culture which have a meaning but not a verbal meaning – for example, shaking hands and other forms of greeting, blessings and curses, symbolic gestures used in ritual and in certain kinds of dancing. Conventional gestures are usually intended to communicate, and are normally given and received with full awareness; they are coded either iconically or arbitrarily.

Saitz and Cervenka (1972) studied the gestures used in Colombia and the U.S.A.; some gestures were used with the same meanings in both cultures, while others were different. Some which were common are:

Gesture	Meaning
head-nod	agreement
shake fist	anger
rub palms	anticipation
clapping	approval
raise hand	attention
yawn	boredom
rub hands	cold

beckon	come
extend hand	invite to dance
point	give direction
thumb down	disapproval
shrug shoulder	disinterest
pat on back	encouragement
action of shooting self	*faux pas*
outline female body	attractive female
rub stomach	hungry
wave hand	goodbye
shake hands	greetings

The message conveyed by one of these gestures may be modified by the way it is performed. At a greeting, for example, intimacy is indicated by its 'warmth', the amount of contact, pressure, and proximity, while status is indicated by who salutes first or bows first or lowest. These gestures are complete messages in themselves, and do not combine to form complex sequences, as in sign languages. While conventional gestures vary between cultures, there is some similarity in the way greetings, for example, are performed. Ekman and Friesen suggest that there may be culturally universal signs for bodily functions like eating, love-making, walking, sleeping, etc. Gestures are also commonly used for curses, blessing, and protection against evil spirits. Certain gestures are widely used in this way, a raised hand for blessing, palms together for devotion, pointing finger gestures for curses or protection, for instance, the 'horns' (sticking out the first and fourth fingers). While all of these signs can be translated into words, the words do not convey the emotional intensity that these gestures commonly have. Religious rituals make use of these and other gestures, e.g. the sign of the cross, which have meaning through association or analogy. Conventional gestures are used in certain kinds of dancing and theatre, where there may be as many as sixty different arbitrary gestures. These are used as well as iconic gestures such as embracing and gestures indicating emotions.

Deaf and dumb languages are not really cases of non-verbal communication. However, they are not exactly verbal either, since they are not based on letters or sounds and have a distinctive syntactic structure. Use may be made of finger-spelling for difficult words – signs are used for letters of the alphabet. Most of the signs are arbitrary and they are linked together in sequences to form complex messages. The vocabulary is large, and communication is rapid – Helen Keller could sign at eighty words per minute. The deaf and dumb languages in different countries are as different as the languages of those countries (Stokoe, 1972). American Indians and Australian Aborigines, and others, also have sign languages. Although there are sixty-five groups of American Indian languages, these all have similar features, and the different groups can understand one another. However, inter-cultural communication by gesture is better achieved by means of iconic signs, and by the common gestures for greetings, directions and so on described earlier, which are also used by deaf people as a kind of manual shorthand.

Conventional signs are often developed by occupational groups because verbal communication is unsuitable for some reason. In broadcasting, for example, speech is impossible, and there are gestures for 'start', 'two minutes left', 'cut him off, he is talking rubbish', etc. Tic-tac men on racecourses are able to signal betting information at a distance. In a number of occupations numerical information is conveyed over a distance by means of finger signals. Prostitutes, homosexuals, masons, and others can signal their identity by conventional gestures, for example special hand-shakes.

Gestures and emotions

The hands are not adapted as areas of communicating emotions as the face is; nevertheless emotions are to some extent displayed in the hands and other parts of the body. The general level of arousal is reflected in all parts of the body, in the form of diffuse, and generally meaningless movements. Probably one of the main messages conveyed by hand movements is the level of excitement of a speaker. It is not known how far more specific emotional states are communicated. Anxiety, for example, may be conveyed by tense, strained hands, clutching each other, or the arms of a chair. In these cases the general emotional state results in gestures, which are not intended to communicate, and which people often try to conceal.

How can the encoded meaning of a gesture be discovered? Psychoanalysts like Felix Deutsch and George Mahl make interpretations of the gestures of patients during psychoanalysis; for example, a patient's putting both legs on to the couch was interpreted by Mahl as committing herself to treatment. The main evidence taken into account is the verbalization which typically accompanies a particular gesture, together with the occasions on which a person uses a gesture, and the kinds of person who use it. However, NVC is often used to send information which modifies or contradicts what is in the verbal channel, so the verbal accompaniment must be used with care.

Ekman and Friesen (1968) studied the gestures of a patient before and after treatment. She used twenty repeated hand movements before treatment and thirty-four different hand movements after treatment; her gestures after treatment were more varied but less frequent. Films of these gestures were shown to judges, and there was over 70 per cent agreement on the meaning of some but not all. For example, 'chair-arm-rub' was interpreted as emotional and restless, 'head-toss' as argumentative. This shows that idiosyncratic gestures for emotions often convey meanings consistently to other people, though there must be some underlying common components or qualities which give them this meaning. We discussed earlier the claim that such gestures can communicate emotions which are not shown in the face (p. 111f).

Freedman and Hoffman (1967) made a valuable distinction between gestures which are linked with speech and oriented towards objects, and those which are directed towards the self. They suggest that the first are intended to communicate, while the second merely release tension. Animals produce 'displacement activities' such as scratching themselves when in states of conflict or frustration, and as we have seen these acts can become ritualized and act as social signals. The same is to some extent true of human emotional expressions. Krout (1954) carried out a very interesting experiment on 'autistic gestures'. These are gestures which do not appear to be intended to communicate, since they occur most if no one else is present; they consist mainly of touching some part of the body with the hands.

He found twenty-four gestures which appeared to be associated with particular emotions where speech or action were blocked. He aroused these blocked emotions in fifteen experimental situations. For example:

Experiment 8

(1) People consider strong feelings of one person for another of the *same* sex strange. Don't they? (Pause for answer)

(2) But, don't *you* sometimes have more than friendly feelings for your best (boy, girl) friend? (Bend forward, point finger) – I mean *more* than friendly feelings. Think it over.

Rationale for experiment 8

(1) Hypothetical emotional attitude: POSITIVE (Affection, Attachment).

(2) Hypothetical conflicting attitude: NEGATIVE (Repulsion).

(3) Hypothetical verbal response: NEGATIVE ('No I don't').

The subjects were asked to delay their reply to the second question, in each case, until the experimenter gave a signal, which was given after a gesture had appeared. They were later asked to decide which statement represented most closely their feelings. A number of gestures were regularly connected with emotions, and nearly all involved touching the self. Examples are hand to nose (fear), finger to lips (shame), and making a fist (anger – males).

Other self-touching gestures are covering the eyes, ear or mouth, movements connected with eating and excretion, auto-erotic movements, grooming, and picking the nose, ears, or teeth. These gestures are mainly used in private or in intimate relationships and are inhibited in public; other people present usually ignore them. Some of them are completely idiosyncratic and convey no meaning to others, some can be decoded by friends or relations, while others are more easily understood. Ekman and Friesen (1969, 1972) find that face-touching gestures ('self-adapters') occur when a person is experiencing shame or other negative attitudes towards the self. They have found, for example, that covering the eyes is encoded and decoded as shame. Although there is little firm data here it is likely that self-grooming is related to concern with self-presentation, picking and scratching the face with self-blame or self-attack, and rubbing with self-assurance. Whether these gestures should be interpreted as an overflow of emotional tensions or as the expression of self-attitudes – a kind of communication to the self – they are not primarily intended to communicate to others. Perhaps touching the self is a kind of emotional equivalent of talking to oneself. Self-grooming gestures are not intended to communicate in themselves – though the results of the grooming are. These are rather different since they take place in specific social situations – greetings, courtship, and when about to appear or perform in public. The reason is presumably that attention is focused on the self-image being presented, including the body-image, on these occasions. Scheflen and Scheflen (1972) point out that these acts appear to be irrelevant to the context in which they occur; however, they represent private reactions to what is going on.

Other gestures express attitudes to other people. Ekman and Friesen maintain that these gestures are truncated inter-personal acts in relation to others, many of them consisting originally of some kind of bodily contact. While emotional gestures consist largely of self-touching, gestures expressing attitudes to others are directed towards the bodies of others. Thus hands across the body represents defence, reaching out movements represent moves towards intimacy, restless movements of hands or legs represent flight from the other, exposure of part of the body may represent sexual invitation, and so on. Posture is an important signal here, and there are various conventional gestures and postures representing deference and intimacy (p. 276f).

The feet move as well as the hands, though the reper-toire is much more limited, and these movements are not attended to much. Ekman and Friesen (1968) studied the foot movements of individual patients; one patient pre-dominantly used 'one-foot floor slide forward and/or back'; a film of her foot movements was rated as 'timid, cautious' whereas the total film was not rated in this way. Yet with other patients ratings for the feet film and the total film were the same. It is not clear whether the information obtained from the feet was simply wrong in this case, or whether it represents part of a complex non-verbal message which in-cluded information about inner conflict.

Gesture and personality

Do individuals have characteristic gestures or gestural styles? It is a common experience that we can recognize people from a distance or from behind by their bodily movements, just as we can recognize them from their faces and voices. It has been found that expressive behaviour varies with mood, for example, a person says and does more when elated than when depressed, but the basic patterns, for instance, of handwriting and probably also of gesture, remain the same.

An extensive study was carried out by Allport and Vernon (1933) of twenty-five young men. They measured movements of different parts of the body in thirty different situations. They did not study specific emotional expressions, but styles of bodily movement such as shaking hands, drawing circles, and walking out of doors. It was found that the subjects were very consistent in the same situation from one occasion to another. There was also a considerable degree of generality between different parts of the body. The similarity between movements due to different groups of muscles was as great as the similarity between different actions by the same group of muscles. People who had large strides also drew large circles, and made larger movements when idle – making up a factor of 'expansiveness'. There was also a factor of 'emphasis', based on voice loudness, writing pressure, and so on.

This study was not primarily concerned with validity, but 'congruence' was reported between expressive behaviour and clinical assessments for four subjects studied. One of them, for example, had bodily movements which were 'predominantly firm, strong, forceful, emphatic, expansive, well-spaced', and in personality was 'assured, incisive, expansive, with capacity for prudent delay and caution'. One or two other studies have been carried out in which judges were asked to match the expressive behaviour and case-descriptions of a number of people. Estes (1937), for example, found that artistic and literary people were quite good at this, whereas university teachers and professional psychologists did rather badly.

There is probably a closer connexion between personality and the emotional aspects of gestures. An aggressive person for example would be expected to make fist and banging gestures. Charlotte Wolff (1945) found a number of patterns of gestures of this kind in mental patients:

(1) *Extreme inhibition*: withdrawal movements, stereotyped movements, hair gestures, general motor unrest, unnecessary movements.
(2) *Depression*: movements are slow, few, hesitating, non-emphatic, use of hiding gestures.
(3) *Elation*: movements are fast, expansive, rhythmical, spontaneous, emphatic, self-assertive, affected.
(4) *Anxiety*: gestures involving the hair, hiding the face, wringing and interlocking of hands, opening and closing of fists, plucking eyebrows, scratching face, pulling hair, aimless fidgeting.

Gesture is also a product of inhibited emotions, as we have seen, and people often have habitual autistic gestures which have a symbolic meaning for them. These may or may not be interpreted by others, depending on how obvious the symbolism is, and how sensitive they are to this kind of communication. Mahl (1968) interprets the habitual gestures of patients in the way described above. Here are some examples:

Gestures	Interpretations
Very frequent patting and stroking of hair; even gets up and preens hair in front of mirror on wall at one point	Narcissistic, complains that people don't pay enough attention to her
A great deal of ring play	Marital conflict; frustrated by life at home
Spasmodic clutching of bodice	Fears of bodily mutilation, illness and death
Frequently takes off glasses	use of denial as defence

Several studies have compared psychiatric patients before and after treatment, or with normal controls. The patients are found to make many more gestural movements, but these are of a stereotyped kind. Drawing and doodling have been compared for different kinds of personality. There is consistent evidence that extraverted, aggressive, and impulsive personalities make large drawings, while introverts make smaller ones. Neurotics make smaller drawings than normals; Wallach and Gahm (1960) suggest that anxious introverts compensate and conceal their true personality by adopting an apparently extroverted style of expansive drawing.

There has been a great deal of controversy over the re-relation between handwriting and personality. If the matching method is used, most people can match handwriting to personality sketches slightly better than chance, and some graphologists can do a little better. However, no relation has been found between measurable aspects of handwriting and aspects of personality – whatever information is used by judges has so far eluded investigators.

The relation between gestures and other aspects of personality depends on several different processes. First, some gestures reflect a prevailing emotional state, such as anxiety, or a general style of behaviour, such as aggression. The gestures are correctly seen as part of the whole. Secondly, people control and manipulate their behaviour, and may even produce the opposite gesture to their true state, as when a nervous person has a loud voice or a firm handshake. Thirdly, a person's gestural style is partly a product of his cultural and occupational background, age and sex, of health, and fatigue, and so on.

Further reading

CRITCHLEY, M. (1939) *The Language of Gesture*. London: Arnold.
EKMAN, P. and FRIESEN, W. V. (1969) The repertoire of non-verbal behavior: categories, origins, usage and coding. *Semiotica* 1: 49–98.

270 The different bodily signals

References

ALLPORT, G. W., and VERNON, P. E. (1933) *Studies in Expressive Movement*, Boston: Houghton Mifflin.

BAXTER, J. C., WINTER, E. P., and HAMMER, R. E. (1968) Gestural behavior during a brief interview as a function of cognitive variables. *Journal of Personality and Social Psychology* 8: 303–7.

BIRDWHISTELL, R. L. (1970) *Kinesics and Context*. Philadelphia: University of Pennsylvania Press.

EFRON, D. (1941) *Gesture and Environment*. New York: King's Crown Press.

EKMAN, P., and FRIESEN, W. V. (1968) Nonverbal behavior in psychotherapy research. *Research in Psychotherapy* 3: 179–216.

EKMAN, P. and FRIESEN, W. V. (1972) Hand movements. *Journal of Communication* 22: 353–74.

ESTES, S. G. (1937) The judgement of personality on the brief basis of behavior. Cambridge, Mass.: Harvard Library.

FREEDMAN, N., and HOFFMAN, S. P. (1967) Kinetic behavior in altered clinical states: approach to objective analysis of motor behavior during clinical interviews. *Perceptual and Motor Skills* 24: 527–39.

GRAHAM, J. A. and ARGYLE, M. (1975) A cross-cultural study of the communication of extra-verbal meaning by gestures. *International Journal of Psychology* 10: 56–67.

HEWES, G. (1973) Primate communication and the gestural origin of language. *Current Anthropology* 14: no. 1–2, 5–12.

KENDON, A. (1973) Review of Birdwhistell: *Kinesics and Context*. *American Journal of Psychology* 85: 441–55.

KROUT, M. H. (1954) An experimental attempt to determine the significance of unconscious manual symbolic movements. *Journal of General Psychology* 51: 121–52.

MAHL, G. F. (1968) Gestures and body movements in interviews. *Research in Psychotherapy* 3: 295–346.

SAITZ, R. L. and CERVENKA, E. J. (1972) *Handbook of Gestures: Colombia and the United States*. In T. A. Sebeok (ed.) *Approaches to Semiotics*. The Hague: Mouton.

SCHEFLEN, A. E. and SCHEFLEN, A. (1972) *Body Language and the Social Order*. Englewood Cliffs, N.J.: Prentice-Hall.

Gestures & bodily movements 271

STOKOE, W. C. (1972) *Semiotics and Human Sign Languages*. In T. A. SEBEOK (ed.). *Approaches to Semiotics*. The Hague: Mouton.

WALLACH, M. A. and GAHM, R. C. (1960) Personality functions of graphic constriction and expansiveness. *Journal of Personality* **28**: 73–88.

WOLFF, C. (1945) *A Psychology of Gesture*. London: Methuen.

14

Posture

The repertoire of postures

Dogs, horses, monkeys, and other animals each have a number of characteristic postures. Rhesus monkeys, for example, have five sitting positions – upright, relaxed, hunched, cat-like, and crouching. They have other postures for threat, sex, grooming, defecation, sleeping, and so on.

There are three main human postures:

standing
sitting, squatting, and kneeling
lying

Each of these has further variations corresponding to different positions of the arms and legs and different angles of the body. Some are used only in particular cultures.

It is possible to draw up elaborate classifications of the components of posture, as Birdwhistell (1970) has done – in terms of the positions of the spine, shoulders, back, stomach, arms, legs, and head. However, posture is used in several different communication systems, and I think it is better to consider separately the repertoire used in each.

In the first place posture is associated with the activity being pursued. Here are examples of how some stick-figure diagrams were interpreted in an experiment by Sarbin

Figure 14.1. Stick figures interpreted: *a* curious, *b* puzzled, *c* indifferent, *d* rejecting, *e* watching, *f* self-satisfied, *g* welcoming, *h* determined, *i* stealthy, *j* searching, *k* watching, *l* attentive, *m* violent anger, *n* excited, *o* stretching, *p* surprised, dominating, suspicious, *q* sneaking, *r* shy, *s* thinking, *t* affected. (from Sarbin and Hardyk, 1953)

(g)

(h)

(i)

(j)

(k)

(l)

(m)

(n)

(o) (p)

(q) (r)

(s) (t)

and Hardyck (1953). However, these postures are not normally used to communicate, though they can be part of an interaction sequence.

Posture is an important means of conveying interpersonal attitudes, and there are two dimensions of posture associated with the main attitudes. Postures are also associated with emotional states, either through direct physiological effects of emotions, or for symbolic reasons. Posture accompanies speech, in a way similar to that of gesture, though more slow-moving. There are powerful social conventions about posture, about which postures are proper in a culture and in particular situations. They may also have symbolic meanings in connexion with rituals.

Interpersonal attitudes

Mehrabian (1972) studied the encoding of interpersonal attitudes by asking subjects to approach a hat-rack, and imagine it to be a person of certain characteristics. Their posture, and other aspects of their behaviour, was then assessed. He studied decoding by presenting a series of photographs of seated persons, varied along a number of dimensions, and asked subjects to imagine they were talking to the people in the photographs. They were then asked to indicate how much they thought the target person liked or disliked them. Scheflen (1965) used a less systematic but more realistic method, consisting of careful analysis of behaviour during psychotherapy and group therapy, where something was known about the attitudes towards others present.

Mehrabian's encoding and decoding studies found two main dimensions of posture (see p. 122).

(1) *Immediacy* consisted of:

> leaning forwards
> touching
> proximity ⎫
> gaze ⎬ Related non-postural variables
> direct orientation ⎭

This style of behaviour is used towards people who are liked, and by females more than by males. The different components of immediacy all have the effect of reducing distance or improving the visibility between two people. There is a further component of immediacy – openness of arms and legs. It has often been suggested that openness indicates a positive attitude, especially in male–female encounters. Mehrabian found some evidence that for females only, while sitting, an open posture was seen as more friendly.

(2) *Relaxation* consisted of:
    asymmetrical arm positions
    sideways lean
    asymmetrical leg positions
    hand relaxation
    backwards lean

The relaxed postural style is used towards others of lower status, more to females than males, to a person of the opposite sex more than to a person of the same sex. A less relaxed posture is adopted by males towards other males who are disliked. A number of these results were obtained by Mehrabian in his highly controlled but rather unrealistic experimental situations, and similar results were obtained by other workers in real-life situations. Goffman (1961), for example, noticed that the most important people at meetings in a mental hospital sat in the most relaxed postures – as well as occupying the best seats, and at the front of the room.

There are probably further postural components of dominance and submission, in addition to the relaxation dimension. The author and his colleagues at Oxford (1970) created dominant and submissive non-verbal styles, by a combination of posture, facial expression, and tone of voice. The dominant posture was erect with the head tilted back; the submissive posture was less erect and with the head

278 The different bodily signals

lowered. Mehrabian, however, working in Los Angeles found that heads were tilted *upwards* to a high status person. It is possible that there is an Anglo-American difference in the significance of head-tilting.

Scheflen and Scheflen (1972) have carried out careful observations of therapy groups and other situations, and present photographs of various interpersonal attitudes being expressed. They suggest that two people of opposite sex often go through a series of postural shifts, similar to those of courtship, as their intimacy increases, and they regard this sequence as a universal structure. The stages are:

(1) Courtship readiness: high arousal, bodily alertness, grooming
(2) Positioning for courtship: facing or side-by-side
(3) Actions of appeal or invitation: gaze-holding, protruding breasts, rolling pelvis, hand on hips, etc.
(4) Use of qualifiers of courting behaviour to arrest the sequence: verbal disclaimers or mentions of inappropriateness of setting, incomplete or bizarre performance of postural moves. The plates show one of their photographs of grooming, also showing high tonus, a female courtship signal, and a masculine stance.

We referred earlier to the possible symbolic significance of postures; Mahl interpreted a patient's position on his couch in terms of commitment to therapy and sexual attitudes towards the therapist. It is certainly possible that postures can represent feelings and attitudes in this way, just as gestures can be intention movements representing more extensive social acts. Postures could represent sleeping, running away, copulating, and so on. Probably such acts if they occur are not intended to communicate; and as yet we do not have much experimental evidence that they take place. Mehrabian's finding that females adopt an open-arm position to someone they like is one of the few in this area (p. 277).

Emotions

Ekman and Friesen (1967) showed films which did not include the head, and asked subjects to judge emotions experienced by the patients filmed. Sarbin and Hardyck (1965) used the stick figure method described earlier. Ekman and Friesen found that while facial expression conveyed more information about specific emotions, bodily posture showed the intensity of the emotion. Again the tense-relaxed dimension of posture seems to be important. What is not entirely clear is how far posture communicates more specific emotional states. In the Sarbin and Hardyck study a number of stick figures were commonly thought to indicate emotions: indifferent, shy, self-satisfied, excited, affected, violent, angry.

Rosenberg and Langer (1965) presented these stick figures to subjects and asked them what the figures represented in terms of colours and direction. They found that the postures had agreed non-verbal meanings, in other words the postures conveyed information about emotional

Figure 14.2. Other non-verbal information expressed as posture

indifferent   extreme anger

states, which could also be expressed in other non-verbal
ways, e.g. by means of colour. The results for two of the
stick figures were as follows:

Emotion perceived	Chromatic colour	Achromatic colour	Feeling	Stability	Vertical direction	Horizontal direction
Indifferent	Yellow (51%)	Grey (85%)	± (56%)	Flighty (76%)	—	Backward (66%)
Extreme anger	Red (75%)	Black (90%)	— (89%)	Flighty (66%)	Down (70%)	Forward (78%)

Extreme emotions can be seen in the postures of certain
mental patients. Depressives have a drooping, listless
posture, sit brooding and looking at the floor. Manics are
alert and erect, their body is in a high degree of arousal.
This is partly a difference along the tense-relaxed dimension,
but it includes other components as well. Patients in anxiety
states are highly aroused too, but here the specific emotion
is anxiety rather than euphoria, and this is shown in their
muscular tension.

Personality

There has been little experimental research on the relation
between posture and personality. However, there is little
doubt that some people do create impressions of their
personality through posture – the stiff, military bearing, the
affected superior posture, for example.

A number of psychoanalysts have offered interpretations
of the postures adopted by patients during therapy, either
lying on a couch or sitting on a chair. These interpretations
are based on the personalities of particular patients. Another
method used is to adopt the posture in question and then
introspect. Some of the postures in the list have been
interpreted in the same way by several analysts, and there
appears to be a tradition of interpretation.

TABLE 14.1. *Psychoanalytic interpretations of postures*

	Posture	Interpretation
Arms	(1) Folded arms, self-wrapping	Self-protection, especially of breasts, withdrawal.
	(2) Bodice of dress clutched	Fears of bodily damage
	(3) Shoulders shrugged, palms out	Passive helplessness
Legs	(1) High crossing (females)	Self-protection, withdrawal
	(2) Uncrossing	Flirtation
	(3) Exhibitionistic leg cross (female) crossing (females)	Flirtation
	(4) No movement in pelvis	Sexual inhibition
Trunk	(1) Stiff, military bearing (males), prim and upright (females)	Imprisoning anxiety
	(2) Vain, affected bearing	Conflict between flirtation and shyness.
	(3) Drooping, listless, immobile	Helplessness, request for help
	(4) Nestling into chair, languid, erotic manner	Expresses sexual impulses

(From papers by Mahl (1968), Scheflen and Scheflen (1972), and others.)

Posture may also play a part in more intentional self-presentation. A man may adopt a stiff, military posture to show that he is a soldier, rather than to imprison his anxiety. He may adopt a quiet and humble manner because he is a monk, an eccentric and relaxed posture to show he is an intellectual, and so on. Posture is probably affected by the body-image. Adolescent girls who are proud of or ashamed of their breasts will adopt quite different postures. People may display or conceal their height, their legs, or other features of their bodies. As the psychoanalytic interpretations suggest, people may also try to protect various parts of their body, and they may try to appear more relaxed than they really are.

Posture and speech

Postural changes can be regarded as a kind of extension of gestures, consisting of larger and slower bodily movements. Scheflen reports that a patient will adopt from two to four postural positions during a therapeutic session. A person repeats his postures when the same emotion or topic comes up, but the code is an individual one, and cannot be decoded without experience of that individual.

Posture is intermediate between gestures and spatial behaviour, in its scale and functions. Posture frames and defines a period of interaction longer than that of a gesture, shorter than that of a spatial position. This is not so much communication as the adoption of a suitable posture for the period of encounter in terms of relationships with others; however, certain postures have come to be associated with particular relationships.

Gestures accompany and support speech in a number of other ways, and may on occasions turn into postural changes – in providing illustration, in synchronizing, in giving comments on utterances being given and feedback on those of others.

Culture

The range of stable human postures is very large, about 1,000 according to the anthropologist Gordon Hewes (1957), who has studied the postures used in different human cultures. In primitive societies there are about 100 common postures, most of them not used at all in more advanced societies – such as standing on one leg, squatting, sitting with legs crossed, and kneeling on one knee. The postures which are used in a particular community depend on such factors as the nature of the ground, whether it is cold or wet, and the clothes worn. In Western countries we have found sitting or lying on the floor unsatisfactory and are accustomed to using furniture.

The ways in which particular attitudes or emotions are expressed vary from culture to culture, but there are common features. For example 'humility' may be expressed in the following ways:

Attitude expressed	Behaviour pattern	Culture group
Humility	Throwing oneself on the back, rolling from side to side, slapping outside of thighs (meaning: you need not subdue me; I'm subdued already)	Batokas
	Bowing, extending right arm, moving arm down from horizontal position, raising it to the level of one's head, and lowering it again (meaning: I lift the earth off the ground, and place it on my head as a sign of submission to you)	Turks and Persians
	Walking about with hands bound and rope around one's neck.	Ancient Peruvians
	Joining hands over head and bowing (ancient sign of obedience signifying: I submit with tired hands)	Chinese
	Dropping arms; sighing	Europeans
	Stretching hands towards person and striking them together	Congo natives
	Extension of arms; genuflection prostration	Preliterates, European peasants
	Crouching	New Caledonians, Fijians, Tahitians
	Crawling and shuffling forward; walking on fours	Dahomeans
	Bending body downwards	Samoans
	Permitting someone to place his foot on one's head	Fundah and Tonga
	Prostration, face down	Tabu peoples
	Putting palms together for the other person to clasp gently	Polynesians
	Bowing while putting joined hands between those of other person and lifting them to one's forehead	Unyanyembans
		Sumatrans

from Krout (1942)

Nearly all these postures involve bowing, crouching, or lowering the body.

For every situation in a culture there are approved postures. There are correct postures for eating, giving a lecture, being interviewed, sunbathing, and riding a horse. A person who fails to adopt the correct posture may be the object of savage disapproval – he is regarded as slack, immoral, uncivilized, or eccentric.

There are special postures for rituals. At religious services the participants have to adopt a series of postures. Often the priest at a ceremony adopts a standing posture, and may raise one or both arms; those being processed kneel or stand with heads bowed. Monks and nuns lie face downwards on the floor when taking their final vows.

Further reading

MEHRABIAN, A. (1972) *Nonverbal Communication*. Chicago: Aldine-Atherton.

References

ARGYLE, M., SALTER, V., NICHOLSON, H., WILLIAMS, M. and BURGESS, P. (1970) The communication of inferior and superior attitudes by verbal and non-verbal signals. *British Journal of Social and Clinical Psychology* 9: 221–31.

BIRDWHISTELL, R. (1970) *Kinesics and Context*. Philadelphia: University of Pennsylvania Press.

CHRISTIANSEN, B. (1963) *Thus Speaks the Body*. Oslo: Institute for Social Research.

GOFFMAN, E. (1961) *Asylums*. Garden City, New York: Anchor Books.

HEWES, G. (1957) The anthropology of posture. *Scientific American* 196: 123–32.

KROUT, M. H. (1942) *Introduction to Social Psychology*. New York: Harper & Row.

MAHL, G. F. (1968) Gestures and body movements in interviews. *Research in Psychotherapy* 3: 295–346.

ROSENBERG, G. B. and LANGER, J. (1965) A study of postural–gestural communication. *Journal of Personality and Social Psychology* **2**: 593–7.

SARBIN, T. R. and HARDYCK, C. D. (1953) Contributions to role-taking theory: role perception on the basis of postural cues. Unpublished.

SCHEFLEN, A. E. (1965) *Stream and Structure of Communicational Behavior*. Commonwealth of Pennsylvania: Eastern Pennsylvania Psychiatric Institute.

SCHEFLEN, A. E. and SCHEFLEN, A. (1972) *Body Language and the Social Order*. Englewood Cliffs, N.J.: Prentice-Hall.

15

Bodily contact

Bodily contact is the most primitive form of social communication; it is found in very simple organisms, and in young children. The other forms of NVC are a later development both of evolution and growth. Primates use a number of different forms of bodily contact – infants cling to their mothers, and engage in rough and tumble play with each other; adults groom each other; presenting, mounting, and embracing takes place between sexual partners, and in dominance hierarchies rival males may bite, strike, and pull fur; greetings consist of genital and stomach muzzling, kissing, embracing, and grooming.

In humans a large area of the brain is used to receive messages from the body surface, and these are used to guide bodily movements. Bodily contact stimulates several different kinds of receptor – responsive to touch, pressure, warmth or cold, and pain. The skin sends several kinds of signals about its condition – by its colour, taste, and smell (e.g. of perspiration), and temperature.

By means of touch the most basic forms of interpersonal attitude can be communicated. To a more limited extent emotional states can also be conveyed. Active touch is quite different from passive touch. Active touch is caused by motor activity, and is a kind of exploratory scanning; passive touch is the reception of signals from an outside agency.

Touching another person becomes a kind of double active touch, in which each is responsive to the other.

There are many possible kinds of bodily contact. It is usually performed *by* the hand, arm, or mouth. It is usually done *to* the hand, arm, head, shoulder, knee, or upper body. And the contact may be of several kinds – patting, hitting, pinching, stroking, shaking, kissing, licking, holding, guiding, embracing, linking, laying-on, kicking, grooming, or tickling. Of all the many possibilities, relatively few are used in a particular culture. In western culture the following are the most common:

Patting, head, back
Slapping, face, hand, bottom
Punching, face, chest
Pinching, cheek
Stroking hair, face, upper body, knee
Shaking hands
Kissing mouth, cheek, breasts, hand, foot

Licking face
Holding, hand, arm, knee
Guiding, hand, arm
Embracing shoulder, body
Linking arms
Laying-on hands
Kicking bottom
Grooming hair, face
Tickling anywhere

It is also possible to touch oneself in a number of these ways, but we discussed this as a kind of gesture (p. 264f).

Touching seems to have a primitive significance of heightened intimacy, and it produces increased emotional arousal. However, the precise meaning of a particular form of touch depends on the culture, and is learnt. Touch often has a sexual meaning, and certain kinds of touch between certain combinations of persons are primarily regarded as sexual signals. On the other hand bodily contact in greetings, ritual, on the part of doctors and hairdressers, and in crowded places, is not regarded as sexual.

It is possible to grade bodily contact between two people by the level of intimacy which is implied (e.g. an embrace ranks above handshake), and by its frequency and duration. The degree of intimacy also depends on how many clothes are in the way.

In other cultures there are a number of further kinds of bodily contact. Within each of these kinds of contact there are further subdivisions, e.g. hand shakes with one hand or two, hand shakes incorporating masonic signs. More commonly there are differences of degree, for example, the firmness of grip and duration of a handshake.

Bodily contact in different relationships

The amount and type of bodily contact which occurs is greatly dependent on the ages, sexes, and social relationships of those concerned. It also has a different significance for different age-groups and in different relationships. While there is a clear biological basis to bodily contact, it is also governed by a strong set of social rules, prescribing who can do what and to whom. These rules are somewhat different in other cultures.

For infants touch is the most important means of communication. Children up to the age of 10–12 continue to touch their parents. They also touch other children of the same sex a great deal, in the course of various kinds of games, friendly fighting, and so on. Touching parents expresses a close and dependent attitude, while touching other children is affiliative or aggressive.

At adolescence contact with parents is much reduced. Jourard (1963) found that few students were touched anywhere beyond their hands and arms by their parents. There is an increasing amount of contact with friends of the opposite sex. In Jourard's survey over 75 per cent of males had been touched by their girl friends on their head, arms, and torso; over 75 per cent of females had been touched on their head, neck, arms, and knees, and over 50 per cent on their legs and torso, by opposite sex friends. During this period there is a return to bodily contact as a means of establishing, sustaining, and enjoying social relationships, now sexual instead of infant–parent.

During adult life bodily contact is severely restricted, and allowed under only socially defined circumstances, of five main kinds. (1) With one's spouse, both during sexual intercourse and more casually as part of everyday domestic life, touch is permitted, and occurs much more often than with other people. (2) With children, up to adolescence. After about twelve there is almost no contact with them. (3) With other relations and friends various kinds of greeting and farewell are allowed, including handshakes, embraces, and kisses on the cheek with members of the other sex, especially after a long absence; congratulations take the form of handshakes and pats on the back; a certain amount of mild touching occurs in flirtation with non-spouses; dancing is an occasion for close bodily contact between non-spouses. (4) Between relative strangers, and in public places, bodily contact is rare. There is a lot of contact in crowds and public transport, but this is not socially defined as touching. A number of professionals touch people in the course of their work – doctors, tailors, nurses, gynaecologists, dentists, masseurs, gymnastics instructors, barbers, beauticians, and shoe salesmen. However, this kind of touch is neutralized and defined as non-social, though it may well be enjoyed socially by some of those who give or receive it. A number of games involve touching, e.g. rugby football and wrestling. Certain ceremonies and rituals involve special kinds of touching, as at christenings, weddings, and graduations. (5) Encounter groups are partly designed to fulfil the need for more bodily contact, and include a number of exercises involving it.

There are great cultural differences in the amount and type of touching. Some anthropologists distinguish between contact and non-contact cultures. Contact groups include the Arabs, Latin Americans, Southern Europeans (Greeks, Turks), and a number of African cultures. Non-contact groups include Northern Europeans, Americans, Asians, e.g. Indians and Pakistanis. Watson (1972) found that people from contact cultures also face each other more directly, and look at each other more during interaction; some contact cultures stand close (Arabs), but so do some non-contact cultures (Indians, Pakistanis). This is illustrated by Jourard's study of the frequencies with which couples touched each other at cafés: in San Juan (Puerto Rico) they touched 180 times per hour, in Paris 110, in London 0.

There are a number of African cultures where it is normal to hold hands during a conversation, or to intertwine the legs. Class differences in touching have been found in a number of countries – in Anglo-Saxon countries there is more bodily contact in the working classes than in the middle or upper classes. This may in turn be due to different patterns of child-rearing: Hore (1970) found that working-class mothers touched their children more than middle-class mothers in Australia; this is part of a general pattern of greater NVC and less verbal communication among working-class people.

Bodily contact and interpersonal relationships

The most important use of touch is to communicate, and enjoy, interpersonal relationships.

Sex

The ultimate goal of sexual motivation is intercourse and the procreation of children. The forms of bodily contact involved are highly arousing and highly rewarding, and they lead to very strong attachment to the partner, which has the biological advantage of providing a stable home for the children produced. The bodily contacts related to sex are similar in all cultures, and have a biological basis. There are also variations, and there are cultural rules about what people may do, when they are unmarried, engaged, and married. There are a number of different kinds of bodily contact of progressive intimacy. Desmond Morris (1971) suggests that in Western culture couples normally go through the following twelve stages of intimacy, always in the same order, though one or more may be omitted: (1) eye to body, (2) eye to eye, (3) voice to voice, (4) hand to hand, (5) arm to shoulder, (6) arm to waist, (7) mouth to mouth, (8) hand to head, (9) hand to body, e.g. the female's breasts, (10) mouth to breast, (11) hand to genitals, (12) genitals to genitals. Some go to a further stage – mouth to genitals. These steps are usually initiated by the male, but he must wait for a positive response from the female before proceeding to the next step. This hierarchy is a very interesting example of meaning structure (p. 58f), and is more clearly structured than any other group of non-verbal signals. Morris suggests that when a form of bodily contact is socially formalized – as in hand to hand introduction (4), and goodnight kisses (7), a couple can move to a point of greater intimacy than is normal for them. He also points out that dancing is a kind of disguised sexual intimacy – in which complete strangers are able to move at once to a high degree of bodily intimacy. This did not happen until the invention of the waltz – which was regarded as outrageous – and has now largely ceased with the invention of various kinds of jazz dancing which do not involve bodily contact.

Mary Henley (1973), in an observational field study, found that men touched women much more often than women touched men – and much more than people touched others of the same sex. She interpreted this not as a demonstration of intimacy, but as an assertion of male power; she points out that in a number of other relationships the high status person touches the low status person, e.g. doctors touch patients. However, males may touch females to express affection too. Jourard (1963) found that both sexes will reveal more things about themselves to females than to males; touch and self-disclosure are both intimacy signals. Perhaps male–female touching expresses power and affection simultaneously, and this is embodied in the social convention that males normally take the initiative in such matters.

Nurturance–dependence

Touch is the most important channel of communication at first for infants. A number of studies have shown that infants who do not have enough bodily contact become anxious and disturbed. It seems likely that they have an innate need for the right kind of touch, as monkeys do, and that contact with the mother is one origin of the maternal bond. Most children seek attention by crying, and stop when picked up. Later they raise their arms, signalling their desire to be picked up. However, Schaffer and Emerson (1964) found that some infants ('non-cuddlers') actively resist physical contact and obtain comfort from being able to see their mothers, or to hold her skirt. One of the goals of contact with the mother is being fed, but Harlow's experiments (1965) on monkeys showed that baby monkeys became more attached to an artificial monkey with the right kind of skin than to one which produced milk. Mothers respond to infants by cradling, caressing, cuddling, carrying, rocking, and tickling, and most of them are in turn responsive to this. To a lesser extent fathers and siblings treat infants in a similar way. During the first year of life games of tickling and other forms of bodily contact are the main means of relating to infants. It has been found in different studies that parents touch their children more between ages one and two, when they are first walking, but that touch declines after this age; girls are touched more than boys.

Affiliation

A lot of animal and human behaviour can be classified as affiliative, that is, directed towards establishing friendly relations with peers. There is a rather fine distinction between affiliation and sex, though affiliation stops short of the later stages of sexual intimacy. The biological purpose of this form of motivation is probably to restrain aggression and bring about co-operative behaviour in groups. In apes and monkeys affiliative behaviour has its origins in bodily contact with the mother and siblings, develops into rough-and-tumble play with other young animals, and is expressed in adults by long periods of grooming, as well as by co-operation and mutual help. In humans the origins are similar, but much less bodily contact occurs in adults: the goals of affiliation appear to be conversation and co-operative work and play rather than grooming. There is a limited amount of bodily contact, of a socially defined kind – greetings, pats, and touches. Attitudes of affection are expressed by the amount and intensity of these signals.

Aggression

As in the case of sex, aggression is expressed primarily by bodily contact. Aggression is the innate response to attack, frustration, and competition for resources. Animals use horns, teeth, or other parts of their anatomy designed for aggressive purposes. However, threat displays are more common than actual fighting: there is a built-in appeasement mechanism which prevents members of the group from damaging each other unduly. Human infants scream, kick, and beat with their fists; aggressive tendencies may become strenghtened during childhood, but restraints on aggression are acquired as well. Boys up to about ten spend a lot of time in friendly wrestling. Girls fight less, though they may pull one another's hair, and they make more use of verbal aggression. Parents spank their children, young adults engage in rough games like boxing, judo, or rugger, and there is institutionalized aggression in war, though this does not involve much bodily contact nowadays. In some cultural groups there is aggression between adult males – in some criminal groups, and at one time in the Wild West for example. In each of these cases the form of aggression, and how far it is permitted to go, is controlled by cultural rules.

Bodily contact is the basic way biologically of expressing interpersonal attitudes. In animals and children there is a great deal of these forms of bodily contact. However, in adults they become replaced, to a very large extent, by other forms of communication of a more symbolic kind, using the distance receptors of vision and hearing, and also language. However, these signals derive their emotive power from their origins and links with bodily contact, and symbolize bodily contact – as clenching the fists stands for punching, and extending the arms stands for embracing.

Touch as an interaction signal

Some forms of bodily contact are used as interaction signals, which do not primarily communicate interpersonal attitudes.

Greetings and farewells

These include bodily contact in most cultures. This is also the case with apes and monkeys: they smack their lips and touch each other; one may present for copulation and the other mount, regardless of their sex; a chimpanzee may hold out a hand and touch the other's head, shoulder, or genitals; a pair of apes may embrace each other enthusiastically. This indicates a biological basis for bodily contact in greeting; Lorenz (1952) suggests that ritualized greeting ceremonies have the purpose of preventing aggression; lip-smacking, for example, invites grooming and acts as an appeasement signal. There are great variations between different human cultures in how greetings are performed (p. 78) but they have a common structure and common elements – including some form of bodily contact. In India, however, the commonest form of greeting does not include touch, and in Britain daily greetings do not. The most common forms of greetings are (1) hand to hand, (2) mouth to cheek, (3) an embrace, (4) mouth to mouth and an embrace, in increasing degrees of intimacy. As mentioned above, a higher degree of bodily intimacy than normal is attained on these occasions. Farewells are similar to greetings, and are carried out in a similar way after an encounter.

Congratulations

Congratulations often include bodily contact – when someone has achieved some success in sport, or career. The signals used are exactly the same as for greetings. An interesting form of congratulation is the embracing of footballers after a goal has been scored, and similar episodes in other games. This is curious, since men do not normally embrace, and this is associated in Britain with homosexuality.

Attention signals

Touch, usually on the arm or shoulder, is often used to attract someone's attention, to indicate that the toucher wants to start an encounter.

Guiding

When walking with someone, one may show them the way, without interrupting the conversation. This may be done by small shifts of bodily direction, or by taking the arm or elbow.

Ceremonies

These usually include bodily contact. As we described earlier (p. 176f) ceremonies have three stages of separation – transition – incorporation. At the height of the ceremony, usually during the transitional period, a symbolic act of bodily contact is performed by the priest, or whoever is empowered by the community to carry out these ritual functions. It is accepted that this person, by performing these symbolic acts, has the power to bring about certain changes of state in the initiates. The commonest form of touch is laying a hand or hands on the initiate's head. It is not clear why this is done: it may be to symbolize the continuous chain from St Peter, or other spiritual source. In healing and ordination a number of priests or elders lay their hands on at once, perhaps to increase the spiritual forces being activated.

Ceremony	Bodily contact	Symbolic meaning
graduation confirmation ordination healing	places hands on initiate's head	passes on continuous chain of authority
healing ceremonies	anoints with oil or other substance	application of medicine
wedding	places ring on bride's finger	ring stands for marriage bonds
monk taking vows	puts his new clothes on him	clothes represent his new status
prize-giving	presents cup or other prize, shakes hands	prize is mark of group's recognition for success
adolescent initiation	inflicts physical damage	test of manhood

There is further bodily contact by friends and relations before and after such ceremonies. There may be handshakes or embraces beforehand; these would be regarded by anthropologists as 'separation' i.e. farewell signals, but may be regarded by those involved as preparations or good wishes for the ceremony. Afterwards there are greetings – for the person in his new status as an adult, graduate, married man, etc. These are more than greetings, they are used to establish a somewhat different relationship with the person in his new social position.

It is interesting that fans of pop stars or other heroes want to touch the body or even the clothes of their hero. (It happened to Jesus too.) This suggests that bodily contact is believed to convey spiritual power in some way, and this may be the real reason that touch is used in ceremonies.

Encounter groups

These groups were first conducted at the Esalen Institute, Big Sur, California, and have subsequently spread to other parts of the world. A number of different versions have been devised. The main purpose of the groups is therapy or training, by means of various individual and inter-personal exercises, many of them involving bodily contact and intimate relationships with other members of the group. For some people the groups are an end in themselves, since they enjoy the bodily contact and intimacy and they feel that ordinary life is too inhibited and restraining in these respects.

Here are some examples of the bodily contact exercises used at Esalen, as described by Schutz (1967):

(1) *To help people who are withdrawn and have difficulty in making contact with other people*

   (a) 'Blind milling.' Everyone in the room stands up and wanders round the room with their eyes shut; when they meet someone they explore each other in any way they like.

   (b) 'Break in.' Some of the group form a tight circle with interlocking arms. The person left out tries to break through the circle in any way he can.

(2) *To help people who are unable to express hostility or competition*

   (a) 'The press.' Two people stand facing each other, place their hands on the other's shoulders and try to press the other to the ground.

   (b) 'Pushing.' Two people stand facing each other, clasping their hands, and try to push each other backwards.

(3) *To help people who have difficulty in giving or receiving affection, who avoid emotional closeness*

   (a) 'Give and take affection.' One person stands in the centre of a circle with his eyes shut; the others approach him and express their feelings towards him non-verbally however they wish – usually by hugging, stroking, massaging, lifting, etc.

(b) 'Roll and rock.' One person stands in the centre of a circle, relaxed and with his eyes shut; the group pass him round the group from person to person, taking his weight. The group then picks him up and sways him gently backwards and forwards, very quietly.

What is the effect of encounter group exercises? A careful follow-up study was carried out of 206 Stanford students who attended encounter groups, T-groups, etc., and 69 control subjects. Success was estimated by a combination of criteria – self-ratings, ratings by friends, and so on. The results were as follows:

	Percentage group members	Percentage controls
dropouts	13	—
casualties	8	—
negative change	8	23
unchanged	38	60
moderate positive change	20 ⎫	13 ⎫
high positive change	14 ⎭ 34	4 ⎭ 17

About a third of the group members and 17 per cent of the controls improved, while 8 per cent of the group members were harmed by the experience (for example, needing psychiatric help afterwards) in addition to the dropouts and those who showed negative changes. There were no consistent differences between encounter groups and non-touching groups; differences between individual group leaders were more important (Lieberman, Yalom, and Miles, 1973). From the continued growth and popularity of the movement, these experiences are clearly enjoyed by a lot of people – though whether it has any therapeutic effect on them is another matter. Quite a number of people drop out because they find the exercises too disturbing. Some end the session by being attached to a different spouse from the one they started with – bodily contact is a very powerful source of social bonding. Some lose interest in ordinary life and ordinary society and want to spend their whole time having 'meaningful experiences in groups'.

Further reading

FRANK, L. K. (1957) Tactile communication. *Genetic Psychology Monographs* **56**: 209–25.

MONTAGU, A. (1971) *Touching: The Human Significance of the Skin*. New York: Colombia University Press.

MORRIS, D. (1971) *Intimate Behaviour*. London: Cape.

References

HARLOW, H. F. and HARLOW, M. K. (1965) The Affectional Systems. In A. M. Schrier *et al.* (eds.) *Behavior of Nonhuman Primates*. New York and London: Academic Press.

HENLEY, M. (1973) Status and sex: some touching observations. *Bulletin Psychonomic Society* **2**: 91–3.

HORE, T. (1970) Social class differences some aspects of the non-verbal communication between mother and pre-school child. *Australian Journal of Psychology* **22**: 21–7.

JOURARD, S. M. (1963) An exploratory study of body-accessibility. *British Journal of Social and Clinical Psychology* **5**: 221–31.

LIEBERMAN, M. A., YALOM, I. D. and MILES, M. B. (1973) *Encounter Groups: First Facts*. New York: Basic Books.

LORENZ, K. (1952) *King Solomon's Ring*. London: Methuen.

RUBIN, Z. (1973) *Liking and Loving*. New York: Holt, Rinehart & Winston.

SCHAFFER, H. R. and EMERSON, P. E. (1964) Patterns of response to physical contact in early human development. *Journal of Child Psychology and Psychiatry* **5**: 1–13.

SCHUTZ, W. C. (1967) *Joy*, New York: Grove Press.

WATSON, O. M. (1972) *Proxemic Behaviour: A Cross-Cultural Study*. The Hague and Paris: Mouton.

16

Spatial behaviour

Spatial behaviour consists of proximity, orientation, territorial behaviour and movement in a physical setting. As
we have seen already, there are physical limitations on
proximity and orientation due to the characteristics of our
organs for sending and receiving signals. However, there is a
range within which variation is possible, and this variation
signals interpersonal attitudes. Changes in spatial position
are also used as interaction signals, and there are considerable
variations due to culture and to personality. Spatial behaviour is of particular interest to us since it follows a
number of simple quantitative laws, like events in the
physical world, so that spatial behaviour has a clear underlying structure.

Types of spatial behaviour

Proximity

This is the distance between two people. It can be regarded
as a case of NVC by one of them under certain conditions,
or it can be taken as joint behaviour by both – for purposes
of cross-cultural comparisons for example. A variety of
research methods of differing degrees of realism have been
used. Pairs of people who are interacting can be sampled
and observed in free social situations, like a children's

playgroup, and their proximity estimated. A subject can be left in a waiting room with someone who appears to be another subject, but is actually a confederate who does not move though he replies to conversation. After a few minutes the distance between them is measured. Or a target person can be moved towards the subject, in a series of small steps, until the subject feels uncomfortable. Mehrabian asked subjects to go up to a hat-rack as if the hat-rack was a person of given age, sex, or social status. Another method is to ask subjects to move cut-out figures to the positions they would be expected to adopt under certain circumstances. This has the advantage that proximity under a large number of alternative conditions can be surveyed rapidly, but there is little evidence that this method gives valid results. Sommer (1969) asked subjects to indicate which seat they would occupy at tables where others are already sitting, on diagrams of tables and chairs. Distances can be measured by tape measure, or more surreptitiously be counting tiles, or by a floor which is responsive to pressure. E. T. Hall (1959) suggested that there are four zones, in North America:

Intimate	18 inches (for intimate relationships; bodily contact easy; can smell other and feel heat; can see but not very well; can talk in whisper)
Personal	18 inches – 4 feet (for close relationships; can touch other; can see better but not smell breath)
Social-consultative	9–12 feet (for more impersonal relations, e.g. from behind a desk, and more independent work; louder voice needed)
Public	12 feet and above (for public figures and public occasions)

So far we have considered proximity as a steady state. There are also changes of proximity made as social moves in encounters. These can be made slowly or quickly, in different styles and with different verbal and non-verbal accompaniments.

Orientation

This is the angle at which one person faces another, usually the angle between a line joining him to another and a line perpendicular to the plane of his shoulders, so that directly facing is o degrees. It refers to the orientation of the body, not the head or eyes. Again orientation can be regarded as a piece of NVC if there is individual choice. The waiting room, and other techniques described for proximity can all be used for orientation. Another method is to offer a choice of chairs, either in reality, or in a diagram. For example, a subject is invited to go and talk to x who is sitting at the table as shown below. His choice of seat indicates preference

Figure 16.1.

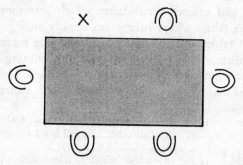

for orientation; the same information can be obtained by observations in real life situations, in pubs and restaurants, as was done by Mark Cook (1970). It has been found in a number of experiments that there is an inverse relation between orientation and proximity, i.e. a head-on orientation goes with greater distance. Proximity and orientation are alternative cues for intimacy, and different combinations of the two are chosen on different occasions.

Height

This is the third dimension of spatial behaviour, though little use is made of it. Height can be manipulated by standing or sitting, using a dais, sitting on the floor, lying on the floor, standing on a chair, wearing high-heeled shoes, and variations of posture. Changes in height are familiar social acts – standing up and sitting down in particular.

Movement in a physical setting

The significance of spatial positions and movements depends on the physical setting, in several ways. (a) Certain areas have the significance of being the territory of some person or group, e.g. behind a counter or desk. Moving into another person's territory is a special kind of social act. Leaving one's own territory, for example to welcome someone to it, is another. (b) Certain areas have the significance of having high or low status, for example the dais, high table, and front seats in a lecture or concert hall are of high status. To move into or away from such areas is a definite social act. (c) Certain areas or seats are associated with particular social roles – in a law court, for example, the judge's seat, the dock, the jury benches; at an interview, the candidate's seat, the chairman's seat, and the other interviewer's seats. (d) The parts of a house have distinctive symbolic significance – upstairs *versus* downstairs, sitting room *versus* bedroom, 'front' *versus* 'back' regions. There are rules and taboos about who may enter different rooms. (e) The size and shape of the room, and the arrangement of furniture may act as constraints on how close and at what angle people sit. They may have to sit closer or at a different angle from the one they would prefer. (f) The existence of physical barriers may make it possible for people to sit much closer than they would otherwise – for example, across a narrow table.

Manipulating the physical setting

We can extend the social behaviour connected with the use of space to include the actual manipulation of space by moving objects and furniture, and by architectural design. Territory is established by leaving markers, like coats on chairs, or moving furniture, like desks in offices. It is possible to alter the social interaction of a room by moving the furniture. Sommer was able to increase the amount of social interaction in an old people's home by moving the chairs; instead of the chairs lining the walls of rooms in long rows they were placed in groups round tables. Arrangement of furniture in offices can create status differences (by putting visitors in smaller chairs or on the wrong side of a large desk), barriers (by tables or desks in interviews), can invite co-operation or competition (by adjusting the angles of chairs), create formality or informality (by adjusting the distance and angle of chairs). The physical arrangements also determine whether or not co-workers or neighbours can see each other, or can create vision in one direction only; they can create status differences making rooms or houses of different sizes or degrees of magnificence. Mehrabian found that the presence of a piece of sculpture – a 'conversation piece', a shared focus for attention – resulted in people high in fear of rejection looking at it more, and made interaction easier for them. Goffman (1956) drew attention to a feature of many buildings, the difference between front and back regions, as in hotels, restaurants, and other places where the staff and public occupy different rooms; this too can be emphasized or minimized by the manipulation of space.

Communicating interpersonal attitudes

Affiliation

If A likes B he will sit or stand somewhat closer. In one experiment this effect was quite large: Rosenfeld (1965) asked students to show a seated person that they wanted to be friendly with her; they approached to 57 inches, compared to 98 inches on the contrary instructions. In a similar experiment Mehrabian found that sitting distances varied directly in 5 steps from 68½ inches for a liked person to 110 inches for a disliked person. A number of studies have shown that closer proximities are decoded in terms of liking. In real-life situations friends sit and stand nearer, and friends are allowed to invade personal territory, such as kitchens and bedrooms.

Argyle and Dean (1965) found that in a given situation people seek a certain degree of proximity, lean forward or back to attain it, and feel uncomfortable if they cannot. They proposed that this is the result of a balancing of forces to approach and withdraw: people are attracted to others (as the result of past rewards) and also repelled (as the result of past punishment). Other experiments have shown that such forces fall off with distance, but that the avoidance forces decline faster, so than an equilibrium is found at the point where the lines cross.

Figure 16.2.

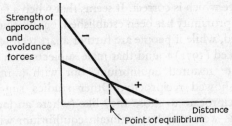

Strength of approach and avoidance forces

Distance

Point of equilibrium

If one person likes another, the approach forces will be stronger and the avoidance forces weaker, resulting in greater proximity (Fig. 16.3).

It also follows from the model that if a person comes too close this will arouse stronger avoidance forces than approach, so that the other will both be disturbed and will back away. Argyle and Dean suggested further that disturbed equilibrium can be compensated for by the use of other

Figure 16.3.

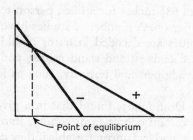

- Point of equilibrium

signals for intimacy; they found that greater distance led to more use of gaze (p. 239f).

However, other experiments have shown that a second process can occur which interferes with equilibrium-maintenance. If A smiles, gazes, or leans forwards, then B will often do the same, to reciprocate or return A's rewards. So according to the equilibrium theory, if A moves forward B should move back, while according to reciprocity theory B should move closer. A number of experiments have been done to see which is correct. It seems that when a fairly high degree of proximity has been established, equilibrium will be maintained, while if people are further apart reciprocity will occur. Breed (1972) found that male subjects with a female confederate restored equilibrium, but with a male confederate showed reciprocity. Other studies suggest that people reciprocate to those they like (where an increase in intimacy is welcome) but maintain equilibrium with those they dislike. Equilibrium-maintainance is seen in those interactions in which one person gradually retreats backwards followed by another who tries, unsuccessfully, to establish a closer degree of intimacy.

Orientation also signals affiliation, though it is a weaker signal than proximity, and it works in a more complex way. Robert Sommer (1969) and Mark Cook (1970) asked subjects how they would sit at tables in different kinds of social relationships. Their results (in percentages) were as follows:

Figure 16.4.

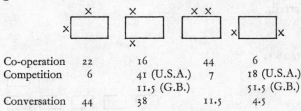

Co-operation	22	16	44	6
Competition	6	41 (U.S.A.)	7	18 (U.S.A.)
		11.5 (G.B.)		51.5 (G.B.)
Conversation	44	38	11.5	4.5

Clearly the side-by-side position is regarded as co-operative, while directly facing positions are seen as competitive; conversation often takes place at 90 degrees. There is a kind of inverse relationship between proximity and orientation – close proximity goes with a more side-by-side orientation. At the same time an emphasis on seeing and hearing is replaced by the possibility of touching. Studies by Mark Cook found that orientation depends on the nature of the situation and the relationship. For example, in an intimate situation, with a friend of the opposite sex, a close and side-by-side position is preferred. Mark Cook's results are shown in Figure 16.5.

Mehrabian (1972) also found that in a hostile situation with another male, male subjects adopted a directly facing orientation, together with a high level of gaze, suggesting vigilance in relation to physical threat. Animals, when frightened of other animals, keep at a distance from them, but keep them under surveillance. While considerations of looking and touching are probably the original basis for these choices of spatial position, the positions acquire standard meanings – side-by-side as co-operative, directly facing as hostile, and so on. Orientation can act as a substitute for proximity, as an affiliation signal: at a more side-by-side orientation proximity can be less – and it is this combination which signals greatest intimacy. For opposite sex relations proximity, and the possibility of bodily contact, are important; in hostile relations being able to watch the other and to keep out of range of bodily contact are preferred.

Figure 16.5.

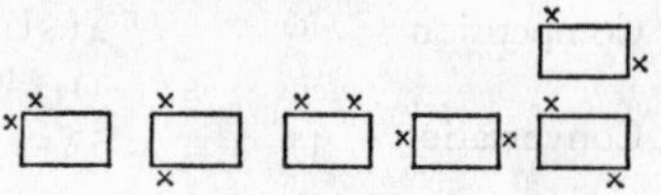

Low motivation

(+) Sitting with a friend of the same sex studying for different exams — 13, 8, 10, 31, 47

(−) Sitting with someone you do not like very much and do not wish to talk to — 5, 13, 11, 9, 67

Medium motivation

(+) Sitting chatting with a friend for a few moments before a class — 51, 29, 16, 1, 12

(−) Sitting with a friend, competing to see who can finish a series of puzzles first — 8, 11, 8, 55, 28

High motivation

(+) Sitting with your boy/girl friend — 32, 8, 65, 4, 0

(−) Sitting with someone of the same sex, with whom you are expecting to have an argument — 22, 41, 5, 11, 22

Dominance

The only direct connection between dominance, or status, and spatial behaviour is that deference is shown to high status people by keeping at a distance from them. A number of sociologists have suggested that a distance of something like twenty-five feet is kept from 'great men' until they invite people to come nearer. A number of experiments have found that proximity is closest between people of the same status.

There is probably some connexion between status and height: it is very common for leaders or people of higher status to be placed physically at a higher level, as on a rostrum. This may be because height is a kind of natural symbol for status, or it may be so that as many people as possible can see the leader.

However, the most important way in which dominance is signalled is by the use of spaces which have symbolic value. A person communicates dominance or high status by occupying one of the most important seats, e.g. in the front row or at the high table, or by occupying positions associated with high status roles, e.g. the head of the table, the pulpit: also by sitting behind his desk rather than coming round to the front of it to meet someone, by having a larger territory, a large desk, etc. Lott and Sommer (1967) asked people where they would sit for various kinds of encounter. The higher status person was usually placed at the head of the table with a lower status person at 90 degrees. When there was a status difference people were not placed side by side and were placed a greater distance apart. Dominance is signalled by the way a room is entered, as several experiments have shown: by entering without knocking or by knocking loudly, or entering immediately after knocking, or by walking in and sitting down uninvited. When saying farewell, especially to an important person, it is common to back away, as if turning the back does not express sufficient deference. This custom is extended at royal courts where visitors have to learn the art of walking backwards.

Interaction signals

Movements in space are used as moves in social interaction. They differ from NV signals of other kinds in that they mainly indicate the beginning and end of sequences of inter-action, for example, the beginning and end of a speech. Spatial movements do not normally occur within periods of interaction. In order to interact with someone it is neces-sary to come near enough for speech to be heard and the face to be seen. Movement towards a person becomes a signal, indicating the desire to interact. This intention is made clear by the gaze, facial expression, and speech that accompanies the spatial move. It may be necessary to obtain the other's approval in order to approach beyond a certain point such as the door to his room or house. At such bar-riers a kind of ritual sequence takes place as he passes into a different zone. Within a larger social situation, such as a party or committee meeting, an encounter with a particular person may be initiated by a shift of orientation, combined with other NV signals, such as a touch on the arm. Thus someone sitting at a dinner table can terminate a boring conversation with the person on his left and start one with the person on his right simply by re-orienting the upper part of his body. This is better than putting his desires into words – 'Please stop talking to me, I want to talk to X.' Similarly encounters are terminated by moving or turning away – accompanied by appropriate NV and verbal signals.

Special phases of an encounter are usually initiated by spatial moves. If someone is going to make a speech he stands up, and others move to positions where they can hear and see him. If a ceremony is going to take place, the priest (or equivalent) takes up a prominent, perhaps raised, posi-tion; the initiates stand in front of him, with their assistants at their side or behind them, others looking on from a distance. If two or more people are going to play a game, they take up opposing spatial positions accordingly.

Spatial behaviour may also signal a particular definition of the situation. Just as orientation communicates co-operative and competitive relationships, so a greater dis-tance indicates the desire for greater formality. This is usually accompanied by other cues like posture and facial expression. A relationship has been found in a number of studies between proximity and a pleasant facial expression: this is interesting as it shows that these two variables act in combination rather than alternatives as orientation and gaze do in relation to proximity.

Spatial behaviour is concerned with establishing the conditions for various forms of communication – being near enough for conversation, or for physical contact. An oblique orientation makes closer proximity possible, but at the expense of not being able to see the other so well. Shifts of position are used to mark the beginning and end, and the main phases of an encounter. The degree of liking felt towards another person is communicated by physical closeness (and by other NV signals); this is probably a case of simple iconic coding, since physical closeness stands for, and makes possible, bodily contact. Similarly deference and social distance are communicated by greater separation. Dominance and status can also be communicated in a quite different way, by using positions in space which are associated with dominant roles, like the head of the table. Territory is indicated in a similar way by the use of markers associated with the self.

Spatial behaviour is part of social skill. In addition to adopting an appropriate spatial position in relation to another person, social skills may involve arranging the space for a group of people. For example, a school teacher can arrange the desks in a classroom in a number of different ways, producing quite different patterns of interaction.

(1) Traditional rows of desks, for teacher-centred sessions with little discussion, or for taking exams
(2) Groups of four desks facing each other, or a library table
(3) A number of pupils in a row behind the teacher's desk, the others facing in a semi-circle, for reading a play
(4) A hollow square, for committee work

(5) Rows of desks, facing on two sides of the room, teacher in middle with slides, tape-recorder etc., e.g. for a language lesson
(6) A semi-circle of desks, for discussion (Richardson, 1967).

Since spatial behaviour is encoded and decoded in terms of interpersonal attitudes, and in other ways, it can be properly regarded as a kind of NVC, though it may not be intended to communicate at all. Moreover it follows simple mathematical laws – for example, liking is directly related to proximity, and proximity is correlated with a friendly facial expression.

Territorial behaviour

Some of the most important aspects of spatial behaviour are connected with 'territory' – establishing it, invading it, and defending it. This doesn't quite fit the categories of communication we have been using in this book; perhaps it comes nearest to self-presentation. Many species of animals display territorial behaviour; a group of animals may regard a certain area as its exclusive preserve, and defend it fiercely against rivals. While there may be an innate basis for this kind of behaviour it has the biological purpose of controlling access to food, water, and shelter. Human beings appear to display a similar pattern of behaviour, in relation to different kinds of areas and resources. One can distinguish three kinds of territory of different sizes.

Personal space

This is the area immediately round the body. It can be measured for an individual by asking another to approach him from different orientations, i.e. head-on, sideways, etc. The points at which he stops the other can be plotted as an envelope: this is his personal space. There is more space at the front than in other directions, and there are considerable individual differences. Fig 16.6 shows the personal space of schizophrenics and normals obtained in this way. It is found that measures of emotional arousal like skin resistance go up as a person is approached from different directions, and personal spaces of the same shape can be confirmed in this way.

Figure 16.6. Personal space of schizophrenics and non-schizophrenics (from Horowitz *et al.*, 1969)

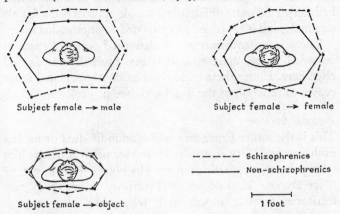

Subject female → male

Subject female → female

Subject female → object

— — — — Schizophrenics
———— Non-schizophrenics

1 foot

Violent prisoners have also been found to have larger body-buffer zones. Kinzel (1970) found that violent prisoners had zones of 22·3 square feet, compared with 7·0 for non-violent prisoners. Their zones were larger behind than in front, and there was evidence that they feared physical or homosexual attack from the rear.

The Argyle and Dean theory predicted that invasion of personal space would be disturbing. The measures of skin resistance show that this is indeed so, and other studies have found an increase in number of gestures which suggest stress. When A's personal space is violated by B, A will turn his head or body away, hunch up his body, and move away. Nancy Russo (in Sommer, 1969) studied the invasion of space in libraries, by sitting close to solitary female readers. Most were visibly disturbed and moved away, especially if the experimenter sat in the next chair and moved it closer. However, this and similar results should perhaps be interpreted in terms of the meaning of the violating act. It broke a rule, and it seemed to invite an intimate relationship without any other NV signals or verbal explanation. It would be useful to know how violation of personal space is decoded under different circumstances. Probably the violation would be interpreted quite differently if a male approached a female or a male, and it happened in a crowded or uncrowded room.

There is, of course, great violation of personal space in crowded buses, underground trains, football crowds and elsewhere. Under these conditions evidently personal space ceases to function in the usual way (see p. 320).

Personal territory

This is the rather larger area which an individual owns, has exclusive use of, or controls. This space often provides him with privacy, or social intimacy. His house, garden, car, or office are one kind of personal territory. More temporary territories include rooms in hotels, tables and seats at restaurants, seats in cinemas, a tennis court, a table in a library. A territory may be established simply by repeated occupation of a particular seat or table. In most homes each member of the family has a bed, a chair, and an area which is regarded as his or her own domain. Some animals mark their territory by leaving scents; humans mark their territories by leaving coats on chairs, books on library tables, or putting their names on doors of rooms. Sommer asked students to show how they would sit at a table to defend it against other users; they chose a position in the centre of a long side, facing towards the door of the room; they thought it was easier to defend a small table, against the wall, at the back of the room. Sommer and Becker (1969) found that places at library tables were most effectively defended by leaving a coat and open notebooks. These techniques are of course also used by people who want to keep compartments in railway carriages, or tables at restaurants to themselves. Altman and Haythorn (1967) studied the establishment of territories when pairs of sailors occupied an experimental room in isolation for a number of days. Each man came to use a certain bed, chair, and area of the room. This was most marked when the pair were incompatible, as that led to social withdrawal from one another. Groups where there was little territoriality in the early part of the isolation period were more likely to fail to complete the twenty days of the experiment – suggesting that territoriality was adaptive in this situation. Studies in mental hospital wards have found that secluded territories are sought by schizophrenics and patients low in the pecking order. Territories can be established by moving the furniture. Men in offices move their furniture to control their relations with visitors. Duncan Joiner (1970) found that more senior officials in the British Government and commercial offices placed their desks to create a social barrier and a status difference between themselves and their visitors; however, in universities neither senior nor junior staff placed their desks in this way.

Various kinds of social behaviour are seen as invasions of territory. This may be purely spatial – sitting at a library seat, it may consist of making a noise, speaking, or looking when the territory occupier wants to be undisturbed. Facilities may be used without permission, or parts of the territory may be damaged, made dirty, or contaminated in other ways. Whether or not there is thought to be such invasion of territory depends on the circumstances. In a very crowded library it would not be an invasion to occupy the next seat to someone else, whereas in an otherwise empty library this would be seen as an invasion. If verbal permission is sought first, an act of invasion will often be allowed, and it will no longer be seen as an invasion.

Home territories

These are areas of otherwise public space which are nor-mally used by the members of a particular group. Examples are the cafés and other places frequented by juvenile gangs. 'This place is ours,' said one of the motorcycle gang. 'This and the Aloha. This is our territory, you're a surfer, come in here and you're dead' (Sommer, 1969:39). Other examples are corners of pubs, clubs, and hotels used by certain groups of regulars. In the case of gangs at least, home territories are defended with violence. This kind of territoriality is similar to that of animals.

Two or three people can establish a temporary home territory by sitting or standing talking to each other. Knowles found that while 75 per cent of people walking down a corridor walked between two wastebarrels, when two people talking stood in the same positions only 30 per cent walked between them. I have carried out a similar experiment on a broad pavement in Leuven, Belgium. Pairs of people stood four feet six inches apart, without attending to one another; they then started a conversation without moving; the number of people passing between them per minute was counted in the two conditions – conversation reduced the number to one-tenth. Knowles and Efran (1973) found that the effect is greatest if the people talking are less than four feet apart, are of opposite sex, of high status, and if there are four of them rather than two. Two or more people in a larger gathering, or in a public place, may indicate that they are for the time being a closed group, by their spatial positions, and also by their arm positions, low tone of voice, and so on. If they are more open to new members they will stand side by side, with a greater distance between them, and look around at others present. When a person passes through a group, especially a closed group, he does so quickly, with lowered head, avoiding eye-contact, and with some embarrassment.

Cultural settings and spatial behaviour

As we have seen, variations in spatial behaviour are limited by how well we can see and hear each other. Nevertheless there are considerable cultural variations both in the preferred spatial conditions for interactions, and in what can be tolerated. E. T. Hall (1959) observed that Arabs and Latin Americans prefer closer proximity than Europeans or North Americans. Watson and Graves (1966) confirmed that this was true for Arabs; they compared the distance between pairs of Arabs from different countries, and pairs of Americans. They found that two Arabs stood closer together than two Americans, and faced each other more directly. Their results are represented in the following figure.

Figure 16.7. The spatial position of pairs of Americans and pairs of Arabs

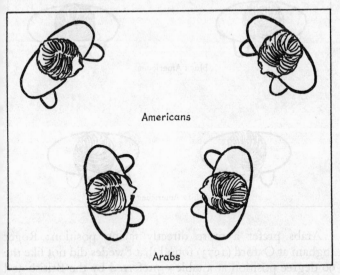

Americans

Arabs

Later research by Watson (1972) found that Latin Americans, Asians, and Indians are intermediate between Arabs and Northern Europeans. Baxter (1970) carried out an observational study of the spatial relations of 859 pairs of people in a natural setting – a zoo in New York. He found that the average distances apart, nose to nose, (usually side-by-side looking at the animals) were as shown below.

Figure 16.8. Spatial positions at the zoo

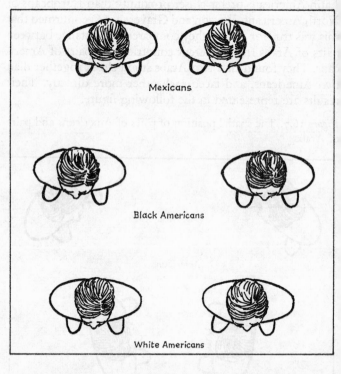

Mexicans

Black Americans

White Americans

Arabs prefer a more directly facing position; Roger Ingham at Oxford (1973) found that Swedes did not like the 90 degree position at a table – preferred by the British and Americans for conversation with friends. The Swedes preferred the directly facing position, perhaps because of a strong need to get feedback on how the other person is reacting.

One of the most remarkable sets of cultural rules about spatial behaviour is that governing how close the members of each Indian caste may approach one another. These rules are still kept in rural areas of southern India.

Brahmins
} 7 feet
Nayars
} 25 feet
Iravans
} 32 feet
Cherumans
} 64 feet
Nayadis

This works additively, so that a Najadi must not come closer to a Brahmin than 128 feet.

There are rules governing spatial behaviour for different situations in any culture. Here are some examples of conventions in Britain and the U.S.A. Mark Cook (1970) found that two people sitting in a pub prefer to sit side by side, with their backs to the wall. At a restaurant or cafeteria on the other hand they sit opposite each other. When they are seated people adopt a considerably greater distance than when standing: 5–8 feet as opposed to $1\frac{1}{2}$–3 feet.

There are rules about seating guests at dinner parties. At parties in general the main object is to enjoy interpersonal behaviour, and closer proximity than normal is allowed. In trains, libraries, and other places where individuals are pursuing their affairs independently, they space themselves out as far away from one another as possible. On lifts, the underground, and crowded buses very close proximity is common, but it is combined with very indirect orientation, and avoidance of mutual gaze, conversation, or other exchange of signals.

320 The different bodily signals

Vine (1973) suggests that under crowded conditions people regard each other as physical objects rather than persons, and the usual non-verbal means for sustaining encounters are reduced to a minimum. This would also explain the high level of anti-social behaviour in cities. In prisons and other overcrowded places people withdraw from social interaction, don't move about much, and avoid quarrels with one another. When there is a social distance between two groups, this is reflected in physical distance.

There appear to be clear social conventions about proper spatial positioning for particular situations and relationships. The author and Margaret McCallin asked judges to rate the appropriateness of a series of staged conversations in which distance and orientation were varied. The most appropriate spatial positions were as shown below:

Figure 16.9. Spatial positions for different relationships

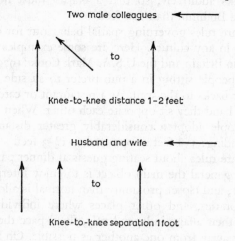

Two male colleagues

to

Knee-to-knee distance 1–2 feet

Husband and wife

to

Knee-to-knee separation 1 foot

Personality

There are a number of relationships between personality variables and spatial behaviour. Some of these can be interpreted as the desire to seek or avoid social relationships, or to seek social relationships of a particular kind. On the other hand they are not instances of 'self-presentation', in that spatial behaviour is not being used as a sign for other features of the person.

Mental patients need more personal space than other people. Results for schizophrenics are shown in Figure 16.6; it has often been observed that schizophrenics avoid other people, keep to their corners of the hospital wards, and keep well apart from one another. Prisoners also need a lot of personal space, and fights between them may be set off by invasions of space which would not worry other people. Neurotics, and all classes of patients studied, have similar needs. Dominant people are found to seek central locations; for example, the foremen of juries often virtually elect themselves by sitting where the foreman might be expected to sit.

It is consistently found that females approach closer than males, and prefer corner or side-by-side seating positions. It is also found that people approach closer to females than to males.

Further Reading

HALL, E. T. (1959) *The Silent Language*. Garden City, N.Y.: Doubleday.
MEHRABIAN, A. (1969) Significance of posture and position in the communication of attitude and status relationships. *Psychol. Bull.* **71**: 359–72.
SOMMER, R. (1969) *Personal Space*. Englewood Cliffs, N.J.: Prentice-Hall.

References

ALTMAN, I. and HAYTHORN, W. W. (1967) The ecology of isolated groups. *Behavioural Science* **12**: 169–82.
ARGYLE, M. and DEAN, J. (1965) Eye-contact, distance and affiliation. *Sociometry* **28**: 289–304.

322 The different bodily signals

BAXTER, J. C. (1970) Interpersonal spacing in natural settings. *Sociometry* **33**: 444–56.

BREED, G. (1972) The effect of intimacy: reciprocity or retreat? *British Journal of Social and Clinical Psychology* **11**: 135–42.

COOK, M. (1970) Experiments on orientation and proxemics. *Human Relations* **23**: 61–76.

EFRAN, M. G. and CHEYNE, J. A. (1973) Shared space: the co-operative control of spatial areas by two co-operating individuals. *Canadian Journal of Behavioural Science* **5**: 201–10.

HOROWITZ, M. J., DUFF, D. F. and STRATTON, L. O. (1969) Body-buffer zone. *Archives of General Psychiatry* **11**: 651–6.

GOFFMAN, E. (1956) *The Presentation of Self in Everyday Life.* Edinburgh University Press.

INGHAM, R. J. (1973) Cross-cultural differences in social behaviour. D.Phil. thesis, University of Oxford.

JOINER, D. (1970) Social ritual and architectural space. Bartlett School of Architects, unpublished.

LOTT, D. F., and SOMMER, R. (1967) Seating arrangements and status. *Journal of Personality and Social Psychology* **7**: 90–5.

KINZEL, A. F. (1970) Body-buffer zones in violent prisoners. *American Journal of Psychiatry* **127**: 59–64.

KNOWLES, E. S. (1973) Boundaries around group interaction. *Journal of Personality and Psychology* **26**: 327–31.

RICHARDSON, E. (1967) *The Environment of Learning.* London. Nelson.

ROSENFELD, H. M. (1965) Effects of an approval-seeking induction on interpersonal proximity. *Psychological Reports* **17**: 120–2.

SOMMER, P. and BECKER, F. D. (1969) Territorial defense and the good neighbour. *Journal of Personality and Social Psychology* **11**: 85–92.

VINE, I. (1973) Social spacing in animals and man. *Social Science Information* **12**: (5): 7–50.

WATSON, O. M. (1972) *Proxemic Behaviour: A Cross-Cultural Study.* The Hague: Mouton.

WATSON, O. M., and GRAVES, T. D. (1966) Quantitative research in proxemic behavior. *American Anthropology* **68**: 971–85.

17

Clothes, physique & other aspects of appearance

Clothes, badges, and forms of decoration are entirely under the control of the wearer; physique, hair, and skin are partly so. Appearance is prepared, with more or less care, and it has a powerful effect on the perceptions and reactions of others (and some effect on the wearer). Appearance, then, can be regarded as a sphere of NVC. Knapp (1972) gives the following illustration of the manipulation of appearance.

'Picture the following scene: Mr and Mrs American awake and prepare to start the day. Mrs American takes off her "nighttime" bra, and replaces it with a "slightly-padded-uplift" bra. After removing her chin strap, she further pulls herself together with her girdle. Then she begins to "put on her face". This involves an eyebrow pencil, mascara, lipstick, rouge, eye-liner and false eye lashes. Then she removes the hair under her arms and on her legs and places a hairpiece on her head. False finger-nails, nail polish, and tinted contact lenses precede the deodorant, perfume, and endless decisions concerning clothes. Mr American shaves hair on his face, puts a toupee on his head and carefully attaches his newly purchased sideburns. He removes his false teeth from a solution used to whiten them, gargles with a breath sweetener, selects his after shave lotion, puts on his elevator shoes, and begins making his clothing decisions' (p. 63–4).

These manipulations of the body image are directed by ideals about what bodily appearance is attractive, or (in other societies) threatening, holy, or desirable in other ways. In Western society attractiveness is one of the key dimensions of appearance, and we shall see that it has a great effect on the behaviour of others, both for males and females. In a survey of which kinds of females were considered attractive Iliffe (1960) found that there was a remarkable degree of agreement between 4,355 British judges of different ages, sexes, social classes, and regions. On the other hand it is familiar that different shapes of female bodies and faces are in fashion at different periods and in different countries.

The body a person has, or perhaps the body image he succeeds in presenting, has a marked effect on his feelings about himself and on his behaviour to others. Jourard and Secord (1955) found that males were more satisfied with their bodies when they were large, and that females were more satisfied when they were smaller than average, but when their busts were larger than average. Singer (1964) found that attractive female students made use of their physical assets, by sitting in the front of classes and going to speak to instructors more often. On the other hand Stroebe and colleagues found that there was quite a small correlation between ratings by self and by others for attractiveness: this means that many people are generally considered more attractive than they realize, and others less so.

Different aspects of appearance

Clothes

Clothes are primarily intended to protect their wearers from cold, heat, and rain, and probably to conceal parts of the body. However, in all societies clothes are used to send information about the personality, status, and group membership of the wearer, and also about his or her sexual availability, aggressiveness, and other interpersonal attitudes. Clothes take a great variety of forms in different parts of the world and periods of history. They may be designed for protection against the elements; they may be minimal as in the Sudan, or they may completely cover the wearer, as the clothes of Arab women did until recently. They may be uniform for all members of the same rank or group, or great individuality may be encouraged. While Western countries insist on the wearing of clothes, many primitive societies do not, and there is nothing indecent about nudity. In the West various degrees of nudity are allowed only under special conditions – at home, on the beach, at the art class, and now in the sauna bath.

Personality characteristics are signalled by style of clothes; several factors have been found, like conformist *versus* rebellious, amount of decoration, use of saturated hues, and large design size. There are certain limited aspects of personality which can be encoded in clothes in this way. Status and group membership are encoded quite differently, by the arbitrary styles of clothes associated with different social groups. Thus the same item may communicate in two ways; a tie may be red, blue, black, or represent a college or club, thus conveying arbitrary meanings, and it may be neatly tied, loosely knotted, or with one end over the shoulder – indicating personality qualities analogically. Clothes also convey inter-personal attitudes, for instance, of sexuality, aggressiveness, or humility, by either of these forms of symbolism

We shall discuss below experiments showing how clothes and other signals create impressions of, for example, attractiveness or high social status. Clothes have an effect on the wearer, as well as communicating to others. The effect on the wearer of clothes suggesting higher social status or greater glamour are familiar. It has been found in a number of experiments that wearing a uniform has the effect initially at least, of 'de-individuation', i.e. making people less aware of themselves as individuals and less socially responsible.

Badges and decoration

Clothes may come to indicate group membership or occupation; badges are special additions designed for this purpose alone. A familiar British example is the school, college, or club tie, which indicates the wearer's school etc. to the limited circle able to decode the signal. Wedding and engagement rings indicate marital status. Small crosses (which usually indicate Catholicism), trade union pins, Scottish tartans, and other national and regional signs, are other examples. Women in western society, and both sexes in more primitive societies, wear beads, head-dresses, or other decorations, whose aim is mainly to increase the beauty of the wearer – they may also signal her wealth or sexual desirability and availability. In primitive societies the scalp, teeth, bones, or horns of victims may be worn as trophies.

Hair

Hair is rarely left to grow wild, but is cut, and dressed. It is possible to dress the hair in a great variety of ways, and some of these are acceptable in each cultural group. Each has a social meaning, though these meanings differ at different periods: for example long hair in men has been regarded as masculine and as effeminate at different times. At the present time length of hair is very important to young males – some attach great value to having it long, while many of their elders regard long hair as outrageous. Some young men find that to acquire girl friends they need long hair, while to acquire a job they need short hair, so they have a wig. One anthropologist, Hallpike (1969), has suggested that long hair has a widespread symbolic meaning in many societies: it indicates being outside society, beyond social control, and is worn by outcasts, wild animals, intellectuals, hippies, and ascetics. Cutting the hair represents re-entering society or living under a disciplined regime (like monks, or soldiers). On the other hand shaving the head, or wearing the hair extremely short, has been used by skinheads and other rebellious groups. It has been suggested that lack of control over hair symbolizes and communicates a state of society where there is lack of control over the members. But there is still the problem of why such intense feelings are attached to length of hair. A Freudian interpretation is that cutting the hair symbolizes castration, and long hair sexuality. In an American study by Freedman (1969) it was found that many women regarded bearded men as masculine and mature, and felt more feminine towards them; bearded men were more tense with other bearded men. These results suggest that while there are clearly fashions in the meaning of hair, there are also deeper meanings in terms of rebellion and sexuality.

The face and skin

In primitive societies like some Australian tribes, the face is often decorated by 'cicatrization' – deep scars. Duelling scars were fashionable among German students until quite recently. The face can also be decorated by tattooing and painting. It can be mutilated by making holes for ear-rings or nose rings, by flattening the nose, or putting circular plates in the lips. In modern societies men may have different kinds of facial hair, while women use cosmetics for their lips, eyes, and cheeks, and wear ear-rings. Plastic surgeons often carry out 'cosmetic surgery' on noses and sagging skin. Experiments have recently been done in giving plastic surgery to criminals with disfigured faces; it has been found that removing scars, tattoos, or other disfigurements had a considerable effect on the recidivism rate (Kurtzberg et al., 1968). The personality is particularly associated with the face, and the appearance of the face is manipulated to convey information about the person. In primitive societies masks are often worn, which conceal the identity and the emotional state of the wearer. This can have the effect of producing uninhibited behaviour, as at a masked ball, or of the wearer playing the role suggested by the mask. In modern societies women often partly conceal their faces by means of long hair and hats.

The eyes are looked at more than other parts of the face. The eyes are given a lot of cosmetic attention by women, they can be framed by spectacles or concealed by dark glasses, and the pupils can be enlarged by belladonna.

In most societies most of the skin except for the face and hands is covered up by clothes. The neck, arms, feet, and lower legs are often left visible by women. In warm weather, and for sports, more is left visible. The body can be decorated by scars, tattooing, paint, or mud. In the U.S.A. about 10 per cent of males are tattooed, mostly on the hands, and usually by themselves. J. H. Burma (in Roach and Eicher, 1965) found that a large proportion of delinquents were tattooed, and that most of them wanted it removed. However, it acted as a signal of group membership, gave them status in the group, and made them feel tough. All that other people in modern society do to the skin is to sunburn and sometimes paint and remove hairs from it. Particular care is paid to the more visible areas, hands and feet, and the nails may be carefully cut and painted. A particularly important aspect of the skin is its colour. In most societies a dark skin results in lower social status, except inside black groups themselves. Nevertheless many people try to make their skins darker by sunbathing, since tanned skin is regarded as more healthy and more attractive.

Physique

Physique can be described in a number of ways, but three dimensions have been found to be associated with various aspects of personality:

Ectomorphy – Thin and Bony
Endomorphy – Fatness
Mesomorphy – Muscularity

As we show later (p. 336), there are correlations between

these dimensions and personality, and decoders interpret physique in the same way – ectomorphs as quiet and tense, endomorphs as warm-hearted, agreeable and dependent, and mesomorphs as adventurous and self-reliant. However, fashions in physique vary between different times and places – various parts of the body are thought nicer if they are larger, smaller, or of a particular shape.

Physique can be manipulated, within limits. In some primitive societies bodies are extensively deformed by binding the feet to make them smaller, as in China, binding the head to make it more oval, as in parts of Africa. While there has been a trend towards less bodily deformation in modern societies, there is still a lot of binding of waists, mainly female, by corsets, and a lot of supporting and padding of bosoms. Fatness is controlled by slimming, muscularity increased by exercise, and the general appearance of the body manipulated by the stance adopted – with shoulders back, and so forth.

As we show later (p. 337), men who are tall have a definite advantage in getting jobs and being promoted in our society; women, however, prefer to be short. Height can be manipulated to a small extent by wearing higher or lower heels, 'walking tall' or stooping, setting the hair in different ways, and wearing hats. Apparent size can be changed by wearing more or less voluminous clothes.

Signals sent by appearance – information about the self

The main purpose of manipulating appearance is to send messages about the self. A person chooses the clothes which he buys, and he chooses which he wears on a particular occasion. As we shall see, people have a clear idea of the social meaning of different items of clothing, so they must be choosing clothes at least in part because of their social meanings, that is the signals they can send about the wearer. This information need not be correct, but it is what the wearer wants others to think about him. Of course such communications only work up to a point, and appearance may not be sufficient. It may be necessary to produce more substantial grounds for prestige than merely looking the part.

Individual identity

We saw that birds can identify the calls of their mates from several thousand very similar calls (p. 23f). Human beings can recognize voices, but can identify one another more easily by appearance – much of which is the object of deliberate manipulation. People present a consistent appearance; G. P. Stone (1970) found a number of people who deliberately dressed in a consistent and distinctive way in order to be recognized.

Group membership

This may be indicated by the adoption of shared styles of dress, badges, etc. The signals used may indicate the group's ideas or social position, for instance its social status, degree of westernization, or rebelliousness. Some of the signals used – badges, uniforms, and special hair cuts – have arbitrary meanings. In Britain during recent years membership of various movements among young people – teddy boys, mods, rockers, skinheads, and hippies – has been clearly indicated by means of appearance. The mods adopted a more middle class, feminine style, while the rockers were aggressively masculine and working class in appearance.

Age and sex

A person's age and sex need to be known by others, since they affect the way they will treat him. While these are communicated involuntarily, the cues concerned can also be manipulated. There are very clear social conventions about the clothes, hair, and grooming of males and females in most societies. It is possible to pass for the opposite sex, but there are severe penalties for doing so. Similarly there are conventions about the correct appearance of people of different ages. Here it is possible to suggest that one's age is somewhat greater or less than it really is, but the uncontrollable features of face, hair, and skin are likely to fail to confirm the manipulated signals and make the wearer look ridiculous.

Status

Status is one of the most important sources of variation. Rank is shown by uniforms in the army, and by distinctive clothing in many occupational hierarchies. Social class is less definite – it represents a person's position in the community and his associated life style. Mary Sissons (1970) at Oxford found that a person's social class could be judged quite accurately either from a still photograph of his clothes, or a recording of his voice, or from a photograph of his face. Social class is symbolized in ways that keep changing, and the clothes that convey status change quite rapidly – a case of the 'circulation of symbols' (p. 341). Veblen (1899) maintained that clothes portrayed social status by the amount of conspicuous consumption involved, and by being unsuitable for manual work. Goffman (1956) has observed that there are great temptations for people to misrepresent their social class, but that this is prevented by the use of symbols which it is difficult to fake – wearing very expensive clothes or jewellery, or objects which are very scarce, keeping hands or body in a condition which requires time, money, and avoidance of work.

Orthodox Jews have a status hierarchy which is based on frequency of religious observance, and intensity of religious emotion, not on wealth or occupation. There are six distinct levels in this hierarchy, which are recognizable by appearance – by the state of the beard and side locks, the kind of hat and the kind of coat worn (S. Poll, in Roach and Eicher, 1965).

Occupation and social roles

Policemen, postmen, monks, and others wear distinctive uniforms. Other occupations are partly recognizable, at least in broad social and occupational categories. Where two groups wear different clothes this often indicates the existence of different roles, change of dress by a group often indicates a change of role, and where all members of a group dress alike the role is well defined (S. Bush and P. London in Roach and Eicher, 1965).

A film star might be mistaken for a model or a member of the royal family, but not for an all-in wrestler or farm worker. There are other social groups which are recognizable by their characteristic appearance – tramps, hippies, revolutionaries, and members of some political and religious groups. It is important for members of these groups to be able to recognize each other. Within an organization there are usually uniforms or semi-uniforms. These are partly *roles* rather than occupations, since a nurse could become a patient or a visitor. In a university science department it is fairly easy to distinguish the academic staff, students, secretaries, and technicians. Members of working organizations indicate by their appearance how they define their job: for example, a foreman may look more like a manager or more like a shop-floor worker. A person may indicate his role in a particular situation by his appearance – a barrister puts on a wig, an academic puts on a gown, to indicate the role he is about to play. On ceremonial occasions it is common for the king, priest, vice-chancellor, or whoever is in charge to put on a special costume. This indicates that he is acting not on his own behalf, but is using the authority vested in him and symbolized by his ceremonial gear.

The other participants may feel that the role performer has special status, powers or holiness when he is dressed up. Priests usually wear robes which are both impressive and in strong contrast to those of the laity (E. Crawley, in Roach and Eicher, 1965).

In an extreme case, the witch doctor becomes invisible under a mask and takes the role of the spirit represented by the mask. White laboratory coats, dinner jackets, shirt sleeves and academic dress may be used as signals in this way.

Personality characteristics

These are also communicated by appearance. This is because individuals with certain kinds of personality also prefer certain colours and other features, and it is also due to more deliberate self-presentation. People who are sociable and extraverted prefer brighter and more saturated colours. Conformists also conform in the clothes they wear. People wear clothes for a number of reasons not connected with communication, but these can be decoded by some observers. Flugel (1930) suggests that some people wrap themselves up warmly in compensation for a lack of love. He reports that twenty-four out of fifty students said that they would wear more clothes when homesick.

Appearance is also manipulated with a more or less clear idea of what information is being sent, or with more deliberate self-presentation. Gibbins (1969) studied fifteen- and sixteen-year-old grammar school girls in the north of England. They were asked to judge photographs of six outfits of clothes, taken from magazines, on seven-point scales. There was a high degree of agreement on the kind of person who would wear the clothes in terms of the following variables:

snobbish
fun-loving
rebellious
shy
gay

and a behaviour pattern such as

> number of boy-friends
> sexual morals
> whether she smoked
> whether she drank
> hobbies (sporting *versus* artistic)

The girls were also asked which clothes they liked best: these were those that corresponded most closely to a girl's own self-image. Statistical analysis of the ratings produced a main factor of fashionability combined with favourable evaluation. Wearing clothes that send the right messages has to be learnt during socialization. Stone suggests that children go through three stages here:

(1) *pre-play*, wearing clothes chosen by mother
(2) *play*, dressing up in fantasy costumes
(3) *game*, wearing peer-group-approved uniforms, indicating the identity as a group member and as an individual.

We have already discussed a number of other appearance cues that convey information about social station, age, and so on. When a person is keen to emphasize part of his identity he will stress the corresponding cues. Often people want to indicate that they are not wholly identified with a role, or that there is more to them than just this role. They may express 'role-distance' by adopting an appearance that is slightly inappropriate to the role, and sends additional information about other roles occupied or about personality.

Appearance contains a lot of different cues and messages which between them may convey quite a full picture of a personality. For example, someone might convey an impression of high social status, eccentricity, Scottish origin and bad-temper – or gaiety, sexual attractiveness and religiosity. In these ways appearance communicates personality, including its conflicts and complexities.

Appearance plays an important part in establishing and

maintaining a self-image. Appearance reflects the self-image, and produces corresponding reactions from others, thus confirming it. T. K. Miller and others (in Roach and Eicher, 1965) report an interesting experiment in which twenty-six female mental hospital patients were helped to design and make some attractive clothes. They were then shown how to model them, and did so before a large number of other patients. The patients felt that they looked better, and felt better than before.

There are individual differences in extent of concern with appearance. Adolescents and others who are personally insecure (i.e. have not formed a stable self-image) are greatly concerned. The reason is that their self-image is still dependent on how others react to them, which in turn depends on their appearance. Similarly the socially mobile, and other newcomers to groups, are concerned about being socially accepted, and thefore with their appearance. On the other hand many old people, some men, and most schizo-phrenics are very little concerned about appearance; indeed schizophrenics can often be recognized by the way they wear their clothes.

There are very interesting sex differences in concern with appearance. Among animals the male of the species is usually the more magnificent; and in primitive societies the males often dress up in a more decorative way. Since the late eighteenth century, however, there has taken place what Flugel called 'the Great Masculine Renunciation', and men have since been dressing in a drab and uniform way, though with some reversal in the late 1960s. Women dress in a more colourful and varied way, there are rapid changes of fashion, and their clothes are lighter and less constricting. While women's clothes emphasize their sexual charms, they are also more affected by considerations of modesty than male clothes, producing the conflict between decoration and modesty described below.

Interpreting physical cues

There are several stages in the decoding of bodily cues. First, inferences may be made about a person's true height, physique, etc. if it is suspected that bodily cues are being unduly manipulated. Secondly, physical cues may be conceptualized in terms of more global physical dimensions like 'attractive', 'sexy', or 'athletic'. There are cultural conventions about which kinds of bodies are classified in these ways, and we have seen that there is considerable agreement within cultures about which people are attractive.

Thirdly, inferences can be made from physical cues to personality characteristics. Probably people who classify others as 'muscular' or even 'tall' are not thinking simply in terms of these physical dimensions, but have a set of associated personality traits in mind. Physique is also decoded in terms of personality traits: Wells and Siegel (1961) showed silhouettes of three physiques and obtained ratings on the personalities of the target persons. The fat person was rated as, among other things, more warm-hearted, sympathetic, good-natured, agreeable, and dependent on others; the muscular person was seen as stronger and more adventurous; the thin person was seen as more tense and nervous, pessimistic, and quieter. Other studies of the actual correlation between physique and personality show that the subjects in this experiment were largely correct in their views – except that there is only a rather weak statistical relationship, corresponding to a correlation of about 0.30.

Other studies have found that tall people are seen as intelligent, that people who wear spectacles are seen as intelligent, that girls with thick lips are seen as frivolous. In these cases there is either no relationship at all between the physical attributes and personality, or there is only a very small one; for example the height – IQ correlation is about 0·15.

Hamid (1968) showed coloured photographs of girls wearing different clothes to decoders. There was a high level of agreement in the way in which they were judged, but little agreement on the faces alone. Girls with short skirts, bright dresses and make-up were seen as sophisticated, immoral and attractive; those wearing spectacles were seen as conventional, shy, religious, and less attractive and sophisticated.

Dion and colleagues (1974) found that persons who are seen as physically attractive are also thought to possess a number of favourable personality characteristics – to be sexually warmer and more responsive, sensitive, kind, interesting, strong, poised, modest, sociable, outgoing, etc. They are thought to be more competent, to have better jobs, and happier marriages – but to be worse parents.

Fourthly, the final degree of decoding physical cues is into social responses. Some physical cues produce such responses – taller people are promoted, for example to be President of the U.S.A. (the taller candidate is nearly always elected), to be a Bishop in the Church of England, and to imaginary jobs in experimental studies. More attractive people evoke a wide range of favourable reactions – they are more popular as children, and are thought by their teachers to be more intelligent. In Singer's study there was a correlation as high as 0·40 between the attractiveness of first-born female students and the grades they were given, with IQ held constant. As we saw, this was partly mediated by the girls drawing attention to their charms. Physical attractiveness is of course extremely important in mate-selection; some experiments on this are described in the next section.

A number of experiments have studied behavioural reactions to a confederate wearing different sets of clothes. A more smartly dressed person is more likely to be followed when crossing the road against a 'don't walk' notice, is more likely to be helped if asking the way, or asking social sur-

vey questions (e.g. Lambert 1972); an attractively dressed
female was able to obtain coffee at a snack bar without
money, and to draw money from a bank where she had no
account (B. R. Little, unpublished study).

Perhaps more disturbing is a simulated jury experiment by
Efran (1974). He found that when photographs of the
defendant were provided, more attractive female defendants were much less likely to be found guilty and the
recommended punishment was less severe, when they were
being judged by male jurors; with no photograph the
judgements fell between those for the attractive and those
for the unattractive defendants.

Appearance and interpersonal attitudes

Appearance is also used to signal attitudes towards other
people – in particular sexual availability, aggression, rebelliousness, and formality.

Sexuality

It is widely believed that clothes have a sexual role, both in
concealing the sexual organs and in drawing attention to
them, and generally making the wearer sexually more
attractive. The conflict between modesty and decoration
leads to all kinds of ingenious compromises in female dress,
particularly in the area of the breasts. In previous times
the male organs were similarly concealed and magnified
by the codpiece. For women at least, sexual attractiveness is
one of the most important aspects of appearance – both in
their own eyes, and in that of others. Many women signal
their attractiveness, but are clearly not sexually available.
Why do they do this? Perhaps to produce favourable but
not sexual responses from men, perhaps to sustain their
self-image.

The physical attractiveness both of males and females is
very important in the selection of mates. Elaine Walster and

colleagues (1966) invited 752 students to a freshman dance, and randomly assigned each to a partner; attractiveness was assessed on a seven-point scale by a group of young experimenters. It was found that physical attractiveness was the most important predictor of how much each person was liked by their partner – for males as well as females – with correlations of about 0.40. In this and other studies it was found that physical attractiveness is more important for females – both in affecting the reactions of others and in affecting their own feelings about themselves. It was not found that students liked partners most if they were of the same level of attractiveness as themselves – less attractive people liked attractive partners.

Sexual attractiveness depends partly on clothes, partly on hair, grooming, skin, and physique. Most aspects of appearance on which attractiveness depends can be controlled in the ways described earlier, including plastic surgery for noses and breasts. Attractiveness, like other aspects of appearance, can to a large degree, be regarded as a sphere of NVC, which is under voluntary control.

Aggression

Animals often put on threat displays, for frightening and inducing submission in other animals. This is normally done by males towards other males. In primitive societies it is common for men to dress up in impressive and terrifying war costumes, painting themselves from head to foot in paint or mud, and wearing head-dresses or masks. Until recent times men went to war in handsome uniforms, and the swords and spurs were worn on other occasions too. To dress in a threatening way is now rare in civilized countries, though members of motor cycle gangs wearing black leather clothes with studs, swastikas, and knives are an example.

Rebelliousness

Since there are clear social conventions about appearance

in every social group, one dimension of appearance i
conformity. Some people wear exactly what they are sup
posed to wear; others show some degree of independenc
and originality; others deliberately dress outrageously. Th
hippy style is a current example of this – long and dirt
hair, weird and ragged clothes – though of course there is
high degree of conformity to the anti-fashion. Revolu
tionaries also indicate their opposition to conventiona
society by means of their appearance. There are severa
strands of meaning here, (1) symbolic expression of lack o
control, (2) rejection of conventional norms, (3) an asceti
rejection of middle class values of material success an
display, and (4) communication of an aggressive attitude.

In the U.S.A. the change of attitude of Negroes in the mid-
sixties was communicated by a sudden change in appearance,
especially the Afro-Asian hair style (see p. 198 f).

Women's fashions require conformity within certain
limits, but independence and originality within those
limits. There are conventions about appearance on particular social occasions; in the Gibbins (1969) study the
subjects were agreed on whether the clothes being judged
were suitable for church, shopping, a formal dance, an
ordinary dance, or a party. Clothes vary along a formal–
informal dimension, corresponding to a range of social
situations. By dressing in a particular way a person suggests
the kind of situation he is accustomed to, or prefers, or
expects to find himself in – he is defining the situation by
his appearance, and thus influencing the behaviour of others.
Appearance is deliberately managed and manipulated,
though some people work very hard at this form of communicating while others care very little. However, many
people, perhaps most, have little consciously formulated
idea of what it is they are trying to communicate. They go
into clothing shops and select something that 'suits' them,
and decide what is 'appropriate' for a particular occasion.
They may discriminate in terms of verbalized categories,

such as 'young', 'fashionable', 'smart', or 'drab'. Or they may not have any verbal translation for the image they are going to present.

Culture and appearance

Cultural variations in appearance are enormous. In some primitive tribes people wear nothing but a string of beads, in other places they wear so much as to be totally invisible. There are rapid changes in conventions about appearance. In western culture at the present time female fashions change very rapidly, male fashions more slowly. Some aspects of appearance change faster than others; male ties and shirts undergo changes of fashion, while other aspects of male clothes change very slowly. But why are there changes in fashion at all? The most widely accepted explanation is that members of an élite seek social status and sexual attractiveness; other people imitate them to gain status and attractiveness themselves; the élite then change their appearance to distinguish themselves from imitators. However, the élite do not invent new fashions themselves; they adopt styles of clothing and other behaviour which have been invented by others, fashion designers in this case. The new items become the new status symbols and the old ones lose their symbolic value. At the same time social changes bring new people and groups to the top, and their choice of styles becomes accepted. Fashions grow and evolve out of previous fashions. There may be long-term trends, for instance towards informality, or cycles, for instance in length of skirts. The residues of earlier fashions, like slits in jackets once designed for riding horses, are often retained. It is difficult to resist changes in fashion, since a person who adopts an out-of-date appearance is universally regarded as ridiculous; fashion has a powerful effect on the perception of appearance, and in the meanings conveyed by different appearances.

Hurlock (1929) surveyed 1,500 people, and found, amongst

other things, that 25% said that they changed their style of clothes because of fear of disapproval, 100% of men would wait for a new style to be accepted while 19% of women would adopt it at once, 40% of women and 20% of men said they would follow a fashion in order to appear equal to those of higher social status, about half said they changed their styles when their social inferiors adopted it, 29% of women and 8% of men chose their clothes so as to appear conspicuous, men said they dressed to win the approval of the opposite sex, women dressed for the approval of other women, and both thought appearance more important when with strangers than when with friends. It is doubtful how far respondents would be able to give accurate answers to these questions, but even so the results are very interesting and give some support to the imitation of élites theory. However, some social groups introduce 'chic' fashions of their own, though these too stem from leaders of fashion and social diffusion, for example, the clothes worn by pop singers. Some social groups are very resistant to fashion, for example, the aristocracy and the traditional working class (Polhemus, 1973). In England working-class men wear dull clothes, avoid ostentation, and the older men are suspicious of smart clothes. Class differences though are much smaller than before (Zweig, in Roach and Eicher, 1965). There are also rules of combination – football boots would not be worn with a dinner jacket – since only some combinations are allowed.

Clothes have been compared to a language by Roland Barthes (1967). There are a number of sets of alternatives, which cannot be worn at the same time, e.g. different kinds of shoes and boots. Information is conveyed by what is chosen out of each set, and more information is conveyed by an unusual choice. Leaving out some item, like shoes, also conveys information.

Each item has meaning by itself. This may be arbitrary

and digital, as in the case of badges. It may be arbitrary and
a matter of degree, as in meanings derived from similarity
with a person imitated. It may be analogical, as beards stand
for achieving manhood, and low necklines for sex. There
can be more elaborate symbolism, as in the masks worn in
primitive rituals. Information is also conveyed by the way
items are combined: for example, a dark suit may be
combined with a red tie. And information is conveyed by
the manner of wearing: for example, a uniform may be very
smart or very scruffy. In all these ways people can send quite
involved messages about themselves and their attitudes to
other people, including conflicts and other complexities.

Further Reading

BERSHEID, E. and WALSTER, E. (1974) Physical attractiveness.
Advances in Experimental Social Psychology 7: 158–215.

FLUGEL, J. C. (1930) *The Psychology of Clothes*. London: Hogarth
Press.

KNAPP, M. L. (1972) *Nonverbal Communication in Human Interaction*. New York: Holt, Rinehart & Winston.

STONE, G. P. (1970) Chapters 25 and 43 in G. P. Stone and H. A.
Farberman (eds.) *Social Psychology through Symbolic Interaction*,
Waltham, Mass: Ginn, Blaisdell.

References

BARTHES, R. (1967) *Elements of Semiology*. London: Cape.

DION, K., BERSHEID, E., and WALSTER, E. (1972) What is
beautiful is good. *Journal of Personality and Social Psychology*
24: 285–290.

EFRAN, M. G. (1974) The effect of physical appearance on the
judgement of guilt, interpersonal attraction, and severity of
recommended punishment in a simulated jury task. *Journal
of Experimental Research in Personality* 8: 45–54.

FREEDMAN, D. G. (1969) The survival value of the beard.
Psychology Today 3: 36–9.

GIBBINS, K. (1969) Communication aspects of women's clothes
and their relation to fashionability. *British Journal of Social and
Clinical Psychology* 8: 301–12.

GOFFMAN, E. (1956) *The Presentation of Self in Everyday Life* Edinburgh: Edinburgh University Press.

HALLPIKE, C. R. (1969) Social hair. *Man* 4: 256–64.

HAMID, P. N. (1968). Style of dress as a perceptual cue in impression formation. *Perceptual and Motor Skills* 26: 904–6.

HURLOCK, E. B. (1929) Motivation in fashion. *Archives of Psychology* III.

ILIFFE, A. H. (1960) A study of preference in feminine beauty *British Journal of Psychology* 51: 267–73.

JOURARD, S. M. and SECORD, P. F. (1955) Body-cathexis and personality. *British Journal of Psychology* 46: 130–8.

KURTZBERG, R. L., SAFAR, H., and CAVIOR, N. (1968) Surgical and social rehabilitation of adult offenders. *Proceedings of the Seventy-Sixth Annual Convention of the American Psychological Association* 3: 649–50.

LAMBERT, S. (1972) Reactions to a stranger as a function of style of dress. *Perceptual and Motor Skills* 35: 711–12.

POLHEMUS, T. (1973) Fashion, anti-fashion and the body image. *New Society*. 11 October.

ROACH, M. E. and EICHER, J. B. (eds.) (1965) *Dress, Adornment and the Social Order*. New York: Wiley.

SINGER, J. E. (1964) The use of manipulation strategies: Machiavellianism and attractiveness. *Sociometry* 27: 128–50.

SISSONS, M. (1970) The psychology of social class. In *Money, Wealth and Class*. London: Oxford University Press.

STONE, G. P. (1970) Appearance and the self. In G. P. Stone and H. A. Farberman (eds.) *Social Psychology through Symbolic Interaction*. Waltham, Mass.: Ginn-Blaisdell.

STROEBE, W. *et al.* (1971) Effects of physical attractiveness, attitude similarity, and sex on various aspects of interpersonal attraction. *Journal of Personality and Social Psychology* 18: 79–91.

VEBLEN, T. (1899) *The Theory of the Leisure Class*. New York: Viking Press.

WALSTER, E. *et al.* (1966) Importance of physical attractiveness in dating behaviour. *Journal of Personality and Social Psychology* 4: 508–16.

WELLS, W., and SIEGEL, B. (1961) Stereotyped somatotypes. *Psychological Reports* 8: 77–8.

18

Non-verbal vocalizations

Introduction

As we saw earlier, many species of animals communicate with each other by means of sound. Birds, for example, have special calls giving warning of predators, for seeking a mate, for recognition by members of their family, and for claiming territory. Human beings also make some use of non-verbal sounds – laughing, crying, moaning, and hissing for example, though we use our voices mainly for speech. There are two kinds of NVC involved. First, there are various aspects of voice quality, unrelated to the contents of speech: these include tone of voice, which communicates emotions and attitudes to other people, and type of voice and accent, which send information about personality and group membership. Secondly there are vocal features more intimately connected with speech – completing its meaning by means of pitch, stress, and timing, providing a commentary on the verbal contents, and governing the synchronization of utterances.

All vocalizations are based on sequences of sounds, each sound consisting of a distribution of frequencies of different intensities. We abstract and decode certain aspects of these sound sequences as phonemes, which are put together as meaningful speech. However, we also abstract and decode other aspects, such as emotion and accent. We saw earlier that bird-song can also communicate several kinds of messages at once – species, identity, warning of predator, of a particular species, at a particular distance. This is a very good example of using the same sending and receiving system to send several quite different kinds of signal simultaneously. We can clarify these different signals as follows:

Figure 18.1.

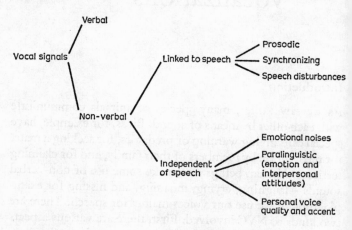

Emotions

Certain aspects of vocalization have been found to express emotions. These are:

Speed
Loudness
Pitch
Speech disturbances
Voice quality, e.g. breathing, resonance.

Research on the encoding of emotions has used the method of asking subjects to read verbal materials *as if* they were angry, happy, and so forth. Other experimenters have induced actual emotional states; for example, anxiety has been induced by interviewing subjects on topics which are known to be disturbing for them, or they have been made angry, and so on. The vocalizations produced have then been subjected to physical measurement, for loudness, speed, etc.

Research on decoding has used various techniques to eliminate the effects of the verbal content. Tape-recordings have been prepared in which speakers recite the alphabet or read numbers in different emotional states, or read the same neutral passage, such as Davitz's 'I am going out now. I won't be back all afternoon. If anyone calls, just tell them I'm not here.' Another method is to use an electronic filter which eliminates the higher frequencies and hence the verbal contents – though it is my impression that some of the non-verbal contents are lost too.

Scherer (1974) carried out three studies in which auditory stimuli were produced on a Moog synthesizer, varied along a number of acoustic dimensions, and subjects were asked to decode them in terms of emotion. The main results are shown below:

Concomitants of acoustical dimensions

AMPLITUDE VARIATION	Moderate	Pleasantness, Activity, Happiness
	Extreme	Fear
PITCH VARIATION	Moderate	Anger, Boredom, Disgust, Fear
	Extreme	Pleasantness, Activity, Happiness, Surprise
PITCH CONTOUR	Down	Pleasantness, Boredom, Sadness
	Up	Potency, Anger, Fear, Surprise
PITCH LEVEL	Low	Pleasantness, Boredom, Sadness
	High	Activity, Potency, Anger, Fear, Surprise
TEMPO	Slow	Boredom, Disgust, Sadness
	Fast	Pleasantness, Activity, Potency, Anger, Fear, Happiness, Surprise

Lalljee (1971) carried out a study in which sentences were spoken in different ways and then decoded. His results are similar to Scherer's, but he also found that filled and unfilled pauses affected perceived emotions. Utterances with a large number of filled pauses (ums and ers) were interpreted as anxious or bored, utterances with a large number of unfilled pauses as anxious, angry, or contemptuous.

Another aspect of speech is voice quality. Donald Hayes has found that a rising tone is evaluated positively (that is, as cheerful), a falling tone as negative (as depressed) and a steady note as neutral (see also table above).

One problem is that people express emotions in different ways, for example, while most people speak more quickly when anxious, those who are normally anxious speak more slowly. And while most people when depressed use a low pitch, others use a whisper of higher pitch. If a person expresses emotions in an unusual way, it would be expected that others would have difficulty in interpreting them. Davitz, in the experiments described below, found that speakers varied from about 25 per cent to 50 per cent in the accuracy with which their performances were recognized correctly.

There has been some controversy over the extent to which listeners can identify emotions correctly from content-free materials. In fact they can identify on average 30–45 per cent correctly, which is slightly lower than the corresponding figure for facial expression, if a range of fourteen emotions is used. They can also make broad discriminations if the upper frequencies have been removed by a band-pass filter. A series of studies were carried out by Davitz (1964) and his colleagues, using tape-recordings of neutral sentences, read to express ten or fourteen different emotions. It may be objected that actors may not express emotions naturally, but the investigators made an effort to put their performers into each emotional state in turn, by imagining appropriate situations. Some emotions are easier to judge than others;

Levitt, one of the Davitz group, found that the emotions most easily recognized from tone of voice were fear and anger (p. 114). Emotions which are often confused are love and sadness, pride and satisfaction. Some judges are better than others at recognizing emotions from tone of voice – with accuracy scores varying from 20 per cent to 50 per cent in the Davitz studies. They found that listeners who are best at this are best able to judge facial expressions, and to express emotions in face and voice. They are also more intelligent. Sensitivity could be increased quite quickly by simple training procedures, using a tape-recorder.

Interpersonal attitudes

There is some overlap here with emotions, since no distinction is made in the voice between anger or love as emotional states, and as attitudes directed towards particular individuals. The Davitz studies, for example, did not distinguish between the two, and included admiration, affection, amusement, anger, boredom, despair, disgust, dislike, fear, and impatience – all of which can be directed towards others. In a series of studies by the author and colleagues (1970) a number of interpersonal styles were created, using tones of voice (while counting numbers), facial expressions, and head orientations. We had no difficulty in creating tones of voice corresponding to friendliness, hostility, superiority, and inferiority. Mehrabian (1972) found that tone of voice contributed slightly less than facial expression, but much more than the contents of speech, to impressions of interpersonal attitudes (p. 127). In another group of studies Mehrabian and his colleagues studied the voices of people who were trying to be persuasive. They spoke faster, much louder, with a greater range of pitch and loudness, and at a more regular speed. Such speakers were perceived as more persuasive. But did better speakers actually persuade? A number of experiments have varied the number of speech disfluencies and other aspects of speech. More fluent speakers are regarded as more competent, but not as more credible or trustworthy, and there is no evidence that they are actually more persuasive.

Voice and personality

Inferences can be made about personality characteristics from voice alone, though these inferences are often incorrect. To a limited extent voice cues are the result of deliberate encoding: a person may change his accent. The aspects of voice which are related to other aspects of personality are:

Loudness, pitch, and the other cues for emotion
Personal voice qualities, like resonance, breathiness
Accent, related to class or region.

Social class

In Britain and in many other countries there are class differences in accent, as the result of historical processes, such as the Victorian public schools' propagation of one particular accent, and the B.B.C.'s of another. A number of experiments in England and the U.S.A. have shown that class can be inferred from accent alone. Mary Sissons, at Oxford found that accent and clothes were the two best single cues to class. Many people try to modify their accent towards that of a higher social class, but this is difficult to do. Ellis (1967) found that speakers' real class could still be judged, with a correlation of 0.65, when they were imitating upper-class accents. Another study found that under stress people are liable to regress to an earlier accent. On the other hand, Labov (1972) found that when people use careful speech, or are asked to read, they modify vowel sounds in an upper-class direction. This is particularly true of the lower social classes; upper-class people when speaking informally shift their accents downwards to a rather small extent. In England it has been found that there is a hierarchy of accents of different status – 'received pronunciation', then Yorkshire and other respectable regional accents, and then the accents of Midlands industrial towns. Finer judgements of status can be made from intermediate accents. There is some evidence about the vocal characteristics of these accents. The middle-class and educated accents are more clearly articulated, use more intonation, and are less blurred. Consonants are sounded more clearly and there is less stumbling over words. This is not the whole story, since there are additional features of accents which are quite arbitrary, and serve solely as indicators of social class.

Racial and cultural groups

There is no doubt that racial and cultural groups can be recognized by accent. Most people in Britain can distinguish Scottish, Welsh, and Midland accents, for example, and some people can make much finer discriminations of locality. More interesting is the effect of accent on the impressions formed of the speaker's personality. A series of studies have used the 'matched guise' technique of asking for judgements of recordings of the voice of the same speaker using two different accents. Anisfield and colleagues (1962) in America found that a speaker using a Jewish accent was rated as shorter, less good looking, and lower in leadership – by Jews as well as by Gentiles. They were also rated as higher in humour, entertainingness, and kindness by Jews but not by Gentiles. Lambert (1960) in Montreal found that speakers using a French-Canadian accent rather than an English-Canadian accent were rated as more intelligent, likeable, dependable, good looking, tall, kind, and ambitious – both by English and French-Canadians. Research by Kleiven in Norway elicited stereotypes, but these were not so evaluatively loaded – since he chose some scales favouring each group.

In these and other studies it was often found that the

same stereotypes were shared by both groups, where one group was a minority group or the object of unfavourable attitudes. Evidently in these cases there is a two-stage process: the accent is used to identify the group membership of the speaker, and stereotypes about this group are then applied to him. Other studies have produced similar results by simply asking for the characteristics of different groups. However, this method rather forces subjects to express stereotypes which they may not have and which may be of little importance when further information is available. Gardner and Taylor (1968), in another French-Canadian study, found that listeners would apply stereotypes to speakers unless the speakers made it very clear from the context of their speech that the stereotypes did not apply.

Lambert (1960) and others have found that accents are rated along three main dimensions – competence, integrity, and attractiveness. Cheyne (1970) and Giles (1971) found that while received pronunciation was judged most competent, various regional accents were regarded as higher in integrity and attractiveness – particularly by listeners from the region in question.

A person's accent stems mainly from the cultural milieu in which he was brought up. However, most people are exposed to more than one accent, so that which they adopt reflects their attitudes towards and their degree of identification with the groups in question. Furthermore, people often change their accent according to whom they are speaking to. School children are often 'bilingual' in this way, using different accents at home and at school. While such convergence is common, there are some who diverge from the accent of the person they are addressing – for example, a lower middle-class person may adopt a more working-class accent in the presence of upper middle-class people. Such shifts, like shifts of posture, or spatial positions indicate a person's desire to align himself with or set himself apart from another.

Demographic characteristics

Voice varies with age, though much more for males than for females, and so acts as a cue for age. There are familiar sex differences in voice quality though there are some who deviate from the normal voice for their sex. A number of studies have inquired how well occupation can be inferred from voice. The only people who are recognized better than chance are clergymen, and in a pre-war British study, actors. The relation between occupation and voice is presumably due to special speech training for these professions.

Individual personality

Individual humans like individual birds are clearly recognizable by their voices. Some of the impressions created by a person's voice are based on the emotions he seems to be undergoing. Lalljee (1971) found that there are quite strong differences between the ordinary speaking voices of different people in terms of the level of anxiety, anger, or cheerfulness that judges rate them as displaying.

Hunt and Lin (1967) found that judges scored well above chance in judging the personalities of two speakers, in relation to their self-ratings, for the following traits:

Forceful	– Gentle
Assertive	– Reserved
Realistic	– Idealistic
Bold	– Cautious

However the judges did no better than chance on

Agile	– Slow
Orderly	– Casual
Serious	– Humorous
Co-operative	– Competitive

It seems that some traits are more recognizable from voice than others. In some cases the ways in which traits are coded in the voice have been found. Scherer (1970) found that Americans could identify only sociability correctly from voice – in terms of the speaker's self-image, using the cues of loudness, resonance, lack of breathiness, and lack of gloom. Germans could identify assertiveness correctly in German speakers. There is some connexion between dominance and loudness, low pitch and resonance. It has been found that high achievers speak faster, with more intonation, higher pitch, and sound more confident and self-assured.

The voices of mental patients have been studied by Ostwald (1963) and others, using a speech spectrograph. He describes four kinds of voice which he has commonly found among patients and others: (1) the 'sharp voice' often described as complaining, querulous, helpless, or infantile, found mainly in neurotic patients; (2) the 'flat voice', interpreted as flabby, ennervated, sickly, and helpless, found in dependent and depressed patients; (3) the 'hollow voice', with few high frequencies, decoded as lifeless and empty and found in brain-damaged patients and those with generalized weakness, debility, and fatigue; (4) the 'robust voice', booming, impressive, and successful, found not in manic patients but in healthy, confident, extroverted people. Ostwald has found that the voices of patients change during therapy, from deviant voices into louder more robust and resonant ones.

Addington (1968) found that when male speakers (the results for females are different) adopted different styles of speaking, they were thought to have certain kinds of personality, as follows:

Breathy	– younger, more artistic
Flat	– more masculine, sluggish, colder, withdrawn
Nasal	– socially undesirable in various ways
Tense	– older, unyielding, cantankerous
Throaty	– older, realistic, mature, sophisticated, well adjusted
Orotund	– energetic, healthy, artistic, sophisticated, proud, interesting, enthusiastic
Fast	– animated, extroverted

Varied in pitch – dynamic, feminine, aesthetically inclined.

Vocalizations related to speech

Some NV vocalizations are closely linked to speech. Indeed some of them, the so-called prosodic signals, are often regarded as part of speech. Our view is that a wide range of NV signals are related to speech in a number of different ways and can be regarded as part of a total communication system, of which speech is the central part.

Timing, pitch, and loudness are combined to form a pattern for each sentence; in addition other aspects of voice quality are used to 'frame' individual sentences, i.e. to indicate for instance whether these are to be taken seriously or as a joke. Prosodic signals have been studied by linguistic methods, i.e. by the intensive study of the speech patterns of speakers of a language. Most of the early work consisted of studies of rather small samples of speech. We shall draw on the study by Crystal (1969) of three hours' talk by thirty educated speakers of English. He does not report any statistics, but says that there was a high degree of regularity in following many of the rules which he found, though we do not know how closely the rules which he reports are obeyed.

Timing

Utterances vary in speed, for example, a subordinate clause is spoken faster, and a slower speed is used to give emphasis. Pauses are frequent in speech. Pauses of under one-fifth second are used to give emphasis. Longer ones are used to signal grammatical junctures, for example, the ends of sentences and clauses. Other pauses occur in the middle of clauses and may coincide with disfluencies, such as repetitions, and changes of sentence.

Pitch

There are standard pitch patterns in every language for different kinds of sentence. In English, for example, questions beginning with 'How', 'What', etc., are spoken with a falling pitch; but questions with an inversion of subject and verb are spoken with a rising tone. Again it seems that results like this are a matter of probability, and are not universally true. Pitch pattern can be varied to 'frame' or provide further meaning for an utterance. 'Where are you going?' with a rising pitch on the last word is a friendly inquiry, whereas with a falling pitch it is suspicious and hostile. This expresses more than a paralinguistic attitude to the recipient of the question, it indicates additional thoughts on the part of the speaker, and indicates what sort of answer is needed. Pitch pattern can negate the words spoken, sarcastically, or when the word 'yes' is spoken to indicate such unwillingness that it really means 'no'. Changes of pitch can also be used to accent particular words, though this is usually done by loudness.

Loudness

The prosodic system of any language includes rules about the patterns of loudness of words in different kinds of sentence. In English the main nouns and verbs are usually stressed. The same sentence may be given different meanings by stressing different words, as in 'they are hunting dogs', or a sentence may retain the same basic meaning but attention can be directed to quite different parts of the message, as in *'Professor Brown's daughter* is *fond* of *modern music'* – each of the italicized words could be stressed, and this could change the significance of the utterance. In stressing *daughter* there is some implicit reference to a *son* – a case where a NV signal refers or helps refer to an absent object. Speakers can make soft contrast by speaking some words very quietly.

Duncan and Rosenthal (1968) found that the amount of stress placed on words in the instructions given to experimental subjects had a marked effect on their responses. Subjects were asked to rate the 'success' or 'failure' of people shown in photographs. There was a correlation of

0·74 between their ratings and the amount of emphasis placed by the experimenter on the words *success* and *failure* when describing the scale to be used.

Further Reading

ROBINSON, P. (1972) *Language and Social Behaviour.* Harmondsworth: Penguin Books.

MOSCOVICI, S. (ed.) (1972) *The Psychosociology of Language.* Chicago: Markham.

References

ADDINGTON, D. W. (1968) The relationship of selected vocal characteristics to personality perception. *Speech Monographs* **35**: 492–503.

ANISFIELD, M. BOGO, N. and LAMBERT, W. (1962) Evaluation reactions to accented English speech. *Journal of Abnormal and Social Psychology* **65**: 223–31.

ARGYLE, M., SALTER, V., NICHOLSON, H., WILLIAMS, M. and BURGESS, P. (1970) The communication of inferior and superior attitudes by verbal and non-verbal signals. *British Journal of Social and Clinical Psychology* **9**: 221–31.

CHEYNE, W. M. (1970) Stereotyped reactions to speakers with Scottish and English regional accents. *British Journal of Social and Clinical Psychology* **9**: 77–9.

CRYSTAL, D. (1969) *Prosodic Systems and Intonation in English.* Cambridge: Cambridge University Press.

DAVITZ, J. R. (1964) *The Communication of Emotional Meaning.* New York: McGraw-Hill.

DUNCAN, S. D. and ROSENTHAL, R. (1968) Vocal emphasis in experimenter's instruction reading as unintended determinant of subjects' responses. *Language and Speech* **11**: 20–6.

ELLIS, D. S. (1967) Speech and social status in America. *Social Forces* **45**: 431–51.

GARDNER, R. C. and TAYLOR, D. M. (1968) Ethnic stereotypes: their effects on person perception. *Canadian Journal of Psychology* **22**: 267–76.

GILES, H. (1971) Patterns of evaluation in reactions to RP, South Welsh and Somerset accented speech. *British Journal of Social and Clinical Psychology* 10: 280–1.

HUNT, R. G., and LIN, T. K. (1967) Accuracy of judgements of personal attributes from speech. *Journal of Personality and Social Psychology* 6: 450–3.

LABOV, W. (1966) *The Social Stratification of Speech in New York City*. Center for Applied Linguistics, Washington, D.C.

LABOV, W. (1972) On the mechanism of linguistic change. In J. J. Gumperz and D. Hymes (eds.) *Direction in Sociolinguistics*. New York: Holt, Rinehart and Winston.

LALLJEE, M. G. (1971) *Disfluencies in Normal English Speech*. Oxford. D. Phil. thesis.

LAMBERT, W. E., HODGSON, R. C., GARDNER, R. C. and FILLENBAUM, S. (1960) Evaluational reactions to spoken languages. *Journal of Abnormal and Social Psychology* 60: 44–51.

MEHRABIAN, A. (1972) *Nonverbal Communication*. Chicago: Aldine-Atherton.

OSTWALD, P. F. (1963) *Soundmaking*. Springfield, Ill.: Charles C. Thomas.

SCHERER, K. R. (1970) *Non-verbale Kommunikation*. Hamburg: Helmut Buske.

SCHERER, K. R. (1974). Acoustic concomitants of emotional dimensions: judging effect from synthesized tone sequences. In S. Weitz (ed.) *Nonverbal Communication*, New York: Oxford University Press.

Part 4

Conclusions & wider implications

19

Conclusions & wider implications

Why is bodily communication used by humans?

We can communicate far better than animals about many matters by means of language. Why do we not use language for all communicational purposes? Our explorations so far suggest a number of reasons.

(1) Lack of verbal coding in some areas

There are relatively few words for shapes, apart from a few very simple ones. Probably language failed to develop in this sphere since shapes can easily be described by drawing or hand-movements – non-verbally – so that words are not necessary. Certainly shapes can be communicated more effectively if hand movements are allowed.

Another area which lacks efficient verbal coding is personality. Individuals convey information about their own personality non-verbally. Others form clear but mainly unverbalized impressions, and select an appropriate style of social behaviour accordingly. Describing another's personality is difficult – there are a large number of words available, but it is difficult to select the right ones and they may not be understood in the same sense.

Similar considerations apply to the entire interpersonal area. This is handled perfectly well by means of our primitive non-verbal equipment, so that words are not necessary, are not normally used, and are awkward and embarrassing when they are.

(2) *Non-verbal signals are more powerful*

We have seen that NV signals for interpersonal attitudes are far more powerful than initially similar verbal ones. We can speculate on the reasons for this. Animals have a largely innate NV system for interpersonal signals; we have inherited this system in part. It operates directly, and evokes bodily responses which prepare the receiver for immediate action. Verbal signals on the other hand normally convey information about the outside world; the information is considered carefully, and possible implications explored; there is some modification of the recipient's cognitive field, but these do not lead to action unless they are linked through learning to some drive state. Verbal signals *can* lead to immediate action, as when commands are given to well-trained men, but usually the impact of words is weaker and less direct than the impact of non-verbal signals.

(3) *Non-verbal signals are less well controlled and therefore more likely to be genuine*

It is a familiar experience that words do not always convey the truth. It is difficult to obtain internal evidence from the words themselves to indicate whether the speaker is telling the truth or not. In fact people depend on NV cues like amount of gaze and facial expression for evidence.

Non-verbal signals on the other hand are less easily controlled, and are commonly assumed to be genuine. The main exception to this is facial expression, especially in cultures like Britain and Japan, where there are strong conventions about looking pleasant. Tone of voice is controlled, and known to be controlled, by most educated people. But the other NV signals are much less commonly controlled – except by actors and those who have studied social psychology. Other signals, like pupil expansion and perspiration, can only be controlled by modifying the emotional state itself, which is more difficult than just modifying bodily signals.

It seems very likely that more widespread knowledge about NVC will lead to more people manipulating their own behaviour, and possibly their distrusting that of other people, thus destroying part of the value of the NV system. On the other hand greater awareness should have the effect of increasing social skill and sensitivity. It can also be argued that civilization differs from animal life partly in the restraint of many immediate desires, so that people are not constantly giving vent to their aggressive and sexual feelings.

(4) *It would be disturbing to focus attention on some signals or to make them too explicit*

When people are negotiating or sustaining interpersonal relationships, it would be very disturbing for one to state openly for example that he did not like the other very much, or that he thought he was more important than the other, disturbing too if they disagreed about their relationship. Perhaps for this reason the negotiation of social relationships is conducted non-verbally, at the fringe of consciousness, while conversation or task occupy the verbal channel and the focus of consciousness – even though the social task may be far more important. We have seen that negative attitudes are sometimes expressed symbolically in rituals – a further degree of indirectness – in order to release these feelings safely (p. 188f).

Similarly it is very convenient for these matters not to be too explicit: people can make up their minds slowly about others and change their minds, without being committed to definite relationships.

(5) *It is very useful to be able to use a second channel in addition to language*

We have just seen that this second channel carries interpersonal information. In addition the second channel carries a great deal of information which supports language, but which it would be inefficient and confusing to put into words. Synchronizing signals could be put into words by adding 'full-stop', or 'end of message', but this would take time; it is much faster for synchronization to be handled non-verbally. Feedback from the listener could not be put into words without constant interruption and double-talking, so that this information is virtually forced into the visual non-verbal channel. NV signals by the speaker which add to or comment on the verbal message add enormously to the complexity of the messages that can be sent.

The similarities and differences between human and animal bodily communication

There are striking similarities between animal and human NVC, and this is part of the evidence for the innateness of some of the human NV systems. Animals and men are faced by the same basic biological problems, and deal with them in groups by establishing much the same set of social relationships. Both find mates, rear children, co-operate in groups, develop leadership hierarchies, and defend themselves against enemies. Communication is used to establish and sustain these relationships, to express emotional states, to send information about the self, and to send information about the outside world. In both animals and men signals are sent by facial expression, tone of voice, posture, gesture, and so on – though there are a number of differences: for example, we make little use of changes of body colour.

The main difference (apart from language) is that men incorporate these basic signals into more complex social acts, where there is cognitive control and can be some modification of the NV elements. We showed earlier that social behaviour has a hierarchical structure, where the smaller units are automatic and spontaneous, and the larger units contain cognitive plans (p. 50f). This is true of animal communication too, but the hierarchies for man are far more elaborate. This means that human NVC is less direct and that it reflects internal states in a more complex way. For example, smiling may be used as part of a strategy of ingratiation, rather than to reflect pleasure or liking. Man learns more in connexion with NVC. Although there is an innate basis for the facial expressions for emotion, for example, it can be modified as the result of cultural conventions, in this case about when an expression may be shown, or how much. Most animal communications are triggered directly by immediate stimuli and motivational states. Human communications, verbal and non-verbal, are partly the product of cognitive processes, are directed towards long-term goals, and depend in a complex way on the nature of the situation and its rules. As we have seen, social acts may be consciously planned and monitored; where they are more spontaneous the processes involved are similar, though there is less conscious attention to the performance.

In man NVC is affected by language in various ways. The meaning of NV signals may be partly the result of verbal labelling and categorization – as, for example, when people are classified into personality types, and try to present an image of a verbally defined kind. NV signals may have meanings which depend on verbal conceptual structures, as do the signals used in games and rituals. Social acts are the product in part of verbally formulated intentions, and are later explained by verbal accounts or explanations. However, the influence of language can be overstated: as we have seen much social behaviour is *not* mediated by words, and decoding of signals does not necessarily take a verbal form – but produces rather a cognitive and phenomenal state, partly but vaguely labelled, often combined with readiness for action.

Man of course uses language, and we shall discuss below how far there is a clear difference between verbal and non-verbal communication. Where animals can communicate information about the outside world (as opposed to their own feelings and intentions) inefficiently, we can send complex information quickly and with precision. However, these verbal interchanges, as we have seen, depend on several kinds of non-verbal supports, for synchronization, feedback, and so on, and these constitute forms of NVC not used at all by animals. Human social behaviour typically consists of verbal and non-verbal signals, and of a combination of two channels – auditory and visual. Most NVC is received visually; while sounds can be received whatever the position of the ears, visual signals depend on the visual channel being open, on the appropriate direction of gaze. This is why gaze is of central importance in human social behaviour. It is a channel that becomes a very important social signal.

There is some similarity between some human rituals and, for example, animal courtship rituals. Both are used in a somewhat similar way to bring about a changed social relationship. However, the animal rituals are the product of biological evolution, while the human rituals are mainly the product of cultural development – though there may be biological universals behind the standard structure of rites of passage. Other human rituals, such as those for the expression of religious beliefs, appear to have no animal equivalent. This takes us to the use of NVC to express ideas which are beyond the limits of language, which will be discussed below.

Training in bodily communication

A lot of people need training in social skills, and particularly in the NV signals involved.

(1) *Education*

It is becoming recognized that schools place too much emphasis on verbal learning. Training in NVC and social skills is being introduced as part of English, moral education, or modern languages – to teach languages with the right intonation and gestures. Peter McPhail (1972) and his colleagues have devised a set of curriculum materials for this purpose: cards and brochures are used as the basis of role-playing, discussion, and art-work. Here is an example of these materials:

Figure 19.1.

A middle-aged Pakistani husband is walking in front of his wife on a narrow pavement beside the main road. Comments a man in a car, 'None of them knows how to treat women.'

To what extent can you distinguish between showing consideration and having English good manners?

(2) *Professional social skills*

A variety of social skills are needed at work. One method of training, which emphasizes the trainee's non-verbal performance, consists of role-playing followed by video-tape playback. Using this method, trainees become aware of their facial and bodily behaviour, rather than their voices. To get them to concentrate on verbal and non-verbal aspects of speech it is possible to use an audio-tape recording alone. The author and Elizabeth Sidney (1969) developed techniques in this way for training interviewers, which include the use of stooge candidates who present a variety of typical problems, and the use of an ear microphone for feedback during role-playing. However, in this kind of role-playing training, use is made of verbal intervention to label non-verbal behaviour – which is not the way NVC is usually organized.

Another form of social skills training uses 'modelling' – imitating the performance of skilled practitioners, seen either in person or on film. Again it may be necessary to use verbal intervention, to draw attention to certain aspects of the model's performance. And simply watching other people is not enough – the learner has to have a go himself. Research on training teachers at Stanford showed that watching a filmed model was valuable, especially if there was verbal commentary on it; role-playing, with verbal feedback and video-tape replay was also effective. However, with modelling *and* video-tape playback, verbal intervention is unnecessary (McKnight 1971).

Unless some kind of special training is given, people simply have to learn by experience, by trial and error. Yet it is found that performance is often not improved by experience – in one investigation it was found that foremen actually became *worse* by experience. An interviewer might fail to put candidates at their ease, a manager might not succeed in creating the right relationship with his subordinates, through failure in the use of non-verbal signals.

A lot of professional social skills training is designed to increase sensitivity to interpersonal phenomena. Research by the Davitz group found considerable variations in ability to recognize emotions from tones of voice, and also found that this was correlated with the ability to recognize other NV cues (p. 349). On the other hand most investigators have detected rather little relation between the ability to encode and decode NVC. Professional experience does not necessarily produce sensitivity.

Using one-minute films of children being taught, Jecker Maccoby, and Breitrose (1965) found that experienced teachers were little better than beginners at perceiving whether or not children had understood. However, both Davitz, and Jecker and Maccoby found that increased sensitivity could be taught quite quickly by running through a series of stimuli and studying the essential cues.

(3) Treating mental patients who have inadequate social skills

Failure at the social skills of everyday life is a source of mental ill-health. Peter Trower and Bridget Bryant, at Oxford (1974), found in a survey of undergraduates that there were two common types of difficulty: first, meeting strangers, especially those of the opposite sex, at parties or dances, and, secondly, establishing more intimate relationships, looking others in the eye, talking about the self, and so on. Studies of mental patients show that many of them have inadequate social skills – though this may be an effect rather than a cause. We have found that neurotic patients with interpersonal difficulties show a variety of NVC failures – looking or sounding hostile or uninterested, projecting an inappropriate self-image, and various other peculiar kinds of facial, postural, spatial, or gestural behaviour.

We have been treating such patients for some time, using methods similar to those described above, for interviewer training. These methods include (1) role-playing of difficult situations, with stooges, followed by video-tape and verbal feedback; (2) practice at expressing interpersonal attitudes and emotions, using an audio or video-tape recorder; and

(3) training in groups of patients, with some degree of competition to overcome particular NV failings. A controlled follow-up study showed that neurotic patients with interpersonal difficulties improved more by this kind of treatment than a comparable group who received twice as much psychotherapy. Many of these patients responded to treatment quite rapidly, in up to six sessions (Argyle, Trower, and Bryant, 1974).

(4) *Training for inter-cultural encounters*
See page 97f.

Historical changes in the use of NVC: McLuhan and Huizinger

Marshall McLuhan and Johan Huizinger have drawn attention to historical changes in NVC. McLuhan maintains that historical change is partly due to developments in communication technology. His slogan 'the medium is the message' can be taken in a narrower or a wider sense. In the narrower sense, every medium has special properties – for example, film can provide close-ups, theatre cannot, TV has the property of immediacy while film has not. In the wider sense, McLuhan maintains that the development of a medium of communication has far-reaching social consequences, in terms of individual perceptions and thinking, social relationships and manufacturing processes. McLuhan distinguishes between 'cool' and 'hot' media of communication. In a cool medium the receiver has to participate either by his own actions (as in conversation) or by filling the missing parts of the message from his own imagination (as with TV, cartoons, telephoning, or reading work like that of James Joyce). In a hot medium the message is clear, unambiguous, perhaps redundant, as with the cinema, radio, most writing (apart from poetry), and lectures. (This classification is McLuhan's and is rather arbitrary.)

McLuhan maintains that auditory and tactile communication is cool, since there is participation by the
receiver, while visual communication is hot. He sees the
invention of the alphabet and of printing as producing an
undue shift towards the visual, and as creating a split
between the two modes. He suggests that modern civilization has been considerably influenced by the invention of
printing, which resulted in (1) uniformity and repeatability
in communication, (2) syllogistic and linear thinking, since
a book distorts its contents into an unnatural linear sequence,
(3) mass production and assembly lines, in printing and
elsewhere, leading to new consumer–producer relations,
(4) the separation of head and heart, reason and imagination,
science and art, (5) emphasis on the visual sense, at the
expense of the auditory and tactile; the decline of the spoken
word, (6) loss of 'the magical world of the ear, with its multi-
dimensional resonance, and a denuding of consciousness',
(7) the specialization and segmentation of persons into
impersonal roles, and the break-up of the closed, oral, tribal
group. He also believes that (8) reading results in indi-
vidualism, and the inner-directed Renaissance man, and
that (9) printing makes possible mass communication, mass
movements, power and nationalism.

In these ways, it is alleged, the development of printing
had widespread social consequences, greater than those of
the printed *contents*. This is what is meant by saying 'the
medium is the message'. However, the suggested causal
sequences are entirely hypothetical, and there is no clear
empirical evidence to support them. There are other obvious objections to all this – surely the contents of books
(such as ideas and facts) are important too, and surely there
are other causes of historical change in addition to communication technology.

McLuhan maintains that the next great change in communications technology was TV, and that this corrects the
distortions resulting from print. He maintains that TV is a

cool medium, requiring viewer participation in completing the poorly defined picture and in adding to the information presented. It corrects the sensory imbalance by using all the senses, and the presentation is simultaneous and continuous, not chopped up and linear. The constant use of close-ups focuses attention on the actor's mental states and creates a desire for deep involvement with people. TV broadcasts, for instance, live from battle fronts, give the feeling that what is happening is here and now, so that people feel they belong to a 'global village' where they can keep in touch with the rest of the tribe. He does not see us returning to a primitive style of life, but as moving forward to a new electronic age, which, however, has some of the properties of a more primitive, village life.

Though there is little or no empirical evidence in support of most of these ideas, they are nevertheless of great interest. And the distinction between hot and cool is clearly very similar to that between verbal and non-verbal, where the verbal is hot and the non-verbal cool. It is also similar to Susanne Langer's distinction between discursive (prose and logic) and non-discursive communication (poetry, music, and ritual) (1942) (p. 384).

Huizinger emphasizes the importance of play in society. By play he means voluntary activities undertaken for fun – that is, set apart from real life (though they can be very serious) – which are disinterested and not aimed to satisfy basic wants, and which take place in a special and limited time and place. They often take the form of a contest, and inside the game special rules operate. Huizinger maintains that play is responsible for most aspects of cultural growth, and that play principles operate in ritual, philosophy, art, and elsewhere. He further suggests that there has been a great decline in play since earlier historical periods. In antiquity there was a great deal of religious ritual, in classical times there were games, circuses, and conspicuous, irrational consumption of all kinds; in the Middle Ages there were chivalry, tournaments, courtly love, heraldry, and a great deal of jesting and buffoonery; in the Renaissance the arts and architecture made great use of mythical, allegoric, and symbolic figures; the Baroque and Rococo periods developed highly fanciful forms of decoration, clothes, and wigs. It was in the nineteenth century that 'all Europe donned the boiler suit', and in many spheres of life the playful, irrational, symbolic aspects of life were replaced by technology, realism, and serious games.

This interpretation of certain historical trends has several implications for NVC.

(a) We have already noted the changes which have taken place in men's clothes. In earlier times clothes were far more flamboyant, part of the tradition of boasting and braggadocio; men also wore symbolic devices like coats of arms. Although clothes still communicate, they do so in a much milder and subtler manner.

(b) There has been a decline in the amount of game and ritual activity which is set apart from life, and has a special symbolic character.

(c) There has been a decline in the extent of fancifully elaborated social relationships such as courtly love, and chivalry: social behaviour has become simpler and less symbolic.

Huizinger's ideas can be linked to what we said earlier about the reduced use of NVC in Britain, America, and other modern countries (p. 81). It appears that recent advances in technology have been accompanied for some reason by a decline in NVC. What is likely to happen in the future? McLuhan suggested that exposure to TV compared with print encourage the use of NVC, so that this might bring about a shift to greater concern with non-verbal signals, especially in the face, though there is no evidence that this has occurred. Similarly it would be expected that the widespread use of the telephone would increase sensitivity to vocal signals. The educational developments which we discussed in the last section, if they become widely used, should create a greater awareness, expressiveness and sensitivity to NVC. There has been an interest in some circles in trying to promote the use of NVC in society, and a recent series of lectures and performances at the Institute of Contemporary Arts in London was arranged partly for this purpose (Benthall, 1975). A number of developments among young people are concerned with particular aspects of NVC – encounter groups, political action, and avant garde art forms based on the human body.

Bodily communication and language

Structuralists like Lévi-Strauss maintain that many sets of ideas and objects can be regarded as communication systems, that they have the same basic properties as language, and reflect the structure of the human mind. NVC is more obviously a communication system than, for example, kinship systems, myths, or the courses of meals. In this section we shall explore the similarities and differences between verbal and non-verbal communication.

There are a number of obvious similarities between the two forms of communication. Both consist of social signals which have much the same meanings for senders and receivers, both are rule-governed, and in both cases signals that break the rules of sequences or fall outside the cultural repertoire of signals are meaningless.

Chomsky (1957) pointed out that language is quite unlike a series of predictable stimulus–response linkages. Most sentences that are uttered have never been spoken before, and it is more appropriate for a linguist to make explicit the rules which will generate all possible sentences in a language. (As we showed earlier, there are also predictable, statistical, aspects of language, p. 54.) A number of workers in this field have wondered whether NVC could be treated in a similar way, whether it functions like a language.

The vocabulary of NVC

Birdwhistell, as we have seen (p. 251f), produced a vocabulary of 60 kinemes, though he failed to show that they have shared social meanings. In the course of this book we have presented an alternative vocabulary of NVC – the seven facial expressions for emotion, different degrees of proximity, and so on. For many of them we showed that there is an agreed social meaning, and that the decoded and encoded meanings are the same.

There are a number of further problems.

(*a*) As Birdwhistell recognized, the meaning of NV signals does vary to some extent with the context, and with the preceding sequence of interaction.

(*b*) There is more than one system of NVC, and the same signal may appear in each. For example, a smile can (1) express an interpersonal attitude, or (2) an emotion, or (3) be part of self-presentation, (4) accompany speech or (5) be part of a ritual, e.g. greetings.

(*c*) While some stimuli are discrete, like the seven facial expressions for emotion, others are continuous, like proximity and orientation, though it is possible that they are treated in terms of a few distinct categories.

Combination into larger units

Speech has a clear hierarchical structure – sounds, words, sentences. Verbal and non-verbal signals occur simultaneously in conversation, and there is some correspondence between the two hierarchies, in that the smaller verbal units are associated with smaller NV units (words – hand movements) and the same is true of larger units (long utterances – postural positions). All social behaviour has this hierarchical structure, in which longer sequences are composed of smaller units, where units at each level are complete in themselves, where the smaller units are automatic and the longer are the product of planning and intention. While language is composed of discrete units (words, etc.), social behaviour is more continuous; the units of behaviour are larger or smaller and to be found in the eyes of the observers and interactors.

Non-verbal signals can, however, be combined in a number of ways, to produce communications with more complex meanings. (1) Animals combine facial and postural expressions with direction of gaze and spatial position, indicating who is the intended recipient. An alarm call may contain information about the identity of the caller, and the predator, the degree of danger, and the caller's position (p. 38). (2) Emotions and interpersonal attitudes are usually expressed by a harmonious set of signals via facial expression, tone of voice, and so on. If an inconsistent pattern is presented, this total signal is regarded as odd or funny, particular attention is paid to the negative elements, and a state of conflict may be inferred (p. 115, 128f). (3) Self-presentation usually involves a complex message – a combination of roles and traits, with emphasis on particular components, as in the case of a Scottish, upper-class, but intellectual, and religious dentist. (4) The combination of cues can be used to assert causal or other propositions, as in advertisements and progaganda – suggesting that there is a connexion between coffee and relaxed gaiety, or Conservative government and prosperity. (5) More complex combinations and sequences are used in art and religion to express basic attitudes to life.

Parts of speech

Gesture languages have clear similarities with verbal languages. Nouns, standing for objects or persons, can be communicated by pointing or by illustrative gestures. Verbs, standing for actions, can be communicated by the actions themselves, or reduced versions of them like in-

intention movements. Adverbs are represented by the way
these actions are performed, prepositions (in, under, etc.)
by gestures. These parts of speech can then be put together
in sequence, representing sentences. It is interesting that
the main parts of speech can be represented so easily.

However, for other kinds of NVC there are no obvious
equivalents to parts of speech, though there are distinct
classes of NV signals. First there are the different bodily
areas involved – face, hands, and so on. Each area has
special properties as a communicative system, described in
earlier chapters. Secondly there are NV signals, within
each area, communicating different kinds of information –
illustrating speech, governing synchronization, expressing
emotions. However, there is nothing like verbal grammar
ruling how the different kinds of units are to be combined.

It remains to be seen whether there exist groups of NV
signals which have the same meaning to interactors, and
for which there are rules governing their combination and
sequence.

Rules of sequence

Languages have grammatical rules governing the sequential
arrangement of words. Roland Barthes (1969) has shown
that some NV systems have somewhat comparable rules –
for example, the sequence of types of dish in a menu, the
possible combinations of different articles of clothing.
Highly structured social events, like greetings and other
rituals, have rules of sequence. Some of these rules appear
to be basic, like the three-phase structure of rituals; others
follow cultural conventions, like the behaviour expected at
meals and interviews. However, there is a difference between
these rules and verbal grammars, in that the NV rules are of
a statistical character, rather than definite and all-or-none.

Chomsky showed that language cannot be generated by
'finite-state' grammars, i.e. where rules specify which word
shall follow the words before it: more of a language can be

generated by 'phrase-structure' grammars, where links between non-adjacent words are recognized, and where bracketing operations must be carried out first in interpreting a sentence. Two sentences may have the same sequence of words, but a different phrase structure – as in the phrase 'old men and women' (Lyons 1970). Do similar principles apply to NVC? There is no close similarity but there are certainly rules relating non-adjacent moves. For example, the nature of a farewell is related to the nature of the greeting at the same encounter. There is also the phenomenon of 'embedding' – the actual period of greeting itself has a minor greeting and farewell. More generally, periods of an encounter may be bracketed by NV signals, and interrupt the rest of the encounter, which is resumed later. The NV signals accompanying speech follow phrase-structure which is closely related to that of the words, and indeed may indicate the phrase-structure of the words.

There are good reasons for thinking that social behaviour, including its non-verbal elements, is rule-governed. Interactors are aware of the rules (if only when they are broken), and monitor their own behaviour to conform to them. Clarke (in press) has found that there are rules governing the sequences of *utterances*; again there is some resemblance to the grammatical rules linking words, and again account has to be taken of phrase structure. However, the whole sequence is generated by two people now, not one, and usually they will not have an agreed sequence to run off, except perhaps in greetings and other set-piece encounters. As with social behaviour in general there are *two* sequences of behaviour, which are knitted together by rules governing the detailed order of events, and which have to be synchronized to make a mutually acceptable social relationship (Argyle, 1969). Clarke points out that non-verbal acts may substitute for verbal acts in such sequences. For example 'yes' and a head-nod are equivalent, so are 'look over there' and pointing, and compliance with a command may take the form of doing or saying something. Thus the rule-governed sequence of utterances can be partly replaced by NV signals.

Deep structure

As with language the same signal can have more than one meaning, for example, a smile or a raised finger. To make the meaning of an ambiguous sentence clear the deep structure needs to be specified; to make the meaning of an ambiguous non-verbal signal clear the sequence of events and the structure of the situation needs to be shown. A person raises his finger, the meaning of this signal depends on whether he is an umpire at a cricket match, a bidder at an auction sale, or in some other situation, and on the place of this act in the sequence. A sequence of overt behaviour may or may not be an instance of ingratiation or of hustling (i.e. pretending to be very bad at a game before playing for money) – there can be more than one deep structure here. Situations can be said to have structures, knowledge of which will clarify the meaning of non-verbal signals. By the structure of a situation is meant the basic set of relations and purposes of the participants, for example the power relations between two people, whether they are primarily engaged in task or sociable activities, whether there is mainly a positive (for instance, co-operative) or negative (for instance, competitive) relationship, and whether they are of the same or opposite sex. Thus a tutorial is unequal, task, co-operative, and may be of same or opposite sex; a date is (nearly) equal, sociable, positive, and opposite sex. Probably the rules of situations result from structure; the rules of tutorials simply reflect the purpose of this situation, and perhaps prevent it shifting into a different kind of situation, such as a date. Unless two people keep to the same rules, they cannot have a game of tennis, or chess; neither can they have a date or a music lesson. (Some combinations are, however, possible e.g. a date and a tutorial, though not a music lesson and psychoanalysis.) In addition there may be more complex rules associated with particular formal activities, like auction sales and cricket. Although the 'structure' of situations may make clear the meaning of non-verbal signals, it does not have much in common with the 'structure' of sentences.

Situational rules have at least three kinds of origins: (1) There may be universals of a biological origin; for example the parts of the body used for sending signals, some of the signals that are sent, e.g. facial expressions, the sense organs used for receiving these messages, and the implications for the kinds of behaviour appropriate for mothers and infants, courting couples and in other relationships. In addition there may be more complex universals, such as the common elements found in greeting in different cultures (p. 80). These may have their origin in innate structures related to appeasement, or other basic interpersonal processes. (2) In every culture there are a number of standard situations – eating a meal, having a conversation, working, making love, and so forth, which are universal features of life. Cultures develop rules to govern these situations, as a result of trial and error over the course of social history. (3) Similarly, norms or conventions are built up and slowly change, governing styles of behaviour in situations. These differ from rules in degree; deviation from norms is less disturbing, and norms are more arbitrary, less closely linked to situational structure.

Social situations are like games in some ways, except that games are always competitive. There are rules, and a variety of moves are possible within the rules. It would not be possible to play without some understanding of the basic ideas and purpose of the game. The same is true of behaviour in specific social situations and relationships. A move at chess must conform to the rules; to understand or predict that move it is necessary to understand about the pieces, goals, and basic ideas of chess; a move may follow from the immediately preceding move, but it does so in an immensely complicated way. Rules of games are more formally codified than the rules of most social situations, but both sets develop historically, through successive revisions into a closely co-ordinated set which generates satisfactory play. Games allow the possibility of strategic play, where one player misleads and outwits another; Berne (1966) has suggested that the social behaviour of neurotics is often like this, when they play games in this sense. In games, players who break the rules are penalized or sent off: Scheff (1966) suggested that this is what happens to schizophrenics – and others have suggested that they break the rules in order to be sent off to an easier life.

Non-verbal universals

Are there universal rules governing NVC in all cultures, corresponding to linguistic universals? A number of such non-verbal universals may be suggested, though it must be emphasized that they are tentative hypotheses, and in any case operate in a statistical manner.

(1) Communication takes place through the audio–vocal and visual–gestural channels simultaneously.
(2) Proximity and orientation should enable these two channels to be used.
(3) Only acts in the cultural repertoire may be used.
(4) An act by A must be responded to by an act by B appropriately in terms of time relations, i.e. without a period of non-response and without interruption. (The precise time relations vary across acts and between cultures.)
(5) An act by A must be responded to by an act by B appropriately in terms of content, e.g. B should not laugh or cry unless A's act warranted it, and should not reply on a different topic – without giving some explanation or excuse.

(6) Interactors should keep to the rules of the same social game, such as social conversation, bargaining, or interviewing, or negotiate a change of game. (The precise rules will vary with the culture.)

(7) Single embedding is allowed, for greetings and farewells, or definition of a period of encounter; otherwise a sub-sequence should be completed before another is started. A period of topic change can be embedded, started 'by the way I forget . . .' and encoded by 'now – you were going to tell me about . . .'

(8) Established interpersonal and role relations should be maintained, unless a change is negotiated.

(9) Interactors should sustain a certain degree of positive attentiveness and positive attitudes to one another.

(10) Interactions should follow the principle of exchange of rewards (reciprocity).

Evidence for some of these rules was provided by the rule-breaking experiments described in Chapter 3.

Other aspects of linguicity

There are a number of other aspects of 'linguicity', such as those listed by Hockett (1960). On these criteria, certain kinds of NVC have linguistic properties, but more often they do not. Does NVC have arbitrary meaning? Sign languages do, but most kinds of NVC have iconic or intrinsic meanings. Do NV signals have external reference, to objects or events outside the communicator? Illustrative gestures do, but most NV signals represent states or intentions of the communicator. Are there discrete and standard units of communication? This is true of sign languages: other signals usually vary along continuous dimensions – though decoders may use only a small number of categories, as with facial expressions. Language is a 'digital' system of communication, most NVC is analogical, especially when communicating emotions and interpersonal attitudes (Watz-

lawick et al. 1967). Is there intention to communicate? In
the case of illustrative gestures there is; often there is no
such intention, or the signals, for instance those accompanying speech, play an unacknowledged part in larger units of
communication.

Does NVC reflect the structure of the mind?

Structuralists maintain that all aspects of human culture
reflect the basic structure of the human mind. Mepham
(1972) says of science for example '. . . the scientist always
lives, loves, and dies within the net of signifying systems
which have their origin not in his rational contemplation
of the world but elsewhere, in that which speaks through
him, and in his being in the world'. We have seen that NVC
is affected, to a limited extent, by verbal labelling (p. 82f).
We have seen in this section that there are certain similarities between verbal and non-verbal communication. If
the system of NVC taken as a whole can be said to express
anything, it is the nature of human social interaction and
relationships.

Merleau-Ponty (1964) observed that the mapping of
words onto the world is not arbitrary, but depends on a
number of basic facts about the world – *'l'être sauvage'*: for
example, stars and roses are never categorized together.
Similarly the system of NVC, while it varies to some
extent between cultures, contains a number of universal
features, which are either innate to man, or necessary
aspects of social life.

Beyond language

Language is a very effective means of communicating
information about physical objects, and public events in
the outside world. It is good at describing and influencing
behaviour. Language appears to have developed for these
purposes, though it is also used for others, for example for

384 Conclusions & wider implications

sociable chat. As we have seen in this book there are other spheres where language is less effective, either because there are no suitable words – as in the case of shapes – or because language has rather little impact – expressing emotions and interpersonal attitudes.

There is another important sphere – the expression of the subjective experiences of life, and their interpretation in terms of basic attitudes to life, philosophies of life, and religion. Susanne Langer (1942) has suggested that there are two kinds of communication, one based on logic and language, the second designed to express and articulate feelings by means of non-verbal symbolism. Similar dichotomies of two kinds of thinking, or communication, have been put forward by Polanyi (1958) and others. Such a division is given unexpected support from the research on the difference between those people who break gaze to the left and to the right (p. 246). Left-shifters appear to have dominant right hemispheres, and to be interested in music, the arts, and other activities involving intuitive thinking; right-shifters appear to be left-hemisphere dominant, and engage more in verbal, rational thinking. This suggests that the non-verbal processes being discussed are localized in the right-hand half of the brain.

Music is one means of expressing emotions and attitudes, which could not be adequately put into words. Music can be regarded as a communication from the composer to the listener, and can be looked at from an encoding–decoding point of view. Hampton (1945) asked for listeners' reactions to a number of compositions for which the composer's intentions are known. Thus Part 5 of the second movement of Beethoven's Eroica Symphony was correctly identified as expressing 'sadness, despair or grief' by 93 per cent of subjects. A similar study was carried out by Semeonoff (1940) with compositions intended to convey visual images. Thus Sibelius's Finlandia was correctly judged as describing a 'wild and rugged' scene by 81 per cent of listeners, and the 'elephant' from the Carnival of Animals by Saint-Saëns was correctly identified by 46 per cent.

Music has several different kinds of meaning.

(1) *Emotions*

Music is very commonly decoded in terms of emotion as the Eroica Symphony was in the study described above. The emotions aroused may be evocation of particular social situations, or relationships, as in 'tender memories' and the blues.

(2) *Visual imagery*

This is experienced by many listeners. Vernon (1930) found that sounds may produce coloured images ('synaes-thesia'), for example, the trumpet is scarlet, the flute blue, the oboe green. Music also produces images of shapes – sharp or flat, flowing or spiky, ascending or descending, for example, and listeners can easily draw shapes resembling the musical experience. In programme music there is clear communication of more complex visual images.

(3) *Movement responses*

Listeners often refer to being 'physically stirred', or say they feel like dancing. They also make bodily movements while listening. Vernon (1930) points out that:

> 'Many also hear and think of music muscularly. They raise their heads or contract some other muscle when the music rises, or they perceive it in terms of their hands at the pianoforte or other instruments. Thus several of my audience noticed that their fingers tried to follow those of the pianists, others felt that they wanted to dance, especially in strongly rhythmic music.'

There are physiological reactions too – the heart rate is increased by loud and exciting music.

But is there a further message, beyond emotions, images, and bodily movements? It will be noted that many of the verbalized reactions given are not emotions in the usual sense – triumphant, dreamy, tragic, dignified, graceful, or yearning. Research by Valentine produced verbal descriptions such as 'The joyful uplifting of the oppressed soul that feels itself released from depths of anguish . . .' (Beethoven: Pastoral Sonata). 'Very powerful and stimulating, as if the composer is fighting against something, and when I am listening I feel like that too, and eventually there is triumph and peace of mind after great emotional disturbance' (Hindemith: Piano Duet).

It looks as if what is being expressed in such music is an elaborate sequence of inner experiences including various emotions. It is because music can represent these experiences so well that it has been called 'the language of the emotions'. Susanne Langer suggests that music and emotional experience have the same temporal structure; both have periods of 'motion and rest, attention and release, of agreement and disagreement, preparation, fulfilment, excitation, and sudden change'. She suggests that music does not arouse the emotion itself, but expresses it, that the listener contemplates the actual emotion from a distance.

The visual arts are another means of expressing subjective feelings of a number of kinds. Studies of the decoding of particular aspects of works of art have produced a number of interesting findings. For example, it has been found that the emotional responses to colours are determined almost entirely by the combination of hue, saturation, and lightness. Thus happiness is signalled by a combination of blueness, saturation, and lightness; warmth is signalled by redness, darkness, and saturation. However, saturation was much more important than hue – although there are few words for saturation and plenty of words for hue (Wright and Rainwater, 1962).

There are also bodily reactions to works of art. When there are human figures in a picture, the observer may empathize with them; that is he may imagine their feelings or bodily actions and start to share these feelings or to enact similar behaviour himself. Or he may find the people in the picture sexually attractive or awe-inspiring, and react in a complementary way. Lipps (see Valentine, 1962) suggested that observers may emphasize with line diagrams – vertical figures are seen as standing up, oblique figures as falling over, the bottom part of figures as propping up the upper parts, and so on. The nature of the surface is important for sculpture and ceramics, because people touch it, want to touch it, or imagine themselves doing so. Some modern art is intended to be experienced in this way.

The visual arts often convey messages which are beyond language. Kenneth Clark, for example, in his *Civilisation* (1969) drew attention to the 'heroic energy, confidence, and strength of will and intellect' in twelfth-century architecture, to the 'dignity of man' found in Renaissance Florence, and to the 'worship of nature' manifested by Constable and Turner. Poussin painted classical landscapes, showing an earthly paradise inhabited by great men, giving us a vision of a poetic past or an idyllic future. Works of art contain abstract messages, which are subjectively important and meaningful, but which carry no conviction when put into words – unless they are put into poetry. These messages are not capable of logical proof or empirical verification. Their 'truth' is self-evident, if it is accepted, from contemplation of the work of art in question. When paintings proclaim the worship of nature, they are telling us that the natural world should be admired. Some of these more abstract messages are conveyed by pictures of the human form, or face. This suggests that a whole philosophy of life, an attitude to the world, can be conveyed facial by expression, and other non-verbal signals.

Drama conveys even more complex messages. Usually there is a lot of talk in drama, but recently a form of drama has developed which contains very little dialogue, or where the dialogue is deliberately pointless. The Theatre of the Absurd tries to draw attention to the failure of language as a means of communicating important matters, on the grounds that it has been devalued by the mass media, advertising, and political propaganda, and has lost contact with life. The dramatists of the Absurd express this by portraying failures of communication. These dramatists point to the absurdity of living an inauthentic life, out of touch with ultimate realities. They also point to the absurdity of the human condition when the decline of religion has deprived us of our view of ultimate reality. All that we can do is to face the most basic facts of life and death, and life with one another (Esslin, 1961).

We discussed ritual as a means of expressing religious beliefs earlier. Religion does not consist of verbal propositions about the external world, but of non-verbal propositions about subjective experiences and their implications for the direction of behaviour. Perhaps it is a mistake to try to discuss theology in words as in sermons, prayers, and theology lectures. As with art and music a non-verbal language is needed. This is available in the form of ritual – which uses acts and objects that call up reactions and express religious feelings. However, bodily signals are not very precise and are not very convenient for discussing detailed religious attitudes or experiences. For this reason religious rituals usually consist of a combination of verbal and non-verbal forms – adding the precision and elaborated meanings of the first to the emotional power of the second. If religion is discussed in words it should be realized that these represent religious attitudes feebly and indirectly – as the programme notes represent the music.

Conclusions & wider implications 389

However, in this area we move not only beyond language, but beyond experimental research into non-verbal communication. There is no reason why such research should not be done, and it may have more profound consequences than the experimental work done so far.

Further Reading

ARGYLE, M. (1969) *Social Interaction*. London: Methuen.
HUIZINGER, J. (1949) *Homo Ludens*. London: Paladin.
LANGER, S. K. (1942) *Philosophy in a New Key*. Cambridge, Mass.: Harvard University Press.
MCLUHAN, M. (1962) *The Gutenberg Galaxy*. Toronto: University of Toronto Press.
MILLER, G. A., and MCNEILL, D. (1969) Psycholinguistics. In G. Lindzey and E. Aronson (eds.) *The Handbook of Social Psychology*. Vol. III. Reading, Mass.: Addison-Wesley.
VALENTINE, C. W. (1962) *The Experimental Psychology of Beauty*. London: Methuen.

References

ARGYLE, M., TROWER, P. and BRYANT, B. (1974) Explorations in the treatment of personality disorders and neuroses by social skills training. *British Journal of Medical Psychology* 47: 63-72.
BARTHES, R. (1964, English translation 1967) *Elements of Semiology*. London: Cape.
BENTHALL, J. (1975) (ed.) *The Body as a Medium of Expression*. London: Institute of Contemporary Arts.
BERNE, E. (1966) *Games People Play*. London: Deutsch.
CHOMSKY, N. (1957) *Syntactic Structures*. The Hague: Mouton.
CLARK, K. (1969) *Civilisation*. London: BBC and Murray.
CLARKE, D. (in press) The use and recognition of sequential structure in dialogue. *British Journal of Social and Clinical Psychology* 14: 333-9.
ESSLIN, M. (1961) *The Theatre of the Absurd*. Harmondsworth: Penguin Books.
HAMPTON, P. J. (1945) The emotional element in music. *Journal of General Psychology* 33: 237-50.
HOCKETT, C. F. (1960) Logical considerations in the study of

animal communication. In W. F. Lanyon and W. N. Tavolga (eds.) *Animal Sounds and Communication*. Washington D.C.: American Institute of Biological Science.

JECKER, J. D., MACCOBY, N. and BREITROSE, H. S. (1965) Improving accuracy in interpreting non-verbal cues of comprehension. *Psychology in the Schools* **2**: 239–44.

LEACH, E. (1972) The influence of cultural context on non-verbal communication in man. In R. Hinde (ed.) *Non-Verbal Communication*. Cambridge: Royal Society and Cambridge University Press.

LYONS, J. (1970) *Chomsky*. London: Fontana.

MCKNIGHT, P. C. (1971) Micro-teaching in teacher training: a review of research. *Research in Education* **6**: 24–38.

MCPHAIL, P. (1972) *Lifeline*. London: Longman.

MERLEAU-PONTY, M. (1964) *Le visible et l'invisible*. Paris: Gallimard.

MEPHAM, J. (1972) The structuralist sciences and philosophy. In D. Robey (ed.) *Structuralism*. London: Oxford University Press.

POLANYI, M. (1958) *Personal Knowledge*. London: Routledge & Kegan Paul.

SCHEFF, T. J. (1966) *Being Mentally Ill*. Chicago: Aldine Atherton.

SEMEONOFF, B. (1940) A new approach to the testing of musical ability. *British Journal of Psychology* **30**: 326–40.

SIDNEY, E., and ARGYLE, M. (1969) *Training in Selection Interviewing*. London: Mantra.

VERNON, P. E. (1930) The phenomena of attention and visualisation in the psychology of musical appreciation. *British Journal of Psychology* **21**: 50–63.

WATZLAWICK, P., BEAVIN, J. H. and JACKSON, D. D. (1968) *Pragmatics of Human Communication*. London: Faber.

WRIGHT, B., and RAINWATER, L. (1962) The meanings of colour. *Journal of General Psychology* **67**: 89–99.

Indexes

Author Index

398 Index

Subject Index